MW00659093

Balkan Fascination

AMERICAN MUSICSPHERES

Series Editor
Mark Slobin

Fiddler on the Move
Exploring the Klezmer World
Mark Slobin

The Lord's Song in a Strange Land
Music and Identity in Contemporary Jewish Worship
Jeffrey A. Summit

Lydia Mendoza's Life in Music
Yolanda Broyles-González

Four Parts, No Waiting
A Social History of American Barbershop Harmony
Gage Averill

Louisiana Hayride
Radio and Roots Music Along the Red River
Tracey E. W. Laird

Balkan Fascination
Creating an Alternative Music Culture in America
Mirjana Laušević

Polkabilly
How the Goose Island Ramblers Redefined American Folk Music
James P. Leary

Cajun Breakdown
The Emergence of an American-Made Music
Ryan André Brasseaux

Claiming Diaspora
Music, Transnationalism, and Cultural Politics in Asian/Chinese America
Su Zheng

Bright Star of the West
Joe Heaney, Irish Song-Man
Sean Williams and Lillis Ó Laire

Romani Routes
Cultural Politics and Balkan M´cusic in Diaspora
Carol Silverman

Voices from the Canefields
Folksongs from Japanese Immigrant Workers in Hawai'i
Franklin Odo

Greeted With Smiles
Bukharian Jewish Music and Musicians in New York
Evan Rapport

BALKAN FASCINATION

Creating an Alternative Music Culture in America

Mirjana Laušević

OXFORD
UNIVERSITY PRESS

OXFORD
UNIVERSITY PRESS

Oxford University Press is a department of the University of Oxford.
It furthers the University's objective of excellence in research, scholarship,
and education by publishing worldwide.

Oxford New York
Auckland Cape Town Dar es Salaam Hong Kong Karachi
Kuala Lumpur Madrid Melbourne Mexico City Nairobi
New Delhi Shanghai Taipei Toronto

With offices in
Argentina Austria Brazil Chile Czech Republic France Greece
Guatemala Hungary Italy Japan Poland Portugal Singapore
South Korea Switzerland Thailand Turkey Ukraine Vietnam

Oxford is a registered trade mark of Oxford University Press
in the UK and certain other countries.

Published in the United States of America by
Oxford University Press
198 Madison Avenue, New York, NY 10016

© Oxford University Press 2007

First issued as an Oxford University Press paperback, 2016.

All rights reserved. No part of this publication may be reproduced, stored in a retrieval system, or transmitted, in any form or by any means, without the prior permission in writing of Oxford University Press, or as expressly permitted by law, by license, or under terms agreed with the appropriate reproduction rights organization. Inquiries concerning reproduction outside the scope of the above should be sent to the Rights Department, Oxford University Press, at the address above.

You must not circulate this work in any other form
and you must impose this same condition on any acquirer.

Library of Congress Cataloging-in-Publication Data
Laušević, Mirjana.
Balkan Fascination : creating an alternative music culture in America / Mirjana Laušević.
p. cm.
Includes bibliographical references and index.
ISBN 978-0-19-517867-8 (hardcover); 978-0-19-026942-5 (paperback)
1. Folk Music—United States—History and Criticism. 2. Folk Music—Balkan Peninsula—History and Criticism. 3. Music—United States—Balkan Peninsula influences
I. Title.
ML3560.B28L38 2005
781.62'918073—dc22
2005014887

Audio and video tracks are available online at www.oup.com/us/balkanfascination.
Access with username Music4 and password Book2497.

To Luka and Anja

Acknowledgments

I feel very fortunate to have a long list of people to thank for making this work both possible and enjoyable. If it weren't for Žabe I Babe and Jerry Kisslinger's invitation to a Balkan party in New York my encounter with the Balkan music and dance scene might not have had the impact that ultimately led to this book. The patience, knowledge, and willingness of all the people I have interviewed over the years to open their minds and hearts to me elicits most sincere gratitude. Even if the direct quotes are not included in the text itself, each person's insight did contribute to this work. I am also grateful to EEFC and to all the musicians and dancers who have made my research so full of joy.

In the early stages of research I owe thanks to Dick Crum, Michael Ginsburg, Christos Govetas, Ruth Hunter, Martin Koenig, Steve Kotansky, Yves Moreau, and Ethel Raim, for their generosity, knowledge and direction. Special thanks are due to Lauren Brody, Margaret Loomis, Ethel Raim, Jane Sugarman, and Larry Weiner for "Balkan" hospitality, and to Bob Beer, David Bilides, Martha Forsyth, Ron Houston, John Kuo, Suzanne Leonora, Rachel MacFarlane, Stewart Mennin, Cathy Stately, Judith Verkvist, and many others for their helpful insights and support.

Thanks to Žabe I Babe, Lori Fraser, and Ansambl Teodosijevski for making *Drumovi.* Many loving people and helping hands contributed to this recording in different ways; Rani Arbo, Belle Birchfield, Neely and Phyllis Bruce, Laura Cameron, Chaterine Foster, Jennifer and Peter Hadley, Dora Hast, Kelly House, Peter Irvine, Edward Jessen, Scott Kessel, Donna Kwon, Rob Lancefield, Ingi Loorand, Vesna and Senad Mehinovič, Becky Miller, Keith Moore, Tristra Newyear, Anna-Maria Nygren, Cath Oss, Victoria Pike, Larry Polansky, Laura Risk, Matt Rogalsky, Stanley Scott, Sarah Snyder, Michael Veal, Lisa Wolfe, and David Yih.

At the outset, Wesleyan University provided an intellectual and social home in which I felt comfortable, challenged and inspired, while the University of Minnesota and my wonderful colleagues there supported me in

the final stages of the book's production. The American Association of University Women granted me a yearlong scholarship when I could hardly have survived without it. I am grateful that nothing but pleasant experiences accompanied my research at Wellesley College Archive, various branches of the New York Public Library, Library of Congress, Duquesne University Tamburitzans' Library, Trinity College Watkinson Library, Wesleyan University's Olin Library, University of Minnesota Libraries, and the San Francisco Performing Arts Library and Museum.

Mark Slobin has been a consistent source of inspiration and friendship, and a stalwart supporter. I cannot express enough gratitude for all I've learned from him. For their work and their interest in my work I am grateful to Ted Levin, Jeff Summit, Marc Perlman, and Mike Heffley. Jane Sugarman, Carol Silverman, and Sonia Seaman provided valuable comments and suggestions both as ethnomusicologists and insiders to the Balkan music and dance scene. I am exceptionally grateful to Mark Levy for his thoughtful and nuanced comments on an earlier draft of the book manuscript that resulted in significant improvements.

Many thanks to Ziyia, Kitka, Pitu Guli, Ženska Pesna for letting me use their recordings. Ljubo Živkov went to great lengths to help me get the video footage of Zlatne Uste from Radio Television Serbia. Donna Kwon and Kristin Irving assisted me greatly in obtaining photographs from the San Francisco Performing Arts Library. Michael Ginsburg, Carol Silverman, Mark Levy, and Rachel MacFarlane have been kind to answer many questions. Margaret Loomis helped me sift through thousands of her Balkan camp photos in search of the perfect cover image. Steve and Annie Luttinen, Kim Bahmer, Julie Sabo and Peter Baatrup, Lynn and Bob Dixon, Pat Solstad helped in many ways, not the least of them being taking care of Luka and Anja.

Most important, this book would truly not be possible if it was not for the love, support, and inspiration provided by my family. Cliff and Elsa Eriksen beamed it from New Hampshire; my mother, Nadežda Laušević, heroically moved to a foreign land to take care of her grandchildren and our household whenever time was needed to work on the "book that never ends." It is truly difficult to imagine how this work would have been completed without her help. My brother, Dragan Laušević, relocated us all to Whistler in the summer of 2005 so we could prepare the manuscript while he and mom explored Whistler's playgrounds with the kids. Thanks to Jeff and Jane for letting us take over their house. My late father, Miroslav Laušević, has always been a true source of encouragement. His enthusiasm and pride in my work will stay with me forever. Thanks to Luka and Anja each day is filled with loveliness and joy. Thanks for teaching me about life's priorities. The tender love, dedication, and steadfast support of my husband, Tim Eriksen, have enriched my life and this work in the ways that cannot be described. He is always the first to hear, discuss, and comment on my work. His assistance in the final stages of this book makes it truly a collaborative project. He helped me not only with editing, but also with choosing and digitizing music examples. Thanks. What a joy and a privilege it is to be able to share ideas, to inspire each other, and to work together!

Contents

Balkan Fascination

Introduction

Like most important turns in my life, my introduction to the Balkan music and dance scene in the United States happened quite unexpectedly as the result of a series of seemingly unrelated events. Soon after leaving my native city of Sarajevo in the fall of 1991 to pursue graduate studies at Wesleyan University, I found myself leading a ten-piece band, later named Žabe I Babe, learning to play and sing traditional, rock, pop, and newly composed folk songs from various parts of the former Yugoslavia. For one of the group's favorite songs we needed someone to play a double-headed Macedonian drum called *tapan*. David Yih, an experienced drummer, was willing to learn how to play tapan but, beyond explaining how to hold the drum and what the drumsticks look like, I was not of much help. It was clear that we needed instruction from an experienced tapan player, but there aren't very many even in Macedonia; finding one in the United States seemed like searching for a needle in a haystack. I was proven wrong as soon as I voiced my concern.

"There is a tapan player in New York. Jerry. Jerry Kisslinger. He lives in the Bronx. I can get you his phone number," said Becky Miller, one of the band members.

"Jerry? What would be his real name?" I thought to myself, "Probably Jeremija; an old-fashioned name, which must be why he Americanized it."

"Is he a Macedonian? Or Serbian?" I asked, amazed at the swiftness and ease with which this "impossible" task was accomplished.

"No, he is an American, he plays tapan in this great Serbian brass band in New York called Zlatne Uste," said Becky.

"Zlatne Uste? I don't think it can be Zlatne Uste. That is grammatically incorrect. It must be Zlatne Usne," I explained, "or, maybe, Zlatna Usta."

"No, I am pretty sure it is Zlatne Uste. I have their tape. I think they got it wrong, and after someone told them that it was not grammatically correct they decided to keep the name anyway since they had already printed the T-shirts and done the tape covers with that name."

I recalled hearing interviews with second-generation Yugoslavian immigrants struggling with Serbo-Croatian and getting most of the declinations and conjugations wrong, so I assumed that must have been the case with this band name as well. Serbo-Croatian, with its seven cases and three genders and all the possible declinations and conjugations, is a very hard language to learn, and one cannot blame the children of immigrants brought up in America for not getting it right. The possibility of these people being "non-Serbian-Americans" and still having a Serbian brass band was beyond the limits of my imagination at the time. After all, I had come from a place where the importance of national, ethnic, religious and regional identities and boundaries was, to say the least, being blown out of proportion, and where self-definition, group affiliation, and cultural practice were closely interrelated.

Only a few weeks after this conversation I found myself in Jerry's apartment in the Bronx, sipping turkish coffee, eating feta cheese and *ajvar* (a roasted red pepper and eggplant spread my family and most others back home would make every fall), while he was explaining the basics of tapan playing to David. Jerry did tell me that he was not Serbian, and that his parents were not Serbian either, but since we had come to his place for a tapan lesson and did not have too much time for inquiry I stopped asking questions and simply assumed that in some way he must be "Serbian" or "Macedonian." Otherwise, why would he be offering *šljivovica* (plum brandy) and turkish coffee, how would he know about ajvar and *kajmak*, and why would he play tapan and Serbian brass band music? Before we left, Jerry gave me a flier for the Zlatne Uste Annual Golden Festival, explaining that it was a big Balkan party with good food and many bands playing all night long.

As the day of the "Balkan party" approached, I became increasingly excited. After all, I had not spoken a word of Serbo-Croatian, except occasionally over the phone, in a long time. I was anxious to meet some people from my homeland and to spend at least one night in a familiar atmosphere. I was in for a big surprise.

I remember climbing the stairs to the third floor of Context Studios in New York (28 Avenue A), entering into noise and crowd. I stood in a narrow hallway connecting two rooms, wondering which way to go. People were constantly passing by me, going from one room to the other. Different Balkan-sounding music was coming from each of the rooms. I decided to get out of the way and step into the room to the right of the entrance. In the program that I grabbed at the door, I noticed that the room was called *Kafana*, a word borrowed from Turkish and used in Serbo-Croatian to refer to a pub, although the term can be roughly translated as "coffeehouse." However, I noticed that this Kafana was not fogged up by cigarette smoke, as would certainly be expected in any gathering of people from the Balkans. The room was very crowded. Some people were sitting around small tables, eating, chatting, and listening to music; others were standing, coming and going from one room to the other. A small Bulgarian ensemble was playing in the center of the room. Along the sides were tables overflowing with

food. There was ajvar and pickled peppers, baklava, *japrak sarma* . . . Here and there I could smell šljivovica, and I remember seeing a pastry that looked as if it just came out of my mom's oven.

In the room to the left there was a band up on the stage. The walls were completely covered with beautiful hand-woven carpets and tapestries. It was hot and sticky in the room, which was packed with people dancing circle dances. I began noticing that many of them wore some pieces of folk costume, most often embroidered blouses and leather peasant shoes, called *opanci*. From all I understood about Balkan immigrants to the United States, this was not the scene I expected to see. The men should have been wearing suit pants and dressy shirts, they should be all freshly shaven, with sharp, urban, haircuts, and perhaps here and there I would see a thick golden chain protruding from a loosely buttoned shirt. The women should have been in tight pants or tight short skirts, high heels, stockings, with lots of makeup and at least blow-dried hair. I tried to make sense of what I was seeing by guessing people's life stories and how they "came" here. They must have been here for a while, I thought, since they had lost touch with current fashion in the Balkans. I was surprised that I heard only English around me, except for the people on the stage. It looked as if older people were dressed in folk costumes, rather than the younger ones, which made me imagine that they had immigrated as peasants and kept their costumes for occasions like this. It took me a while to start talking to people, always starting with:

"Hi. Where are you from?"

"From New York, Boston, Philadelphia . . ." were the common answers.

"Oh, where are your parents from?" would be my second question.

I was expecting to hear, "Bulgaria, Serbia, Croatia, Macedonia . . ." But I never got such an answer that night. Instead, I learned the term WASP (White Anglo-Saxon Protestant), as some people would, with a smile, try to explain to me their family origins. I finally realized that the great majority of the several hundred people joyfully dancing to Balkan tunes (played and sung, not by hired immigrant musicians, as I later learned, but by Americans) had no ethnic ties to any of the Balkan countries. It took me much longer to explain to myself what I was witnessing. Who were they? Why were they there? Why did they play, sing, and dance those tunes? Why were they wearing folk costumes and opanci? Where did all these kilims and tapestries come from, and where did they find ajvar in New York?

That night turned out to be the first night of my research. Much like these Americans who had stumbled upon Balkan music and dance at some point in their lives and became enchanted by it, I stumbled upon them and found their enchantment puzzling and fascinating. Had I known more about American culture and lifestyles, had I been better prepared for what I was witnessing, perhaps the whole event would not have been as startling to me as it was being caught by surprise. This was a world in itself, different from anything I had seen in the States up to that point, and certainly far from what I would have expected to be called a Balkan party.

However, the biggest surprise of the evening was yet to come: "Ramo, Ramo, druže moj" (**DVD 1** "Ramo, Ramo. . . ." Filmed at the 1995 Mendocino Balkan Music and Dance Workshops). It was the end of 1992 in New York, and within these walls covered with Balkan carpets and tapestries several hundred Americans were packed tightly, holding hands, dancing a circle dance while singing in Serbo-Croatian "Ramo, Ramo druže moj." I had a flashback to a time when I was little, spending the summer with my family on the Adriatic coast, in a syndicated (government- subsidized) vacation resort. We were dining outdoors on a concrete porch shaded by a grape vine. "Ramo, Ramo, druže moj" was the hit of the summer, played during every meal on the stereo, and then live during dinner. I was six or seven at the time, and it was the first time I remember being deeply affected by a song. I was very intrigued by the story behind the song, trying to understand who Ramo was and why the singer with the crying voice was so sad. Much later I learned that the song had its origin in a Hindi film that was very popular in Yugoslavia in the early 1970s[1], which explains why it sounded so unusual to me. Numerous local musicians and restaurant bands had their versions of the song, but how did "Ramo, Ramo . . ." make it to the States? Why would Americans in New York more than twenty years later be singing, of all songs, "Ramo, Ramo, druže moj" in Serbo-Croatian? What kinds of images came into their minds when they heard this song? Did they understand why the singer was so sad?

I left the Golden Festival with a clear sense of the many questions I wanted to ask, but with little idea of how to pursue answers, and no preparation for the century's worth of historical research that lay before me, detailed in parts II through IV of this book. But first, I shall outline the conventionally ethnographic material. I had learned that there were Balkan bands in most major cities and many small towns across the country, that there were numerous concerts/dance parties throughout the year, that there were many Balkan dance classes where, in the absence of live bands, people would dance to recorded music, that there were at least two annual Balkan music and dance summer camps where one could spend a whole week learning various music and dance styles from the region. I also learned of the many people who danced Balkan dances in the context of "international folk dance," a related scene that was to have great significance to my research. All of these things were completely new to me, and with such widespread activities and locations to investigate, it was hard to determine where my "field" of study would actually be. The community I became interested in was tied neither by the expected shared ethnic heritage nor by a particular location. The existence of this "village" was due almost entirely to a shared interest in a particular music/dance repertoire. In this sense it differed greatly from most traditional fieldwork situations in which the very location of the "field" is, at least, not in question. One of my first discoveries was that these "Balkanites," as they often call themselves, were extremely active on the, then nascent, Internet. Before most Americans even had a home computer, they were already fostering musical community through Web sites, chat rooms, and especially through

an e-mail list serve. The EEFC (East European Folklife Center) list serve became one of the first "sites" for my research. I had access to daily readings on what members of the group had to say about Balkan music and dance, about their involvement in the scene, about particular performing groups, and about song and dance renderings. This helped me recognize a particular sense of humor, learn the in-group jokes, lingo, and general issues of concern, and get a better sense of the group I was working with. I conducted especially thorough monitoring of the "conversations" on the mailing list in the period from 1995 through 1997. I was able, almost immediately, to get a large number of responses to questions that were of a particular interest to me, and to follow discussions that arose on the network without my instigation.

As my research progressed I gradually became involved in the Balkan music and dance scene on several levels: as a researcher, teacher, student, performer, and audience member. At the same time I began conducting ever deepening historical research into the origins of this scene. Since 1993 I have taught Bosnian traditional singing at Balkan Music and Dance summer camps organized by the EEFC (Buffalo Gap, West Virginia 1993; Ramblewood, Maryland 1994, 1995, 1998; Mendocino, California 1995, 1997, 1998) as well as at other privately sponsored summer camps and music workshops in the United States and Britain. This teaching has been very helpful in learning about the expectations, aims, habits, interests, abilities, ethics, and esthetics of the Balkan music and dance enthusiasts. Attending camp classes was equally valuable to my research. Among other things, it provided insight into the kind of knowledge camp participants acquired, and how they acquired it.

Beginning in late 1992 I attended various Balkan music and dance events, not only as an observer, but also as a performer with Žabe i Babe.[2] This helped me to see which aspects of Balkan musical culture are appreciated by which audiences, how events are organized, and what the criteria are for selecting performing groups. Videotapes of concerts, dance parties, rehearsals, and classes became handy tools for analyzing social interactions, bodily practices, and music and dance behavior within the group. The groups' verbal, visual, and acoustical representations of themselves and of the Balkans, through liner notes, packaging, and repertoire choice, have yielded many interesting insights.

It has not been a goal of my work to evaluate or judge Balkan musical texts rendered by Americans, though comparative analysis might be a fascinating undertaking. I became much more interested, rather, in getting a picture of the phenomenon as a whole within the context of American culture and history. What's more, I wanted to avoid evaluation of the musical material produced within the subject group because of the danger of taking on a role of authority, often assigned to me by the very fact that I am a native of a Balkan country. Indeed, in the beginning stages of the fieldwork I was not perceived as a "scholar" who was there to learn, but rather as a "native" who must be there to teach, criticize, judge, and evaluate. My actions were often interpreted as reactions to the music and

dance content of an event. For example, during one dance party I was sitting on a bench watching the dance. A person I had met earlier that evening, and who knew that I was "from the Balkans," approached me with the question:

"Did we make this one up?"

"What do you mean?" I asked

"Did we get the steps wrong? Is this one authentic? Why aren't you dancing?"

"I don't know the dance. I have never danced Greek dances."

Similar exchanges happened several times during my fieldwork, but mostly with people who were, themselves, new to the scene. Those with more experience were more likely to know that "the natives," in the best case, know only a couple of circle dances. But even in situations where my participation, or lack of it, was not understood as approval or disapproval, my very presence in the room made some participants attempt to view themselves through my eyes: "Oh, this must look funny to you! What do you make out of this? Do you think we are all nuts? I guess we sound American, don't we? You know, we are doing this just for fun. . . ." I could not escape being perceived as an embodiment of the "Balkan culture" before which the "Americans" needed to justify and explain their actions.

Over the years of my research and participation in the Balkan music and dance scene I have gotten to "know" so many individuals currently involved in the scene who do not know me. What might have been a sixty-minute interview for them became months and years of listening and thinking about their words for me. I know their biographies, where they live, who they socialize with, what instruments they play, what music they like and dislike, and what they think about issues related to the Balkan scene. I carry in my head the intonation and rhythm of their sentences, and whether I agree with their content or not, they have shaped my thoughts on the subject and, in the end, shaped this work as well. I have established many friendships and meaningful ties with lovers of Balkan music and dance in the United States and have grown to understand and appreciate their endeavors.

Over the course of four years I conducted about sixty formal recorded interviews and talked informally to many more people associated in one way or another with Balkan music and dance events in the United States. I have continued this research less formally in the years since. Among the people interviewed were key individuals in the field: founders of the Balkan Arts Center (precursor to the Ethnic Folk Arts Center), the East European Folklife Center, and prominent Balkan dance and music teachers whose activities were crucial to the development of Balkan music and dance in the United States. These interviews helped me to grasp the development of the scene and its institutional policies. Interviews with many other music and dance teachers and students, as well as leaders and members of prominent or lesser known performing groups, have generally provided for an understanding of the process of transmission of music and dance forms, selection of repertoire, personal insights into Balkan music and dance

forms, and people's motivation for learning and performing them. Musicians and dancers from various Balkan countries who have been involved in teaching and performing in the United States offered interesting insights into issues of representation and cross-cultural learning. A two-page questionnaire, distributed at Balkan camps, enabled me to acquire grassroots responses to the most pertinent questions and to gain statistical confirmation of data culled from numerous interviews. (See appendix.)

While the above-cited methodology was extremely useful in gaining an understanding of the current Balkan music and dance scene, it clearly showed its limitations in recovering the oral history of the "village." As is true of most villages, I discovered that most of the members of this "village" were more interested in tending the grounds and maintaining the house, so to speak, than in understanding when, why, and how the village came into existence, how it got its present- day shape, what it was built for, and who inhabited it before them. Most "villagers" considered the scene to have emerged from the 1960s folk movement and imagined that their ideas and feelings about experiencing "Balkan tradition" were wholly their own or had evolved in recent decades.

Early in my work I did discover, however, that one man, Michael Herman, was widely considered to be the father of this movement and, what's more, that at the age of eighty-four, Herman was still living and leading a folk dance class for elderly people near his home on Long Island. This, I thought, was the person I had been looking for to answer all my questions, at least about the history of the scene if not its significance to American culture and an ethnomusicological study of meaning and identity. But while my meeting with him was fascinating, it left me with few answers and many new questions. I got the distinct impression that Michael Herman was part of an older American tradition, the origins of which were unclear even to him. The beginning of international folk dancing in the United States could not be limited to the enthusiasm and activities of one man, nor could it be explained by him alone. Thus my ethnomusicological study became, in large part, an historical study, demanding that I peel back layer upon layer of history, music, and meaning.

My research quickly went in multiple directions, across a wide time span, and across a range of social groupings. I began my investigation of written sources with the "house library," i.e., various types of in-group material written by and for participants in the scene. These included a long list of folk dance periodicals, magazines, and newsletters from all over North America (*Viltis*, *The Folk Dancer*, *Traditions*, *Ontario Folk Dancer*, *Folk Dance in Baton Rouge*, etc., as well as the more recent *Balkan Tunes* and *Kef Times*), dance and music instruction manuals, songbooks, class syllabi, record covers and liner notes, posters, fliers, photographs, several unpublished papers and a masters' thesis, all done by insiders, and the web pages of various Balkan folk dance and music groups. While extremely valuable as ethnographic documents and analytical material, these sources did not offer much in terms of approaching a history of the movement.[3] Both the content and time frame of these sources corresponded with,

and supported, the information gathered from interview accounts of oral history.

Sources created outside of the group for the general public or reading audiences in other fields of study provided insight into circumstances and ideologies that gave rise to the international folk dance and music movement. My most comprehensive research of daily papers was conducted in the *New York Times*, though other daily papers from Boston, Chicago, and San Francisco were consulted for specific references. I also investigated important archival material at the New York Public Library (both the Main Research Library and the Performing Arts Library), the San Francisco Performing Arts Library and Museum, and the Wellesley College Archive (the latter housing archival material not only from Wellesley College, but also from the Boston Normal School of Gymnastics and the YMCA Normal School for Physical Education in Springfield, Massachusetts). In addition, I researched material at the Trinity (Watkinson) and Amherst College Libraries, the Library of Congress, the Jane Addams Museum in Chicago, and online resources, which have become increasingly available. Rather than systematic research, it was a systematic return to the same sources, each time viewed from a different perspective and with different intentions, that enabled me to notice how various types of distinct information were related to each other and, ultimately, to the rise of the Balkan folk music and dance scene.

The research evolved in roughly reverse chronological order, starting with more recent developments and following leads back to their beginnings, approximating the way in which history is most palpably experienced. As the months passed, the scope of this work expanded decade by decade until it reached a span of over a hundred years. I found myself reading about the history of physical education at the turn of the twentieth century and the introduction of folk dance in public and private school curricula, about the playground, park, and recreation movements, about settlement houses and their folk dance programs, about the late Victorian women's movement, about World's Fairs and "festivals of nations," about United States immigration laws and patterns, as well as many other areas of American and English culture and politics at the end of the nineteenth and beginning of the twentieth century.

As the research progressed I grew increasingly fascinated by my findings. Gradually, names, movements, and activities that had served as keywords for my various library and archival searches came alive. William Morris, John Ruskin, John Dewey, Mary Hemenway, Amy Morris Homans, Mary Wood Hinman, Luther Halsey Gulick, Elizabeth Burchenal, Louis Chalif, Jane Addams, Henry Ford, and many others all began to dance together in my mind. Whether or not they actually danced in the same room is beside the point. Whether or not they ever joined in a Balkan dance was likewise of little importance. What mattered to me was the web of influence they had on each other's thinking and activities, that each was related in one way or another to international folk dancing, and that each was a fascinating representative of a period in American history. Their

writings and personal correspondence told me much about how and why international folk dancing started and spread throughout the country, eventually giving rise to the contemporary Balkan music and dance scene. At the same time I learned much about developing ideas of cultural identity, ethnicity, art, politics, and social practices in a "new" nation.

As I learned more about developments connected to folk dance and music movements, I realized that some of the ideologies that created these movements and motivated their use of international folk dancing had originated much earlier and persisted to the present day. The gathered data was not "falling into its historical place," but kept popping up over and over again throughout this time span. It was at the same time fascinating and strange to read the words of physical educators and settlement house leaders from the turn of the century one day, find the same thoughts in the writings of the folk dance leaders of the mid-twentieth century the next day, and finally have nearly identical words spoken into my microphone by a Balkan music enthusiast as if he or she was the first one ever to articulate these ideas. The lack of awareness of this historical continuum within the modern Balkan scene, and outside of it, is in itself good reason to offer a historical perspective on the subject.

It became clear from my growing historical insight that involvement in international, and later solely Balkan, folk music and dance is not as random and accidental in nature as it appears to many of its current practitioners. Although the people currently involved in this activity have, in most cases, stumbled upon it rather than actively sought it out, there is a complex set of historical and cultural reasons behind their devotion to the maintenance and perpetuation of this activity. If I had focused solely on the contemporary Balkan music and dance scene in the United States, I would have found these reasons primarily in the domains of psychology or sociology, filling particular needs in the lives of mostly urban/suburban white, highly educated Americans of various European origins. My historical research, however, showed the depth of cultural heritage through connections and relationships between seemingly unrelated ideological phenomena. Even for individuals for whom involvement in the Balkan scene constitutes "resistance" or "refutation" of American cultural values, the activity has deep roots in the American cultural mainstream.

Organizing the gathered data into a single chronological narrative has been a challenging endeavor. One cannot apply to this material a simple metaphor of many streams flowing into a river, yielding a new, larger entity. There was not one single river to follow in this research, nor did the streams simply merge and disappear into a new body of water. The visual image I see when surveying the gathered historical data is that of an electromagnetic field in which particles and streams of energy attract, reflect, reject, and bounce off of each other, constantly producing slightly different images. Under these circumstances I am interested in providing an understanding of the very environment in which the dynamic relationships among the constituent parts of the field exist over time and how changes in environmental parameters affect the larger processes within.

Any story can be told in an infinite number of ways, even while bowing to conventional structural demands of language and intellectual understanding. To our Balkanite friends, it is the scene's "Balkaness" that stands out as its most eminent quality and the most significant stream of energy to follow in telling its story. Such a narrative would spend a few decades at most in the United States before leaping the Atlantic to Balkan strongholds of traditional music and dance. But holding the scene up to the light of history, it is its "Americaness" that most fascinates me, and it is this perspective that led me to the narrative structure that follows.

The book is divided into four parts, roughly approximating the periods in the history of international folk dance. Part I, "Ethnography of the Balkan Music and Dance Scene," locates the Balkan scene, provides a profile of contemporary Balkanites, and discusses Balkan camps as central to the maintenance of the scene (chapter 1). Reasons for this particular choice of music and dance activity are explored in chapter 2. While I am intrigued by the challenge and possible interest of presenting my historical research in the roughly reverse chronological order in which it unfolded, I have chosen to backtrack and begin the next section at the "beginning," in the interest of clarity. I do not suggest, however, that I have traced the ideologies and practices that gave rise to the movement from their inception, as there are remarkable precedents reaching deep into American cultural history.

Part II, "Folk Dancing and Turn-of-the-Century America," is devoted to the understanding of various uses of folk dance programs in settlement houses (chapter 3) and physical education and recreation movements (chapter 4). Another reason for backtracking to the early days of the settlement and physical education movements is that their leaders had a clear sense of what they wanted to achieve through folk dancing, and because their ideas and practices led directly into the next period in the history of "international folk dance." As we will notice, there was much common ground between the settlement movement and the physical education and recreation movements with respect to their treatment of folk dance programs. Besides the ideological and methodological overlap, much of the folk dance material itself was shared and a number of teachers were active in both movements. I will discuss them separately because the first was aimed primarily at recent immigrants and the second at "native" Americans.

Part III, "International Folk Dancing from the 1930s to the 1950s," is devoted primarily to the rise of an independent "international folk dance" movement (hereafter referred to as IFD). At this time folk dance clubs and groups were forming throughout the country, and the appearance of Michael Herman and Song Chang at the World's Fairs in New York and San Francisco, respectively, gave a great impetus to the movement. Chapter 5 provides a historical setting for this stage through a discussion of internationalism in America during the Great Depression and New Deal era, and describes this transitional period as expressed through the activities of Mary Wood Hinman and the Folk Festival Council of New York.

The lives and contributions of three major international folk dance leaders, Vytautas Beliajus, Song Chang, and Michael Herman, are discussed in chapter 6. Chapter 7 gives an overview of this historical period, through a discussion of the impact of the World's Fairs of 1939 to 1940 on international folk dancing as a national trend.

Part IV, "The 1950s and Beyond," is devoted to international folk dancing's "Balkan craze" (chapter 8) and the subsequent development of a distinct Balkan music and dance scene (chapter 9).

In the conclusion, I chart the relationships between the four parts of the book, exploring common threads and disjunctions throughout this historical period. Having made these distinctions, I will emphasize that this historical survey does not follow one social group, nor a fixed body of repertoire, nor a single application of international folk dancing in American society. In many phenomena that can be described as postmodern, urban, transnational, or virtual, boundaries are often blurry and difficult to define. How can the ethnographer identify her object of study? Where is the field? Who are the insiders? The points of intersection and disjunction among the institutions, individuals, repertoire, practices, and ideas here described are multiple and complex, and this large number of variables could compel one to question the very justification for such broad research. Yet it is this very breadth that allowed me to identify my object of study, as if I had stepped back to see figures and patterns emerge from a large pointillist painting that, from up close, appeared to be a rather random assortment of colored dots. Such a perspective enables us to see, among all the variables, continuity and a relative consonance on a number of fronts.

Remarkably consonant ideas of "folk," more specifically the concept of international folk dance, ideas of peasantry, and ultimately "Balkan music and dance," surface over the course of a hundred years. The ideologies and institutions that promoted this continuity certainly deserve our fullest attention. Hence, this work can be viewed, in part, as a history of ideas—their emergence, application, modification, and negotiation within various segments of American society. To return to the metaphor of an electromagnetic field, even though what we see changes from moment to moment, there are substantial similarities in motivations and movements, in actions and reactions within the field that can be observed over a long period of time. The field itself may not be visible, but the resultant patterns are clear.

Our exploration will begin with the modern Balkan music and dance scene in the United States, my point of entrance into the world of the book's subject. Chapter 1 offers an introduction to the Balkanites and their world and begins to answer some of the questions that haunted me after leaving the Golden Festival that cold winter night in New York.

PART I

Ethnography of the Balkan Music and Dance Scene

1

The "Balkanites"

What is the Balkan music and dance scene? Who are the Balkanites? What do they do and where do they do it? We begin to approach an ethnography of the scene through a look at the summer camps that are so central to its vitality. A demographic description of the campers—who they are, where they live and work, what they do in the scene and how they found it—is followed by more personal accounts of the scene's role in their lives; their enchantment with "the Balkans" and their people; their relationships to the scene, its repertoire and practices, and to each other.

Locating the Balkan Scene

The Balkan music and dance scene in the United States can be viewed in the context of many similar specialized affinity groups with a particular music and/or dance repertoire at their center. I employ the term "scene" mostly for lack of a better word to describe such a network of people, locations, and activity, but also because the term is used by participants. Throughout the country people are finding alternative artistic and social homes built around a common interest in Irish, Scandinavian, American Old Time, Middle Eastern, Klezmer, Tuvan, and many other traditions.[1] These American affinity groups have much in common, though each has unique features, including repertoire. Locating and situating these scenes is often more complex than is usually the case in traditional studies of local music, due to the often ephemeral nature of scene "membership" and the multiple geographic and virtual locations in which scenes develop and live. The places and faces of most importance to insiders are largely irrelevant and unknown even to people living right next door. Even participants' friends, coworkers, and family members are often oblivious to their involvement in such a scene. Yet, by many, this private identity is held more dearly than their more public identities. An American Balkan music enthusiast might be a computer scientist or a physicist to most of the people he/she

knows, but for friends in the scene it might be hard to imagine what else this person does beyond playing tapan or tuba or singing Rhodope songs.

The Balkan scene is enacted on multiple fronts, including regular participatory music and dance classes and events, band rehearsals, public concerts and recording sessions, annual weeklong camps, weekend retreats, websites and chat rooms, newsletters and other publications, individual and group travel to the Balkans, concert promotion and sponsorship of touring Balkan musicians, and more cloistered activities such as practicing, listening to recordings, and collecting related memorabilia. Scene participants also have opportunities to follow their interest in a host of what might be called "extracurricular" activities, including the use of Balkan folk materials in contexts that are not explicitly "Balkan": folk festivals, jam sessions, choirs, and, indeed, academic research and publication.

Balkan music and dance repertoire figure with some prominence in a number of spheres partly or wholly outside the Balkan scene, most notably the international folk dance scene, discussed in chapters 5 through 7. Other notable examples include Balkan genres and influences embraced by many composers, choir directors, jazz, rock, and folk groups who use this repertoire to color their music expression. Choral groups, sometimes referred to as "world choirs," often incorporate folk song arrangements by socialist era composer/presenters from the Balkans, most notably the Lado and Kutev ensembles. While this is "Balkan music," performed by Americans the songs are treated much as any other sheet music with no special social fabric developing around it, other than that common to choirs. Like the jazz and rock groups, the choirs are clearly part of rather different musical and social circles, marked by networks, attitudes, goals, and esthetics not shared by the Balkanites. Instead of adding Balkan music to their own musical language, the Balkanites construct a large part of their musical and social lives around it. Instead of coloring their music expression they build a paint factory.

The location and activities of the American Balkan scene are distinct, not only from these related American practices, but from the Balkan music and dance scenes in England, Germany, and Japan. In Germany, for example, scene activities are mostly limited to recreational folk dance in which most groups dance to recorded music. In recent years there has been a fashion among German rock, folk, and jazz groups to borrow from various East European musical forms, but primarily within the bounds of their own respective scenes. In England, the preexisting strong choral tradition formed a seed bed for the development of a specifically Balkan scene, more closely tied to various "world choirs" that embrace Balkan vocal repertoire alongside Georgian polyphony, South African freedom songs, and other "world" genres. And in Japan the scene is comprised of many separate "schools" with students' sense of belonging tied more closely to a particular teacher than to shared repertoire, apparently expressing a tendency in Japanese cultural tradition. There the music and Balkan dance are doubly imported. Japanese participants tend to view their activity as, in part, an expression of Americaness, as the tradition came to Japan via the United States.[2]

The size of the Balkan scene is difficult to estimate and varies greatly depending on how the scene is defined. Yves Moreau (1990: 114), a tremendously popular teacher of Balkan dance, estimated that, in 1990, well over 100,000 people participated in Balkan music and dance in the United States alone. Moreau's longstanding experience throughout North America makes his claim quite believable. However, this figure includes all who "take part" in Balkan music and dance, including those introduced to Balkan repertoire as a part of international folk dancing. The group devoted solely or primarily to Balkan repertoire is considerably smaller, and, of these, the group actively involved in the Balkan scene may be only a few thousand strong. According to Rachel MacFarlane, the EEFC has about three thousand names on their current mailing list and about six thousand on a secondary list. Of these, about five hundred people attend the annual camp. On the other hand, none of these estimations include the thousands of people on the fringe who became aware of Balkan repertoire while being part of other music scenes or none at all.

Surveying the Scene

Uses and occurrences of Balkan expressive forms outside of immigrant communities are often interesting, but my focus on the Balkan music and dance scene per se led me to devote my attention to the group of people at the very heart of it, most of whom attend Balkan music and dance workshops and annual camps. From my very first encounter with the scene I was interested in answering the most common ethnographic questions, "who, what, when, where, how," but more interested in the less common question, "why?" These issues may never be clearly or entirely separated from each other, since answers to "who" and "what" often contribute to an understanding of "how" and "why," for example. However, while such separations are somewhat artificial they are generally employed here in the interest of clarity.

My first real experience of immersion in the Balkanites' world was the 1993 Balkan camp at Buffalo Gap, which I approached with an almost childlike curiosity about the classes, teachers, staff, repertoires, parties, and, most of all, participants. I came away with a clear sense that, without getting into the tremendous range of individual personalities and perspectives, there is a high degree of uniformity among the campers. I perceived the participants as members of a clearly defined subcultural group sharing similar ethnic and educational backgrounds, values, attitudes, and lifestyles. Two years later, at the 1995 camp in Ramblewood, Maryland, I conducted a survey (see the appendix for the questionnaire sample) in an attempt to provide multiple perspectives and answers to the basic ethnographic questions.[3]

In designing the questionnaire, I avoided questions with multiple-choice answers, unless the possible categories were clearly defined. This approach created difficulties in processing the acquired data but also enabled

unexpected categories to be created. Some questions were included on the list to allow certain patterns to emerge. For example, I wanted to find out if there were particular recordings of Balkan music or particular teachers that the majority of the sample population clearly favored (see questions 19 and 20 in the appendix). In both cases, such a variety of answers was provided that no single dominant category emerged. On the other hand, the question, "when and where did you get introduced to Balkan music/dance for the first time?" resulted in a few clear groups of answers.

Two other surveys of Balkan music and dance lovers were conducted prior to my study. The first is Yves Moreau's 1985 mail survey of three hundred respondents from the United States and Canada, as well as twelve other countries. Some of the results of his survey are published (Moreau 1990), and this data was used for comparison where applicable. The second is Melissa Miller's survey conducted at the 1994 Balkan Music and Dance Camp in Mendocino, California, with 121 respondents. The results of her research are in an unpublished paper called "Who Are These People, and Why Are They Here?" written for an M.A. degree course in counseling psychology at Santa Clara University. Both researchers had particular interests in conducting the surveys and used different methodologies to acquire the data. Nevertheless, it is often useful to compare the data derived from different samples and through different methodologies.

As an analytical tool, statistical information has been useful to my research, though I am wary of the perceived scientific value attached to numbers and graphs. In an attempt to minimize the effects of reducing people to figures, I have interspersed analysis of the statistical information with personal accounts given in interviews and Internet discussions. The results of the questionnaire are, however, very much in keeping with observations I made in the course of participation and interviews. To provide a clearer understanding of who the Balkanites are, I will begin by discussing the ethnic background, education, gender, age, occupation, and living environment of the respondents.

Profile of the Villagers

Ethnic Background My curiosity about the ethnic background of Balkan music and dance lovers was piqued by my first encounter with them. By the time I conducted my survey I had a pretty clear idea of the ethnic makeup of camp participants. Still, I opted not to provide multiple-choice answers to this question but to leave respondents free to choose the specific method and vocabulary that suited them the best. Four broad categories of ethnic background emerged from the responses, WASP (39 percent), Central and West European (22 percent), Jewish (21 percent), and East European (16 percent). Given the very specific mixtures of ethnic backgrounds that most individuals reported, I needed to create categories that would accommodate this diversity. In some cases, a person is classified under a specific category according to their predominant ethnicity, and quarters or eighths of their ethnic heritage are not taken into consideration.

With the exception of one Asian-American person, all respondents are white and most of them (61 percent) are of a mixed Central and Western European ancestry. Within this group I have distinguished between those who gave detailed descriptions of the specific mixtures of Central and Western European ethnic background and those who have either directly identified themselves as WASPs or who have described their ethnic background as a mixture of English, Scottish, Irish, and/or Welsh. Among the group labeled "East European," most are of Russian, Polish, or Ukrainian descent. A large percentage of the overall sample (21 percent) identified themselves as Jewish, including both Central and Eastern European Jewish backgrounds. It is also likely that there is overlap between the Jewish and East European category. While some people specified whether they were of East European Jewish, West European Jewish, or various mixtures of East European (non-Jewish) ancestry, many stated their ethnic background to be simply Jewish or East European. For that reason, I have retained the two separate categories. Interestingly enough, among the people I have interviewed, a substantially larger percent (41 percent) was Jewish.[4] Only 2 percent of the whole sample is of "Balkan" origin. Only two people (2 percent) did not fit into one of the above categories, one of them being Turkish and another of Japanese and Chinese descent.

Yves Moreau found 32 percent of his sample to have some East European background (mainly Russian or Polish), 15 percent declared themselves to be Anglo-Saxon, and 25 percent described themselves as "WASPs" or "mutts." Only one third (11 percent) of the group with some East European background identified themselves as Jewish. My opinion is that since Moreau's respondents are not only from the United States but also from Canada and from twelve other countries, his data differs considerably from my findings.[5]

Clearly, involvement in Balkan music and dance is, for 98 percent of my respondents, not tied to their ethnic heritage. However, their perception of their ethnic background, or lack of an ethnic background, is an important factor in their choice of this "adopted ethnicity." In my early interviews I asked people about their ethnic background mostly as a matter of interview routine, interested in seeing if it was related to their music and dance interest. Very early on in the interview process I began to notice people's discomfort, even guilt, about the "plainness" of their background. This was particularly noticeable among people who identified themselves as "WASPs," "mutts," "pure Americans," or "of mixed European origin." Representative responses to the question, "What is your ethnic background?" were:

[I'm] really not anything . . . in terms of ethnic anything.

I am not ethnic.

I have no particular ethnic background.

I am a pure lily-white American.

I am just an American.

I am basically a WASP.

These remarks were sometimes accompanied by anecdotes from school days about envying fellow students who could brag about their exotic and colorful ethnic backgrounds. A few people testified that they would even make up a part of their ethnic heritage so that they could "look more interesting."[6]

While some people were apologetic, others laughed at the "purity" or "plainness" of their ethnic background and were often amused that they were involved in music and dance of a region they were not connected to through heritage. Some gave me a dissection of the quarters, eighths, or even sixteenths of their ethnic background on both their mother's and father's side, both to identify themselves accurately and to get to that segment of their ethnic background that stood out. Often, people would focus on the most unusual, distant, or colorful aspect of their ethnic background with replies such as:

I have some Hungarian blood.

I am one quarter Polish.

My great grandfather was from the Ukraine.

Bob, who is one quarter Greek, explained, "Because I was not raised Greek American at all, it was something for me to be curious about. I liked the Greek part of the family. That part of the family stands out; the family was really strong, they knew who they were. . . ."

This feeling appears to be very common for white, middle-class Americans. While looking at the replies people gave for the US Census on their ethnic background, Mary Waters (1990) observed that people not only change the ethnic group with which they identify from one census to another, but that they pick, not the most dominant, but the most interesting/unusual of the possible choices. In her book "Ethnic Options," Waters points out that "having an ethnic identity is something that makes you both special and simultaneously part of a community. . . . And it allows you to express your individuality in a way that does not make you stand out as in any way different from all kinds of other people" (1990: 152). This feeling of being washed out in the vast uniformity of white American society is, to a degree, related to people's choice of Balkan music and dance and is, for some, an important factor in their involvement.

Gender Of the 81 respondents in my sample, 51 (63 percent) were female. In Melissa Miller's survey (Miller 1994) of 121 campers, 80 were women. The percentages were 66 percent women and 34 percent men, which is quite close to the male/female ratio in my sample. More in keeping with the general population, 51percent of the 300 people who responded to Moreau's 1985 questionnaire were women.

Age People between the ages of forty and forty-nine comprised 52 percent of the group. The second largest group (25 percent) consisted of people

between the ages of thirty and thirty-nine. Male respondents were generally older than female ones.[7] The average age of the campers was forty-two (forty-one for women and forty-five for men). Nobody younger than twenty-three responded to the questionnaire, and only one respondent, a sixty-four-year-old man, was older than sixty. While most of the people in their twenties were in their late twenties, those older than fifty were, in most cases, in their early fifties.

At the time when my survey was conducted, the general perception among longtime campers was that the "camp population" was growing older. While keeping in mind the sample variability, the results of Moreau's research support this perception. The average age of Moreau's sample was thirty-six (Moreau 1990: 115).[8] Considering that his research was conducted ten years prior to mine, it is possible that the average age of the campers has indeed increased over the years with a smaller influx of newcomers and the aging of the group membership. The average age of the Balkan folk dancer was quite probably much lower in the 1960s and 1970s, when this activity was particularly popular and widespread among college students. However, in the years since my initial research a growing influx of younger newcomers, as well as attendance by the children of longtime campers, may well be bringing the average down again.

Living Environment A large majority (94 percent) of respondents were raised in, and still lived in, an urbanized area, including cities, suburbs, and small towns.[9] Only 6 percent lived in a rural area. The majority of the "small towns" were identified as "university/college towns." Of the scene members I have met who do live in remote or rural locations, most have moved to these locations from urbanized areas for many of the same reasons they sought the Balkan scene. Beyond music and dance practice in the home, the maintenance of their ties to the scene relies heavily on remote communication and traveling to be with other Balkanites.

Education The educational level of campers in the sample group is extremely high. Only 3 percent reported high school as the highest level of education, while the highest level of education for 44 percent was a bachelor's degree, for 30 percent a master's degree, and for 23 percent a doctoral degree. A remarkable 43 percent of the men reported having doctoral degrees.[10]

To show how exceptional these figures are, I compare them in the graphs below with statistics for the average urban population of the United States, since the majority of the people who responded to this questionnaire live in urban/suburban areas. The comparative data was taken from Table 17, "School Enrollment and Educational Attainment: 1990," of the U.S. 1990 Census of Population, Social and Economic Characteristics. The data was calculated from the portion of Table 17 with the heading "Educational Attainment for Persons 25 Years and Over Living in an Urban Area," a category to which the vast majority of the campers belong. We can see that the higher the degree, the greater the difference between the camp sample and the U.S. urban population sample (graphs 1.1–1.3.)

Graph 1.1 Educational Level: Camp vs. General Population

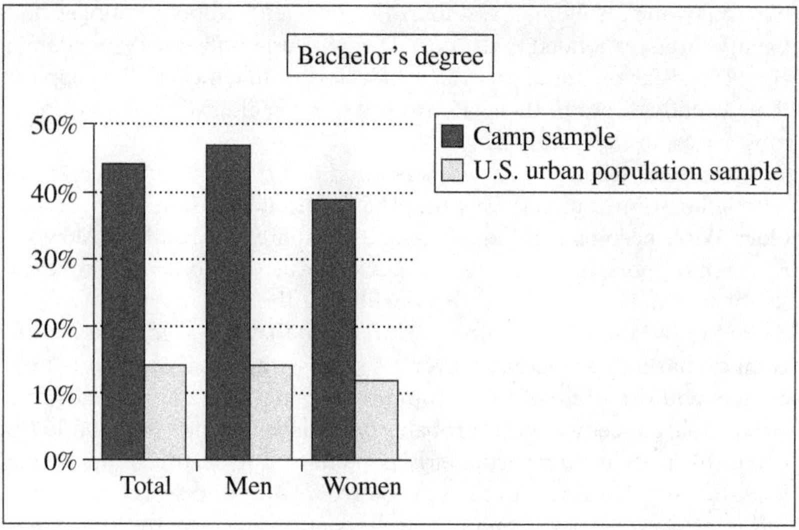

Graph 1.2 Educational Level: Camp vs. General Population

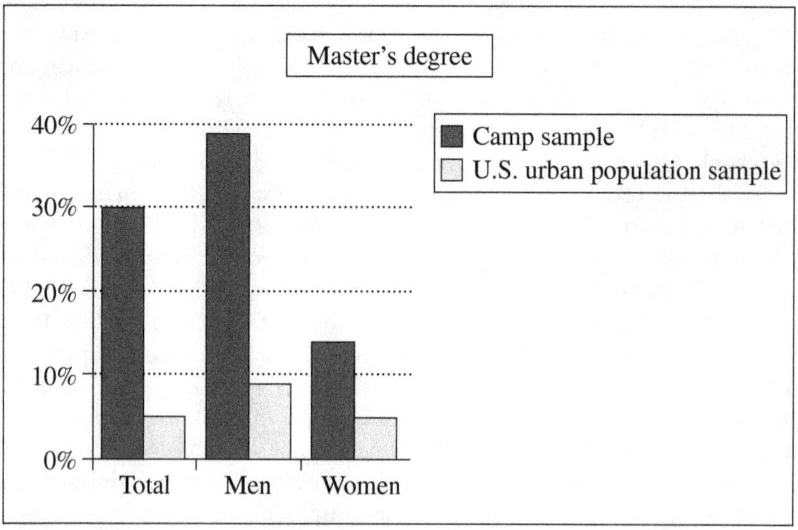

Graph 1.3 Educational Level: Camp vs. General Population

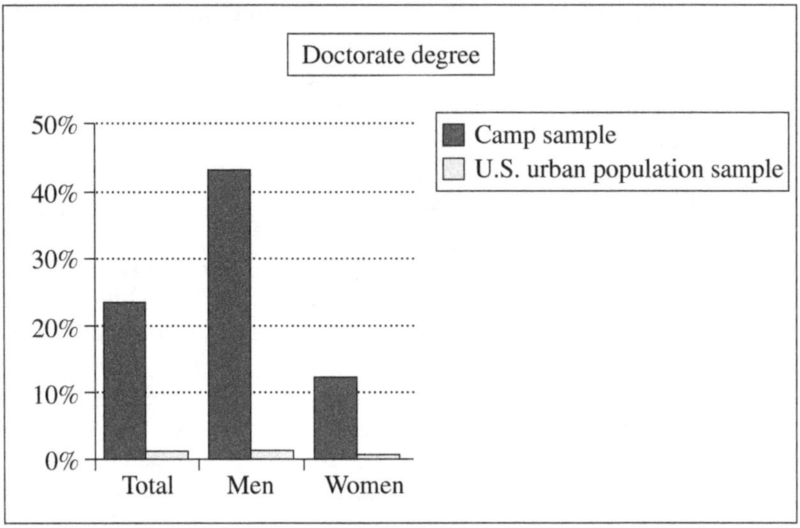

Occupation Although the questionnaire included an open space for response rather than a list of choices, the range of occupations given was extremely narrow. The largest percentage (28 percent) stated science/engineering/ computers as their occupation. While this is the largest occupational category for men (43 percent), for women (28 percent) it was education, including college, high school, and grade school teaching. The next largest category overall was administration/management (17 percent) and medicine/therapy (total 12 percent). The category "other" included students, lawyers, an insurance agent, editor, typesetter, and court stenographer.

Not a single person reported employment in manufacturing, transportation, trade, or unskilled labor.[11] This uniformity of vocations among the campers also demanded a comparison with the general United States population sample. I have chosen the most similar sample for comparison, "employed white persons in an urban area." The actual percentage of the population was calculated on the basis of data provided in the U.S. 1990 Census, Table 81, "Occupation of Employed White Persons: 1990," for the "total urban area."

The differences are the largest in the science/engineering/ computers category, nearly nine times that of the national average for the comparable sample group. There was also an exceptionally high percentage of educators in the camp sample in comparison with the United States urban white population, nearly five times that of the national average, and there were about three times as many people in the area of medicine/therapy. Only within the administration/management category did the camp sample approximate the general white urban population.

Altogether, we can conclude that Balkan music and dance lovers come from a very specific segment of American society: they are mostly white,

urban, highly educated, professional people, among whom the highest percentage is employed as scientists/engineers/computer specialists or as educators. I have found it puzzling that people from such a specific background, even in their occupations, would be drawn to the scene. I suspect it may be related to what many Balkanites self-effacingly refer to as their own "nerdiness." It may not be coincidental that, as in much work in the sciences and various traditionally "nerdy" interests like Star Trek and Renaissance fairs, in the Balkan scene there are lots of facts to be sorted and ample opportunity for the exercise of imagination and curiosity.

"As I was walking down the hall one day. . . ." Beyond getting a sense of who the campers were and where they were coming from, I was interested in knowing how they got there—how they were first exposed to Balkan music and dance. For 37 percent of respondents it was through an international folk dance (IFD) group that included Balkan dances in its repertoire. For a number of reasons these circle dances were often group favorites and, when circumstances allowed, a number of IFD participants devoted themselves solely to the Balkan repertoire. Folk dance clubs, whether IFD or specifically Balkan, have long been widespread throughout the United States, particularly on college campuses. At the height of the IFD movement there was hardly a college in the United States that did not have a folk dance group, and, as some 97 percent of respondents are college graduates, it is not surprising that this was the location of many people's first exposure.

While folk dancing was part of grade-school gym class for many of the current Balkan music and dance lovers, only a few (5 percent) recall learning Balkan dances at that time. Several people explained to me in the interviews that they found folk dancing in grade school uninteresting and could not remember at all what kind of dances were taught. Even those who do remember enjoying folk dancing in grade school do not consider it their own choice of recreational activity and did not consider folk dancing an important part of their lives until they devoted themselves to it during college. However, some people found that the initial exposure to international folk dancing in grade school was important in developing their curiosity about other cultures. People like Melissa see their involvement in folk dancing as a continuum, "from the P.E. classes in elementary school, through Girl Scouts, high school P.E. classes and university folk dance club, to recreational folk dancing."

There is a substantial percentage of respondents whose first exposure to Balkan folk dance was through their folk-dancing parents. The activity has, in some cases, carried over three generations, creating a category of people (15 percent of respondents) who can claim their involvement in Balkan music and dance as part of their family tradition. One of the appeals of folk dancing was that it was "a clean, good activity," as one parent said, "where we could bring our children and do something together as a family."

A very small percentage of the sample (4 percent) were initially exposed to Balkan music through recordings; these tended to be musicians who

decided to learn a Balkan song or a musical style after hearing a recording. This is interesting, considering that most Americans, if they are at all aware of Balkan music, know it through recordings, especially those of the Bulgarian Women's Radio Choir or, less commonly, those of Ivo Papasov, and more recently from broadcasts of "Riverdance" or the soundtrack to the television series "Xena: Warrior Princess," both of which include snippets of Bulgarian music. Recordings of Balkan music were, however, the main factor in drawing many people from the general IFD repertoire to Balkan music and dance.

In my interviews, most first-encounter stories are strikingly similar. For all it is a memorable moment, and even several decades later people remember how the room looked, what they wore that night, even what tune was playing when they first walked in. It is not only the nature of people's first encounters but the particularities of how they spoke of them that fascinate me:

> MARY I walked by this folk dance group at the University of Minnesota and I started dancing every day of the week. It changed my life forever.
>
> MARK One evening I was walking through the student union at the University of Chicago. I looked into this room and people were folk dancing. I did not even know what it was but just thought it was the neatest thing. So, I just became completely obsessed with it, I mean, I danced every night.
>
> RACHEL The very first week there [University of Kansas] I saw a sign up for folk dancing in a dorm. . . . The very first week I went. I was completely hooked. I began folk dancing once a week then twice a week.
>
> CAROL I was just walking down the hall one day when I was a freshman. . . . I heard this music coming out of the room and all these people were dancing in circles. . . . So I decided to come back. I got totally hooked, addicted. I used to go folk dancing every night of the week.
>
> STEVE I remember the first time I went folk dancing. It was a magical moment. It was magic for me. It was at Stanford University, dancing outside. Two girlfriends of mine for some reason dragged me there. I loved it.
>
> LOUIS I remember quite distinctly. I was a freshman in college, University of California, Santa Barbara. . . . There was this little building there and these people were dancing inside, and I kind of stood in the door and watched and they came out and were welcoming and said please come in and join us, and one year later I was teaching the group in the presidential club.

Clearly, stumbling upon a folk dance class was a formative moment in many people's lives. Though first encounters were often serendipitous,

people's attraction to the activity and the urge to keep doing it were usually immediate. This serendipity will be discussed in greater detail in chapter 2, but for the moment suffice it to say that many campers remember their first encounter with Balkan music and dance as an important first step on the path to the "village."

Balkan Camp—An Overview

Throughout the United States, redwoods and pinewoods, lakefronts and riverfronts, hills and valleys ring with strange sounds and shake in unusual rhythms under dancers' feet, but the magic created in these tucked-away places goes largely unnoticed even by locals and passersby. Along with Hungarian, Scandinavian, Klezmer, Middle Eastern, Scottish, Irish and many other camps, Balkan camp is part of a larger phenomenon in contemporary American culture. There are many similarities among various music and dance scenes, not least of them being the organization of an annual music/dance camp. Shared repertoires provide scene members with a common vocabulary and set of references, and each repertoire is tied to values, ideologies, and practices developed over time in individual scenes and their interaction with popular culture in the United States and relevant places abroad. Some of these specifics are developed in relationship to the given repertoire. For example, the Irish music scene might draw more violin, accordion, or flute players who are looking for a different repertoire. Some of the Balkan repertoire taught at camps facilitates bonding among the group members; most Balkan dances are line or circle dances that do not require partners, and group music-making is of particular importance. Many extra-musical factors play a role in the configuration of the scene as well, as the following sections most clearly show.[12]

Despite the relatively small numbers in attendance, camps are at the heart of the Balkan scene. Their importance is felt in a ripple effect reaching and influencing local practice across the country, and even reaching into American culture at large through public performances, written material and other forms of outreach. Attended by many of the most active and influential scene participants, the camps are a microcosm of the trends, ideology, music, and practices in the scene nationwide. They serve as the center of the Balkanites' "village," in which "elders" gather to exchange news and impart knowledge, children watch and learn, and scene culture is perpetuated. What follows is a recollection of first impressions and details of the first camp I attended, as well as a discussion of Balkan camps in general.

Not long after I stumbled upon Zlatne Uste's Golden Festival in New York City, I was asked to teach Bosnian singing at the 1993 Balkan Camp in Buffalo Gap, West Virginia, run by the EEFC. When I arrived on a hot and sticky July afternoon it was almost time for the full staff meeting. A few of us teachers were new to the scene, but most were seasoned campers. The air was so thick with anticipation you could have sliced it with a knife. There was considerable commotion, with people setting up tents or

moving into their assigned cabins. They all carried suitcases but also lugged instruments and tapestries, tables, coffee sets, and other Balkan decorative ephemera. There were screams of joy, even ululation and occasional tears on campers' faces as they ran to greet friends they might not have seen since their last time at camp. Although the camp had not officially begun, the staff meeting was accompanied by background music provided by campers dusting off their *gudulkas*, *gaidas*, and *tamburicas*. Music came from every direction, saturating the soundscape and giving a sneak preview of the week ahead. This was the unique soundtrack to which I was to fall asleep and wake up every day I was there **(CD 1)**.

Nearly thirty teachers were gathered that year to provide instrumental, vocal, and dance classes throughout each day to more than two hundred campers with an insatiable appetite for learning Balkan music and dance. Vocal instruction was offered in Bulgarian, Macedonian, Romany, Bosnian, Turkish, and Greek traditions. In most cases the repertoire consisted of traditional rural songs, although urban folk songs as well as folkloric arrangements of traditional songs were also taught. Instrumental instruction ranged from accordion, clarinet, and violin to classes in *kaval*, gaida, gudulka, tapan, *dumbek*, *santuri*, *tambura*, and tamburica. Campers could also join one of many ensembles: a Serbian brass band, a Croatian Tamburica ensemble, a Bulgarian Bitov, Greek, Romany, or Trans-Carpathian ensembles. There was a place for those who played "traditional" Western instruments, as well as for those who wanted to learn one of the "traditional" Balkan instruments. Many loaner instruments were provided for those who sought to try them out for the duration of the camp.

It is hard to describe the intensity of a typical camp day to the uninitiated. Some campers took classes during each of the five daily slots, breaking only for meals. There being an average of about five classes to choose from during each time slot, one can understand the anguish campers felt trying to choose what to do. No matter how packed one's schedule, there was always a sense that one was missing something important. Lecture-demonstrations after dinner, interviews with new teachers, folklore talks, and informative video sessions about aspects of Balkan culture and lifestyle were all part of the program as well. Outside of scheduled instruction time, people practiced on their own or gathered to play in smaller groups. If they were not catching up on lost sleep during the hour after lunch they would most likely be doing music. It was not uncommon for people to burst into group song while waiting in line for food, at the beach, or even in the sauna. An impromptu music/dance event could happen any time of the day or night (figure 1.1).

While less experienced musicians could get together to practice and go over material they had learned in class, the more experienced musicians could explore, experiment, and improvise with each other. A number of musicians felt so comfortable with their chosen musical language that they could fluently "converse" with each other. I was amazed by the sheer number and variety of dances many campers knew. As soon as a tune was started, regardless of its origin, a line of dancers would form and begin the appropriate steps.

Figure 1.1. Dancing on the table, Mendocino, 1995

Dispersed during the daily classes, the campers all came together at dance parties each evening.[13] Live music for dancing was usually presented in three performance blocks: two organized by teaching staff and, sandwiched in between, one by students who wanted to share their accomplishments. Regardless of who provided the music, dance lines started winding throughout the hall from the moment the music began and continued until the last musician called it a night. This was a great opportunity for new students to try out newly acquired dance patterns. While at the same time they could be seen counting steps and struggling to stay afloat, more experienced dancers would set the pace, gently guiding everybody through the dance. All were undeterred by even the most stifling West Virginia heat and humidity. Holding hands, looking and smiling at each other across the dance floor, and occasionally singing along, the dancers would form large circles that moved counterclockwise around the dance hall (figure 1.2). More popular dances would have several concentric circles or lines winding throughout the dance floor. Being part of such a large dance event can be a mesmerizing experience for both novice and expert alike. As the dance party would come to a close, a smaller, more intimate party would be well underway in what is known as the *kafana*. People enjoy music "Balkan style" there, with food from the grill, Turkish coffee, and drinks. Parties in the kafana often went on until dawn, and as the week progressed fewer and fewer campers were able to get up in time for breakfast.

The camp week had a rhythm of its own, with campers growing not only tired but also closer to each other. The week culminated on the final day with a parade, student concert, lamb roast, and farewell party. A

Figure 1.2. Evening dance party with Steve Kotansky leading the dance, Mendocino, 1997

student concert gave campers a chance to share their accomplishments with each other, each class having an allotted time to perform their repertoire (figures 1.3 and 1.4). Excerpts from a student concert **(DVD 2)** illustrate just a few of the instruments and genres featured one year at one camp (Mendocino 1995).

In the years since my camp initiation I have attended a number of Balkan camps on both coasts, and in many respects the 1993 camp can be considered typical. Still, each Balkan camp has its own unique flavor. There are always "new" trends, hot bands, reliable "classics," old and new teachers offering more exotic or familiar material; there are different proportions of experienced campers and newcomers, different highlights, events, and memories, sometimes different amenities and camp settings. From camp to camp "Balkan" is also defined somewhat differently, sometimes to include Eastern or Central European countries, Klezmer, Turkish and Near Eastern music. Despite these differences, a Balkan camp is still unmistakably a Balkan camp.

Camp as a Learning Center

Like other specialty scenes with their annual summer camps, Balkan camps provide for alternative musical and dance training. While retaining aspects of the formalized instruction native to the Western educational system, camps also incorporate some of the principles native to the tradition of choice. Thus, on the one hand, students still have scheduled classes in

Figure 1.3. Gudulka students in concert, Mendocino, 1997

which they receive step-by-step instructions from a teacher. According to their skill and experience, they are separated into beginning, intermediate, and advanced groups.

Students are expected to make progress during the camp and share their new acquired skills at the end of the camp. Many, accustomed to visual learning, demand transcriptions and charts. On the other hand, learning music by ear rather than from sheet music is a camp experience that many find exciting and new.[14] Many find the idea that they can carry their repertoire inside themselves appealing. Another aspect of this kind of training that participants find refreshing is its social dimension. As a large portion of the repertoire taught at camps is intended for group participation, people can socialize and dance/play/practice together, instead of experiencing "practice" as a lonely, alienating, or "anesthetic" activity.

As the first generation of Balkan campers began having children, they brought them along to camp. Many parents now bring their children along not only to recreational folk dance classes, but also to summer camps where they begin learning Balkan dances and singing or playing an instrument at an early age. For these children, Balkan materials comprise first steps in music and dance education (figure 1.5). In order to take care of the youngest attendees the EEFC started providing full-time instructors to lead children's activities **(DVD 3)**.

Unlike Western classical music, much music and dance in the Balkans is not reserved for the talented few. People of various levels of skill and experience often sing and dance together. This accessibility of music-making to all members of a community is very appealing to many Ameri-

Figure 1.4. Student concert program, Mendocino, 1995

cans who do not want to be "perfect," but to make music in a communal and friendly atmosphere. Specialty scenes and contexts like the Balkan camps provide alternatives to the competitiveness and exclusivity of most classical music education. As Melinda described it in our 1993 interview: "In American culture with Western classical music there is a kind of genius mentality, you are either high caliber, or you are nothing. This community and the band gave me a way to be a musician, gave me a path for expressing myself musically. It was interactive, interesting, challenging music."

Students at the Balkan camps are assured that, whatever their current level of ability, they can participate and enjoy music and dance, without being constantly judged and evaluated on the basis of their "achievement" and career potential. The Balkan music scene is intended, in part, as an oasis from the competitiveness, even cruelty, of the outside world. "The

Figure 1.5. Children at "Gypsy Night." For some children, Balkan music is an inherited option. Mendocino, 1997

scene is very protective, it lets everyone be a musician," Ruth explained (Interview, 1994). While in Balkan villages community members participate in music and dance according to their status, abilities, and desires, at the Balkan camps emphasis is placed on actively encouraging all individuals in their endeavor to learn. "At the end of the class somebody comes up with something they could not do before and we all cheer" (Martha, Interview, 1994). Mutual support between campers is both accepted and expected as a shared value.

While the supportiveness of the Balkan music scene can be highly motivating for some, it can also provide shelter for those who may be more interested in getting support than actually learning the music. Many teachers have noticed that there is a tendency among the students at the camp to be interested in learning new instruments, or new styles, since the initial steps in a learning process are usually the easiest to notice. There is visible and, in a way, measurable progress when a new musical language is first being explored. "There is the excitement of figuring things out. People want instant gratification. Once you get to a certain level you need to work really hard to improve" (Christos, Interview, 1994). It is perhaps due to this reason that only novices and the most devoted performers seem to specialize in a particular regional style (44 percent), while most prefer to study as many different styles as possible. A Bulgarian singing teacher commented on this pattern of exploration of different styles in the following manner:

> I am not pleased that they are doing different styles. I think they can never get one style to be only Thracian, or only Pirin, or only Macedonian. In the end you cannot see one singer and say: 'This is real Pirin, or real Thracian style. They are doing everything, they pay, they come here, they want to come to all these classes. And they are doing great. *I* could not do all these things. (Interview, 1995)

Similarly, there is an inclination to learn several instruments, sometimes all at the same camp. On the one hand new instruments are new territories of knowledge to conquer, and a lot of pleasure can be derived from the challenge. On the other hand, there are people who repeatedly take only beginner's steps, preferring to add to the number of instruments they "know."

Consumerism and a museum mentality are definitely evident in the Balkan music and dance scene. "There is a lot of that collecting mentality. Oh, that tune, I want it," Jane explained. One can collect tunes, step patterns, and musical instruments, just as one can collect folk costumes, or records. There is a strong desire to possess the "objects" of one's fascination. Sometimes people want to learn tunes from different regions of the Balkans so they can have "colorful" program notes for their concerts. Whether or not this collecting appetite is utilitarian, it is often insatiable. People are in the camps to learn *new* material. A lot of excitement is derived from the unfamiliar. And, in self-evaluation, quantity is easier to gauge than quality. Knowing many tunes, many instruments, and many dances marks progress and provides for a sense of authority in the "field." About 25 percent of the survey participants indicated that they studied five or more regional styles, often learning different instruments and/or vocal techniques along with different repertoires. Only 11 percent indicated they had chosen to stick with only one regional style.

Camp teachers have frequently noticed impatience with the learning process. Expectations of what it is possible to accomplish over the duration of the camp are often unrealistic. Here is an excerpt from a conversation between two music teachers:

> There are people in the camp that come with this attitude: "Teach me how to play this instrument in a week!"
>
> Not only that, but, "Teach me how to play like *you* in a week."

Although this is not true of all the campers, some share a belief that as "folk" music, Balkan music must be easy to play and sing, and that there must be a magic and direct way to become as good as their teachers. They want "instructions, they want a recipe to follow. They are more interested in getting instructions from you than a gist of it," one teacher commented. "People in the scene want to be spoon-fed. They do not want the process, they want the product. They short-circuit the learning process and the deep knowledge and the feeling that's attached to that process. They want instant

gratification. I feel it cheapens both them and the culture that they are supposedly representing" (Anonymous, Interview, 1994).

There are many manifestations of the belief that there must be a definitive way to achieve good results quickly and easily. Sometimes students ask teachers to "break the ornaments down," to explain the minutiae of the physical processes happening in a particular ornament. This is in part because they want to know what to do, but it is also partly a symptom of the belief that a logical and literal explanation of the music can substitute for hours of practice and years of listening. Some people resort to instruments that seem to be easy. Drumming classes, whether dumbek or tapan, are often the largest classes at camp since there is a widespread belief that drums are the easiest instruments to play. As a Bulgarian teacher pointed out to me, it is not that students simply want to do the easiest things, but that "they do not have time. They work really hard, but they do not have patience because they want to go back and teach it immediately, and all they have is a week."

Camp attendees have wide-ranging attitudes toward learning and interests to pursue while at camp. Most of the campers (79 percent of my sample) first became involved in the Balkan music and dance scene through dancing. Only 11 percent of the sample started as instrumentalists, and only 10 percent as singers. This is not surprising, considering that the whole scene sprang from dance. Almost everybody at camp takes part in dancing activities even if not partaking in class instructions per se. Dancing as a recreational and amateur group activity does not require the serious time commitment and individual effort that attempting to master a musical style demands. The Balkan music scene remains, to the present day, somewhat subordinate to the dance scene and is of a more recent date. Music performances are, in most cases, connected with dance parties, and music genres that accompany dancing are favored at camp. One of the great advantages of learning at a Balkan or other specialty camp is that students arrive already fascinated by the material, many having danced for years to the tunes they want to learn to play. Since the Balkan scene as a whole is self-sustained, musicians are also highly motivated to get to a level of proficiency that enables them to provide music for dance classes or parties in their local communities, which, as Matthew explained "creates such a high energy. You feed a lot off each other." There is a built-in audience, so to speak, readily awaiting new musicians.

Although most people begin with dance, they then broaden their activity from dancing to singing or playing. The majority in my sample (51 percent) were exploring all three activities at camp. The combination of dancing and playing an instrument is the second most common (19 percent), while singing is still the least widespread activity. I believe this is so for at least two reasons. First, most Balkan vocal genres are not intended for dance accompaniment and do not allow for the whole group to participate. Second, vocal technique is not as easily attainable; more time needs to be put into the basics before one can actually reproduce the sound in a satisfactory way, and it also involves a struggle with lyrics and pronunciation.

While, generally speaking, musicians tend to be much more committed to learning than dancers, people join the music scene with very different aspirations. For some, Balkan music is almost not a choice, and they feel they "simply have to do it." For others it provides more interesting and challenging musical material than, for example, their hometown brass band or church choir. Some find the very learning situation appealing, and are perhaps more interested in being engaged in a focused social activity than they are in the music material being taught. Yet others find that this music allows them to be amateur musicians.

> I did not have time for classical singing. . . . Classical singing if you want to do it well you really have to practice every day. Balkan singing, the voice placement is a lot closer to the natural speaking voice so you do not have to work on your voice placement every day. So, in that sense it fit into my life style a lot better. I can sing a couple of times a week and still be able to do something that satisfies me, instead of classical music where if you do not practice every day you do not sound good. (Melinda, Interview, 1993)

Many people have commented that Balkan music fits their lifestyles. It enables them to do music occasionally on an amateur basis without making them feel like amateurs. The structure of the Balkan scene, particularly the camps, provides direction for people who are inclined to be musicians but who are not comfortable with either the rigor of classical music or the lack of formal structure involved in pursuing most popular music genres. There are songs to decipher and directions to follow, much like in classical music training, but the characteristic shortness of the chosen Balkan repertoire and the unusual nature of the tunes, rhythms, and instruments make for concrete, bite-sized tasks that are found to be immediately interesting and pleasing. Students do not hear themselves so much as beginners as they might in Western classical music, nor are they constantly showered via radio by the "geniuses" of the tradition. "People don't start as musicians, but they want to be musicians," Ruth commented (Interview, 1994). "They embark on that task of 'becoming a musician,' and sometimes a real musician will come out."

Camp and "The Real World"

Balkan camp is sometimes "located" in an imagined Balkan village of yesteryear or some other oasis outside of daily life. The following section will explore relationships between camp and the everyday lives of campers.

> The truth of the matter is that the "village" is vanishing in America. But even as a memory, we choose not to lose some of the best parts of the village. That's why we have these villages we call camps. . . . I think that beyond our fun, some of us have a real intent to HONOR what the village stood for. We want more of the connection that was so taken

for granted at that time (in times of poverty, it was all they had, but it was enough to carry cultures on for centuries). (Jim, EEFC list, March 19, 1995)

This quote raises a number of interesting issues, but, most important, it contains an explicit statement of the often-implicit equation of the Balkan camp with the Balkan village. Whether someone has ever been in a village or not, one imagines that Balkan camp, like the Society for Creative Anachronisms, can enable one to experience "what village life was like." Along with their "back to the basics" lifestyle, camps provide a sense of community, closeness, interconnectedness, and intimacy, the basic values "honored" in this village. Many enjoy this experience of travel in time and space, while for some a more important aspect of camp is that it is a unique opportunity to experience music and dance as an integral part of their lives, for however short a time. Whatever the correspondence between the reality and the commonly held images of life in a Balkan village, life in the camp village expresses values many people feel are missing from their daily existence. For some who have traveled or lived in the Balkans, and experienced music and dance in true villages, camp is the only place where that experience can be approximated. "This camp was so special to me because it was the closest thing in the whole folk dance movement in the United States to the real Balkan experience, real village experience" (Joe, Interview, 1995).

Having once witnessed dancing in an actual Balkan village, many people have found it impossible to dance again at folk dance events back home. Similarly, after attending Balkan camp, many have begun to resent dancing to recorded music at their local folk dance club. On the EEFC list, people talk about "the post-camp syndrome" and "post-camp withdrawal." Mendocino was "fantastic," Betsy wrote to the EEFC list:

> I wish I could have gone without sleep all week—it seems like there was something going on literally 24 hours a day, every day. . . . But now comes the post-camp syndrome. I came home to Minnesota with my head filled with wonderful music and memories of dancing. Last night, I went to our weekly folk dance gathering, and there everyone was, dancing to the same tapes that we do every week, trying to do steps perfectly. I looked around and saw people just moving leg muscles or arm muscles, their faces seriously concentrating. There were few smiles, and little heart or soul.

Betsy's post generated a long and interesting Internet discussion that clearly emphasized the large divide between camps and everyday life. Generally speaking, once having experienced dance as more than just steps, and music as more than the notes, they could not go back to situations in which one is performing a set of tasks and executing the folk dance/music "material." These renditions became viewed as dry and soulless. At camps one could engage in "dancing, rather than just doing calisthenics to a

rhythm." As Bob explained, when the dance takes over half an hour "you start getting a feel for it, then energy starts building up and you get into this trance state where you become a part of a big thing that is moving together . . . you are part of something bigger than just doing steps" (Interview, 1994).

During the nightly camp parties, people have an opportunity to take their time in responding to the music and slide onto the dance floor when their mood and the moment coincide. The dance will carry on with or without them, which is not always the case at smaller local dances. The ability of live musicians to respond to the crowd makes it possible for a dance to last a long time, giving people time to warm up to the idea of dancing. Joining the dance becomes a social interaction rather than a simple exercise of newly acquired steps. "People appreciate the music for its own sake. People dance, not only to do a particular movement or routine, but because they enjoy being together" (Bob, EEFC list, July 15, 1995). It is impossible to recreate this feeling at home since at a recreational folk dance event people "will leave after the evening and return to dishes, kids, laundry, jobs—they can't stay out until the wee hours of the morning. Also, a camp provides sort of a comfortable nest that not only blocks out the rest of the world temporarily, but provides an intimacy that is difficult, if not impossible, to achieve in an evening." Except at camp, folk dancing occupies a space perceived as separate from "real life." Although folk dancing might be a part of one's daily routine, it is still a framed, scheduled activity. It is interesting that rather than imagining how this frame could be removed, people spend a lot of their energy trying to figure out how the framed content can be improved, so that in the allotted time period they can efficiently reach the peak experience.

Of course, the camps themselves are also a framed experience, often referred to as "another world" or "paradise." The following long excerpt from an e-mail post on the EEFC list foregrounds the "otherness" of the camp experience:

> What represents the high point, the acme, the utter pinnacle of what we love about this unreal world of folk-dancing that we all remember somehow and desperately yearn for? The only reason I want more dancers is because I can never forget the warm summer evening out on the Tressider deck at Stanford in the mid-1970s when 250 mostly young people would form endless spirals of unison dancing to exotic music in the moonlight. Yes, it's unreal. It's another world, more like the one I belong in. It's the feeling of the unity of the human spirit. It's the bottle of wine being passed around among the 15 dancers in an intimate shoulder-hold who stuck it out till the last strains of Yovano Yovanke. . . . It's the feverish swirling of a hundred circles of Krici Krici Ticek with live *prims* ringing out. It's the incredible energy of *zurnas* and *tupan* that inspire me to life. It's the living radio dial in the redwoods of Mendocino. It's the endorphins? Forget about tiny struggling folk-dance groups in a small room trying to get the old

bones moving around to match the fading rhythms of a 39th-generation tape of Godecki Cacak. I want my other world. I want my Balkan Camp!!!

While the above passage largely speaks for itself, I would like to emphasize the expressed segmentation of experience. Being at Balkan camp is, for most of its participants, an extraordinary experience, a marker of annual cycles. The accumulation of these time markers provides a sense of continuity, and even a sense of belonging to a particular place. Although the camp in Mendocino Woodlands, for example, is rented to the EEFC for a week's use, the annual return to the place gives to the campers a sense of permanence. Atilla (Group Interview, 1995) expresses this fleeting sense of continuity in the following words: "You see someone, and you say, 'Hi, weren't you here last year?' And the answer is, 'No, I haven't been here for eight years!' 'Oh, gosh, it seems as if I saw you yesterday!'"

The exclusion of the camp experience from the everyday lives of the campers makes them perceive the time lapse between the camps as nonexistent. Personal interactions with fellow campers, although often at least a calendar year apart, also appear to be continuous, as Melissa's statement shows: "These are friends that I have had for twenty-plus years. I see them for one week a year and I feel very close and intimate with those people. I see them one year and we talk: 'What's happening in your life? Blah, blah, blah . . . ' and the next year we pick up where we left off" (Interview, 1995).

Obviously these are alternative communities and friendships. But as Ruth pointed out to me, "I know from my own experience that there are people here who know each other for a long period of time; people marry each other, live together, eat together, play music together, and that's the most community that I've seen in this country. . . . My friends *are* from this music community." The camps are certainly specific social environments in which "there are strong bonds, because of the strong shared experiences among people," as Stewart explained, "and then there are memories; years of memories." Going to the Balkan camps is for some a tradition of several decades, and, as someone on the EEFC e-mail list once wrote, it is indeed a part of "American folklore."

Results of my questionnaire show that 27 percent of the sample had been to the camp five to nine times, and as many had attended more than ten times. Approximately as many (26 percent) had attended three to four times, and only 20 percent of the sample had been only once or twice. There is always an influx of new people to the camp, but most have attended, in this case, more than three times. The Balkanites' regular return to camp over a span of years contributes to the sense of community, family, belonging, and artistic accomplishment that many see as largely missing from their everyday lives, and these camp memories are cherished until the next year. As one musician told me, he would spend "six months preparing for the Balkan camp and six months savoring the last one." The camp time can be effectively compared to ritual time, both in terms of feeling that camp is something one "does" on a regular basis even though one has been

there only several times, as well as in terms of gearing up to it and experiencing it as a culmination of a long period of preparation, as in Carnival time. Although camp itself only lasts for a week, the timeframe expands in people's thinking to be commensurate with all their preparation, anticipation, and the far more than a week's worth of experience and significance camp holds.

The demographic of the Balkan camp has been shifting in the past several years, marking a new cycle in the history of Balkan music and dance in the United States. There seems to be a steady influx of newcomers to the scene who are finding it fresh and exciting. Musicians from various music scenes outside of the folk dance world are finding their way to the Balkan scene along with an increasing number of people who are from the Balkans or who have Balkan ancestry. Mark Levy (e-mail correspondence, October 27, 2004) points out that "the striking upsurge in camp attendance during the past few years . . . presents a puzzling contrast to the general decline in the folk dance movement throughout the U.S." I see in this new crop of younger participants a parallel with the first generation of Balkan camp enthusiasts. It is as if they found a kaleidoscope but managed to turn its end to find their own patterns, making the scene their own rather than participating as if they were visitors or had "joined the club." In this respect the Balkan scene distinguishes itself from a number of American folk scenes that seem to have shifted rather decisively from "tradition" to "orthodoxy"(Soloveitchik, in Kirshenblatt-Gimblett 2002: 136)—a situation that continues to turn young people away despite attempts to attract them. "A traditional society has been transformed into an orthodox one, when what was a matter of course (what was once absorbed and habitual) has become subject to rules, formal teaching, and scrupulous attention to textual authority." Talking about this tendency toward stringency, Soloveitchik points out that performance becomes "no longer, as in a traditional society, replication of what one has seen, but implementation of what one knows." While the Balkan scene is hardly free from manifestations of such a tendency toward orthodoxy, a number of factors contribute to a feeling that the scene is happening "as a matter of course." Not the least of these factors is the lively and inclusive tone set by the EEFC and its board, but I believe there are also attributes of culture and arts from the Balkans that resist, or might imply resistance, to such rigid formalism. While it can certainly be rendered in as stale a form as any other music and dance, its potential to foster intense experience, the value traditionally placed on wrenching emotion, communal enjoyment, and/or the production of sound and movement, may help make the scene more "hip and happening" than others.

Beyond Camp

When the sun rises after a final night of camp revelry, the "village" begins to dissolve like Brigadoon. The magical spot becomes, once again, a simple

campground, the kafana becomes a lounge, and the dance floor a picnic shelter. But the importance and influence of camp hardly ends there, as this village is as much a virtual as a geographic location. The Balkanites carry it with them in a number of ways, from a continuing sense of ritual time to ongoing contact with other campers and involvement in related activities also crucial in maintaining the scene.

The camp experience gives participants fuel to keep the metaphorical camp fires burning throughout the year. Beyond providing opportunities for learning, improving skills, and acquiring new repertoire, camps help create shared repertoires and help Balkanites connect with musicians from the Balkans and with each other. At camp, people from all over the country unite in an intense musical and social experience that enables them to recognize themselves as part of a larger whole. They leave camp eager to seek kindred spirits, and more likely to see kindred spirits in other scene members, even those they have never met. Perhaps the most lasting and wide-ranging impact of Balkan camp can be seen in the activities of local performing groups. If we imagine camp to be the queen bee, the performing groups can be viewed as the worker bees—indispensable in the life of the beehive, working diligently throughout the country for the rest of the year. Their activities include small concerts and dance events as well as larger annual day or evening long events that draw people from all over the country. Two of the largest of these are Zlatne Uste's Golden Festival in Manhattan **(DVD 4)** and the Boston Balkan Night **(DVD 5)**, both of which have become well established and much anticipated traditions.

Performing Groups

Although initiated or given added momentum at camp, much of the learning process takes place beyond its boundaries, in local groups and bands where individuals with similar interests and ability levels join forces in playing together. The formal instruction provided at the camps has not only brought up several generations of musicians, but generated literally hundreds of bands and performing groups throughout the country.[15] In this respect camps exert a tremendous influence on the public presentation and representation of Balkan music and dance in the United States. Performance groups with their origins in camp instruction reach the general public, bringing a significant number of "converts" to the scene and contributing to popular American perceptions of people, culture, and expressive forms from the Balkans.

The results of my questionnaire show that an incredibly high percentage (92 percent) of respondents are members of performing groups. The percentage of performers among campers is likely to be higher than what you would find in any local Balkan music and dance scene. However, performance is an important aspect of involvement in this scene in general, often stimulating research, acquisition of new recordings or new material, and attendance at camps, where new repertoire is learned. The largest group, 39 percent, had been performing between two and five years

(15 percent had been performing for one year, 21 percent between five and ten years, 11 percent between 11 and 15 years, 14 percent 16 or more years).

Most performers, 31 percent, perform only occasionally, one to five times a year, and 30 percent perform once a month. Only 13 percent perform weekly, and 6 percent biweekly. Although 67 percent receive pay for performing, for most people it is neither a career nor the main source of their income.

An important reason to start a performance group is to ensure regular playing. For most Balkanites, music is a hobby that happens after full-time work. Enthusiasm for rehearsing with local musicians tends to diminish in the months following camp, and people find it difficult to get together and play music informally with friends. Having scheduled gigs and concerts gives players the incentive to stick to a rehearsal schedule, to keep playing, practicing and refreshing their repertoire. Shortly after brass band Zlatne Uste's beginnings as a camp collaboration, founding member Michael Ginsburg realized the fledgling group's future was in question. "I phoned everyone . . . to let them know that we had a 'gig.' . . . The next week, everyone showed up for rehearsal" (Ginsburg 2001: 8).

Replies to questions about repertoire acquisition show a tremendous reliance on recorded sound, with 57 percent of respondents listing it as their primary source. The second large category is camp classes and workshops (the primary source for 33 percent of respondents) although, in most cases, people also learn from their tape recordings of these classes. Learning repertoire from sheet music or other musicians is much rarer; only 5 percent of respondents listed either as their primary source of repertoire. Often, people do not feel confident enough to rely on their memory and learn songs from their teachers. Although, almost without exception, people say that they record songs for reference to make sure they are "getting it right," most admit that once they learn a song and start performing it, they rarely turn back to their original tapes.

The desire to perform contributes to many people's involvement in Balkan music and dance. "It is not for money—there is more you are getting from performing than money. You want to perform because you want attention. You want to be in the center. You know, in high school everyone is trying to *play* guitar, but not everyone becomes a *guitarist* or a performer. In this scene everyone is a *guitarist*"(Anonymous, Interview, 1995).

When Balkan parties are organized, as a general rule all the performers are allotted equal time, regardless of how experienced or proficient they are. When I asked a teacher, himself a knowledgeable person and very good performer, whether he would make any comments or suggestions to a group that had given an obviously weak performance at a party, he replied: "No! This is not my place to judge and evaluate, this is my place to share!" Every person is seen to have a right to "express him/herself" and to be received uncritically with equal praise and encouragement. Such egalitarianism is an important factor in attracting new participants both to the scene and subsequently to performing groups.

Performing Balkan music can be considered a safe enterprise, even for beginners. The Balkan scene itself is not only noncompetitive, but people are, as a rule, encouraging and supportive of each other. The "outside" world is largely unfamiliar with the repertoire and styles, and audiences are usually fascinated by the newness of the sound, rhythms, harmonies, and instruments. "It is fun music, you get to play this weird stuff and people clap, and you make a cassette tape, you put your name on it, and people buy your tapes" (Anonymous, Interview, 1995).

There is a certain kind of easiness, almost a groove, leading from one's first attempts to play/sing Balkan music to the stage. Much of the performance takes place within the scene, but the Balkanites' imaginative use of this music and dance potentially loses its quality of innocence in the domain of public performance. Many groups give concerts or lecture demonstrations in schools, often unaware that they are not simply *presenting* their group's repertoire, but *representing* Balkan culture to people who know little, if anything, about it. While some groups are very conscientious about their role in cross-cultural representation, others are often unaware even of the possibility of misrepresentation, and when confronted with the issue, explain that "if it was not for [them] thousands of people would have never been exposed to Balkan music." Some use the term "raising awareness," seemingly unconscious of the fact that the audience's awareness cannot be raised any higher than that of the presenters. Some people even choose to perpetuate stereotypical views of particular Balkan cultures on the stage in order to cater to the preconceptions of their audiences.

A member of a well-known performing group explained to me that part of the reason for her group's focus on Balkan repertoire was the fact that, even if there were Balkan people in the audience, the group was not likely to be accused of misrepresentation, as would sometimes happen when they performed African songs. When there happened to be Balkan people in the audience, they found it "cute and charming that Americans are trying to do their songs. There is no political issue there. But when white women sing a freedom song, and they do not do it right, there will be someone angry backstage saying: 'What do you think you are doing?'"

> For many years the scene was self referential. It was easy for people's egos to get out of control. There was no one from the tradition for them to look at and say: "Gee, I don't sound like that." So, people put themselves up on a pedestal in the confines of their limited knowledge. One thing that people do not do in this scene, they do not defer. There is no deferral. Everyone wants to perform, everyone wants to be on stage and anything goes, it's a free for all. (Anonymous, Interview, 1994)

What is described above is a clash between an in-group value ("everyone can perform and be a musician regardless of knowledge and skill") and its consequences when applied outside of the affinity group. Several American teachers and performers have said, in one way or another, that this clash between egalitarianism and responsibility gets ironed out through

individuals' continued and deepening interaction with the music and the culture it stems from.

> I see a lot of down sides to the performance impulse, but the people who have done best as performers I respect as musicians and as people. . . . People who end up being good musicians almost inevitably get themselves tied to the ethnic communities or to learning about the cultures. There is a difference between being an accomplished musician and just staging things. (Anonymous, Interview, 1994)

It is usually the case that the more people know about Balkan cultures and people the more aware they are of the issues involved in their representation, and considerable educational efforts are being made by EEFC staff and others. Ultimately, of course, it is up to the individuals and their performing groups to decide how they want to deal with these issues.

Relationships with the Balkans

Balkan dance and music gradually becomes a much bigger presence in the lives of many participants after their initial fascination and involvement in learning it. "When this opportunity came along," Carolyn explained in our 1995 interview, "it widened my interest. I mean, there were the foods, the costumes, the culture, and then, of course, we started to travel." Members of our focus group are well traveled. Almost 60 percent of the sample have been to the Balkans (70 percent men and 50 percent women), with 53 percent of men and 33 percent of women having lived abroad for some time.

In part due to advertised folk festivals in Bulgaria and to the openness of the former Yugoslavia to American visitors, these two countries were the most frequently visited by respondents (former Yugoslavia, 37 percent, and Bulgaria, 35 percent).[16] This preference parallels the interests of the early teachers in the Balkan scene over Greek and Albanian music, for example, which were later arrivals on the scene.

A large number of Balkan music and dance lovers have repeatedly visited the Balkans, and some have lived there for an extended period of time. However, most visits were of a touristic nature, between one and three weeks long. Only 14 percent have spent over six months in the region.

Although 41 percent of the sample had not studied a Balkan language, 59 percent had devoted some effort to studying one or more of them. Bulgarian was studied by 29 percent, Serbo-Croatian by 13 percent, Macedonian 6 percent, Turkish 6 percent, and Greek 5 percent. These figures include all levels of proficiency, so, rather than showing the percentage of people who can speak one or more Balkan languages fluently, they show the percentage of people whose interest in Balkan dance and music has led them to try to learn and understand, to some degree, the language of their choice.

Travel is also a huge part of the scene. Focus on things Balkan, as I was once told, can rid you of difficult questions about where to go for a vacation.

> If you're going to have a hobby, it's interesting to have a hobby that reaches out and gathers things in. And so, now, if I do travel to Europe, or Eastern Europe, I know something already, I got a piece of the culture. I am going some place and seeing the roots of something that already fascinates me, and it puts me in contact and gives me knowledge about things exotic, things far away, things totally removed from what I do on a day to day basis. (Louis, Interview, 1995)

For some, the Balkans is an exotic place, different, and removed from daily life, but, in a way, closer to home than any other place on Earth. The "pilgrimage" is sometimes interpreted as an important "initiation rite" that brings the pilgrim in contact with the "sacred soil." It is sometimes thought that "if you've actually been there, then you are somehow better than everybody else in your club" (Melissa, Interview, 1995). The experience is anything but trivial: "I remember the first time I went to Macedonia, which was in 1971, and I was driving the car and I felt this intense need to get out of the car and cry, and kiss the ground. . . . And, don't ask me why!" (Steve, Interview, 1995).

Steve's experience is echoed in Nada's statement: "I remember when the plane was coming down, the plane from Beograd . . . to Skopje . . . Coming down in the plane, circling over the fields, I looked down, I saw the fields, and I burst into tears" (Interview, 1995). I have chosen the above quotes because they clearly, and sincerely, communicate the excitement and almost religious admiration for the land, the actual piece of earth that gave birth to the music and dance these individuals love. The Balkan region is indeed, to many, "sacred soil," to use a term coined by prominent dance teacher Dick Crum.

For musicians and dancers intrigued by any particular aspect of Balkan culture, the desire to go to the "source" is expressed in terms that are almost metaphysical, as being irresistible, outside of one's control. "Something just hit me in my soul and I thought 'I am going to go to Macedonia.' I just knew I had to go there!" This is how Sonia expressed her urge to go to Macedonia after falling in love with Macedonian *čalgija* music. Not only did Sonia go to Macedonia, but she lived there, intensively studying both the music and the culture and actively playing and performing with local musicians.

Traveling to the Balkans seems to be a natural step in the path of a Balkan music/dance lover. However, the reasons for traveling, as well as the impact these trips have had on individuals, differ widely from one person to another. While some are interested in finding what they expect and want to find, others are curious to find out what the place is really like. Perhaps these two attitudes are never as clearly divided as this, but different individuals travel with different expectations and, indeed, different "baggage." What people gain from their travel seems to depend less on the length of their stay or the regions they visit than on their mindset.

What many people expect is to be transported through a time machine into the past to a place where they can experience a "village at work." As

Bob explained in an interview in 1994: "You find a lot of people who have this idea about Greece and Bulgaria, like it is 'folk dance heaven.' And, they have their version of what they want Bulgaria to be. They would like Bulgaria to be this place where everyone goes to Sunday *horo*. Somebody was talking to me today and said, 'You know, I'm afraid it won't be that way?'" Of course, it is *not* that way, and one can either accept the fact that the reality of the Balkans is different from what the average Balkanite imagines, or one can try to find a place where "reality" matches one's imagination. Tours to big folk festivals, like that in Koprivštica, Bulgaria, are extremely popular among folk dancers. Going to a folk festival in a Balkan country enables one to "travel to actual destinations to experience virtual places" (Kirshenblatt-Gimblett 1995: 377). In the Balkan countries, folk festivals provide a representation of the "folk" that matches the image of "happy peasants, dancing in colorful folk costumes" that some American Balkan dance and music enthusiasts long to see. Because of their predictability, folk festivals ensure satisfactory experiences for folk dance tourists. There is certainty that one will meet the "peasant," hear "authentic folk music," and see "real dances" done in a joyous, celebratory environment. In this manner, one can get the desired enjoyment without wasting much time or experiencing the harshness of rural life (outhouses, cold water in the bathroom, and unheated bedrooms).[17]

While the Balkan region is a tourist destination for many, a number of people have found a second home there. Some have lived there for an extended period of time, fluently speaking the language and establishing deep and meaningful relationships with local people. After living for years in Bulgaria, and being married to a Bulgarian man, fluently speaking the language and knowing a great deal about the music and the culture, Lauren is treated, for example, as an insider. "She is ours," as Yuri Yunakov, a Bulgarian musician living in New York, would say.

There are, of course, significant differences between highly educated urban Americans and the Balkan "folk." Involvement in music and dance can sometimes lead to an exaggerated sense of connection and intimacy with a culture and people. When the Americans have little or no connection with people from the Balkans, this feeling of connectedness is mostly limited to the realm of imagination. Many people have realized that, although they love the music, many aspects of Balkan culture are alien to them. When Catherine, a member of Zlatne Uste Balkan Brass Band, went for the first time to the annual brass band festival in Guča, Serbia, she realized how separate her life was from life in the music's homeland. "Suddenly, I saw these people's lives that I have nothing in common with."

Serious problems are not likely to arise in encounters when cultural differences are acknowledged; it is only when real Balkan individuals are treated as idealized and depersonalized pastoral images and are not expected to respond, particularly not expected to demand, express their problems, values, needs, or their own understanding of the encounter. Dozens of Americans told me how disappointing it was to have a Balkan host or teacher ask them for the favor of writing a guarantee letter to the immigration office

so they could obtain a United States visa, or ask to be sent gifts from the States. Getting to know someone, establishing mutual trust and respect, takes time and effort. Involvement in music and dance does not automatically result in cross-cultural understanding, although it is often consciously or subconsciously assumed that there is commonality between members of the culture that created this material and members of the culture that appreciate it. I found that I, myself, was a victim of this belief, and was utterly shocked to discover that members of the Balkan scene could voice, not only intolerance and stereotyping, but even hatred and blatant racism toward particular Balkan people and ethnic groups.

This is not to suggest that most people are unwilling to bridge cultural differences. On the contrary, many have not only established meaningful friendships and contacts during their visits to the Balkans, or while hosting Balkan musicians in the United States, but have also become personally involved in various political campaigns, acted as representatives and spokespersons of minority groups, and perhaps most important, participated in the process of breaking down cultural stereotypes through education. Carol Silverman, Jane Sugarman, Lauren Brody, Eran Fraenkel, Mark Levy, Mark Forry, Sonia Seeman, Bob Beer, Tim Rice, to name only a few, are constantly contributing within the United States to a better understanding of the cultures and individuals whose music and dance they study and appreciate. In addition, several bands in the scene, including Ziyia and Zlatne Uste, are starting to be sought after by Greek Americans, Serbian Americans and others who need music for weddings and other ethnic community events.

In August of 2003 Zlatne Uste returned to Serbia to participate in the annual Sabor Trubača in Guča. It had been thirteen years since their last visit to the festival and four years since the NATO bombing of Serbia. When the band came up on the festival stage there was "an awkward and tense moment as catcalls and whistling (the Serbian form of booing) issue from the audience of thousands standing in the field below. Then, because of a shrewdly chosen playlist and excellent playing, by the second song the people's mood is transformed: singing at the top of their lungs to the popular song 'Djurdjevdan,' the crowd roars their approval. The band has rarely sounded better" [(MacFarlane, 2003–2004: 13); **DVD 6**]. It took not only courage, but also love, conviction, and skill for this group of foreigners, Americans at that, to stand in front of a sea of people and play local music. Michael Ginsburg commented, "For me, our performance was a turning point. All of the difficulties of being in Guca suddenly became trivial. . . . Zlatne Uste did not utter a word on stage. With only music, we were able to positively affect the feeling of a great number of people towards America and Americans, at least temporarily. It was a significant lesson in diplomacy. I do not know if anyone in the State Department took notice of what we had done, but they should have" (Ginsburg, in MacFarlane, 2003–2004: 13).

Such "lessons in diplomacy" are also given by musicians from the Balkans coming to the States, teaching at the camps, forging personal connections with the campers and educating them about the Balkans. As the years

unfold there are more and more native Balkan musicians in the camp from diverse regions and ethnic backgrounds enabling campers to fall in love all over again with the music from the Balkans. The quality of musicianship is raised each year. "Last year," writes Michael Ginsburg in the *Kef Times* (1998:1), "the EEFC brought a piece of the Balkans to camp. . . . What better way to continue that quest towards utopia than to bring to camp some of the people who have provided our inspiration. . . . Esma and Ansamble Teodosievski have touched the lives of everyone who loves the culture of the Balkans. . . . We had meals together, went swimming together, sang, danced and played music together. We learned about who they were and about their lives as Roma in Macedonia. For many of us, the experience was as close to Balkan Heaven as we had ever come" (figure 1.6).

Indeed, it is a speciality of Esma and "the boys" to transform a room, taking the intensity level up a notch with their music and performance **(DVD 7)**.

These ever more common encounters sometimes result in conflict, particularly with regard to how the music should be performed. Many Balkanites would prefer that musicians not play on DX 7 keyboards, trumpets, and drum sets but on unamplified instruments made of wood and skin, like gaida or tapan. Likewise, there has been considerable argument in the scene about the use of amplification. Musicians from the Balkans and some Balkanites tend to like it loud, which has led others to boycott concerts, pay angry visits to the sound man, or retreat to the back of the hall, visibly stuffing cotton in their ears. But perhaps of greater significance than such conflict is the remarkable fact that American and Balkan people are participating together on such a level that something like this can even come up as an issue. Beyond the verbal and behavioral "discussion" that takes place in the context of concerts, there are also other opportunities for debate (in letters to the *Kef Times* and on the Internet) and various attempts at compromise, like providing free earplugs at loud concerts.

Contact such as this is fostering more substantive connections between Balkanites and the Balkans, and the forum for discussion is increasingly relevant to Balkan musicians as well as the Americans. Most people would never otherwise have the opportunity to witness what one camper recognized as a highlight of that year's camp experience, "Listening to Ljubomir Živkov (a Serb from Belgrade) and Raif Hyseni (an Albanian from Kosova) playing music together on the bench above the pool" (Blumenthal, 1999/2000:6). During the NATO bombing of Serbia and war in Kosovo, Lancaster (1999/2000:5) acknowledged a need "to remember or pray for the Balkans—the beloved and beleaguered heartland of the music and dancing we love. We're acutely aware of and humbled by the great privilege we're experiencing here. We're not only blessed with music, dance and friendship, but we're safe, well-fed, and most of us have homes, jobs and families to return to." However concrete or abstract one's connection to this heartland, Balkanites' love of the music and dance makes them at least think about issues most Americans do not, perhaps bolstering claims of "raising awareness."

A deeper sense of understanding and connection to the Balkans is also part of the goal of EEFC staff, who often devote considerable effort to

Figure 1.6. Photo opportunity: Esma Redžepova and Zahir Ramadanov, Mendocino, 1997

cultural education. Examples are numerous. Carol Silverman, who has done intensive research on Rom music, has been trying to break the stereotypical perceptions of Rom people and to educate campers about their personal and political struggles. Sonia Seeman, also an ethnomusicologist who worked with Macedonian Rom musicians in Šutka, took it upon herself to give an example at her workshops of the ways dances are done in Šutka. "Gypsy stuff was viewed as 'wear funky clothes, throw your body around.' . . . I wanted to present another view," says Seeman. Sonia told me that some workshop participants were "shocked" when she showed up in high heels, a miniskirt, and lots of makeup.

Judith similarly described a circle dance she witnessed while traveling in the Balkans, showing how such experiences can provide both a better understanding of Balkan culture and a clearer perspective on the American Balkan scene itself: "It felt very European, the spiked heels on cobbled streets, it was just amazing me! But, I thought: "Oh! We all dress up in these folk costumes, we are so peasant about it!" . . . I thought, 'This is great, she is great, she is kicking my buttkus.' It was wonderful, and I really appreciated it, and realized that music evolves; culture evolves" (Interview, 1995). And as Balkan culture "evolves," it is the aspiration of the Balkanites that their subculture will continue to evolve as well. To many, a critical part of this evolution involves participants' growing understanding of the relationships between their ideas and Balkan realities, and their personal and community relationships with Balkan cultures and people.

2

Why Balkan?

Continuing our ethnography, this chapter examines reasons participants give for being involved in Balkan music and dance (in interviews, e-mails, and publications) and what can be observed in action. Why ask "why?" For the Balkanites, such questioning is not just an attempt to analyze behavior, but often an integral part of that behavior, particularly as their music and dance choices don't "make sense" in terms of their heritage. The dimensions of experience addressed include the social, cultural, historical, psychological, sonic, and spiritual.

"Don't Ask Me 'Why?'"

> Why is it so universally asked whether one is from the culture if we learn a lot about a culture which we are not born into? This is asked with incredulity, and almost the implication that there's something at least downright odd about learning so much about "someone else's culture." . . . I'm really . . . tired of justifying why I am clearly spending a lot of my nonexistent free time learning esoteric languages and folk music. (Bonnie, EEFC list, April 4, 1996)

"Why" questions have often been swallowed up by concepts of "tradition" and "heritage" in "traditional" fieldwork situations. These concepts are so pervasive that we might never ask why, for example, a Bulgarian plays gaida, or why this instrumental tradition is transmitted from generation to generation. Most likely the gaida player would not wonder why either. However, when this music is transplanted to the context of the American Balkan scene, "why" becomes a more obvious question to the researcher, the traditional musician, audiences, and, perhaps most of all, to the Balkanite him/herself. While the previous chapter began to address the question, it only touched on some of the most interesting of the discernible reasons and presented the Balkanites' own thoughts on the matter. Therefore this chapter is devoted to further exploration of the question "why."

Capturing the dynamism of experience in the concrete of words can be like trying to catch shadows in a butterfly net, particularly when it comes to answering questions like "why." What's more, the moment we identify a "reason," the reason itself becomes a model through which to interpret the phenomenon it is meant to elucidate. In the case of the Balkanites, some answers can be found in various forms of popular rhetoric, theories, and models, such as those of alienation, lack of community, American creativity, and multiculturalism. These can be thought of as useful lenses through which to view the world, but they have a tendency to remake the world in their own image. An investigation of the relevant issues yields many clues, as well as some reasonably straightforward answers for the Balkanites' affinity. Still, it is important to keep in mind the dynamism in back of these explanations.

Most of the people I interviewed were quite analytical and verbal about the particulars of Balkan music and dance in the United States, and about their personal involvement and contributions, but the question "why" left them speechless at first. "Why? I could not answer that," Lauren said to me (Interview, 1996). "I tried, believe me! Why am I involved in a culture that is alien to me in so many ways? I don't have an answer." Like Lauren, many have wondered for years why they spend all their "nonexistent free time" doing Balkan music and dance. Friends and family members had asked them the question many times before I began this research. Yet the reply I was first given was, almost without exception, a variation of "I really don't know," often pronounced slowly in a soft, almost whispering voice with the emphasis on *really*, and accompanied by a slight nod of the head which I took as a sign of sincerity. In this manner people communicated the perceived inexplicability of their involvement in Balkan music and dance. As Steve put it, "I first got into it, and 'why' is the question I've been asking myself for the rest of my life." This sequence of experience—attraction/participation/rationalization—was expressed time and again in my interviews. Rather than an "on the spot" construction in response to my questioning, this sequence seemed to articulate something of ongoing significance to members of the Balkan scene, shared by many and deeply felt. It is, in part, the depth of the Balkanites' feeling and dedication that compelled me to explore the reasons "why," detailed below.

Affinity and Community

If there is a line between emotional/aesthetic responses to Balkan repertoire and the social/cultural appeal of the Balkan scene, it is not always clear. Participants' shared affinity for the music and dance lives in a dynamic relationship with the shared affinity for extra-musical values they "recognize" in it or assign to it. "Affinity groups," Slobin writes (1993: 98), "serve as nuclei for the free-floating units of our social atmosphere, points of orientation for weary travelers looking for a cultural home." But our travelers did not simply *find* a cultural home, they are *building* it from available resources. Constructed with materials inherited from the IFD

movement as well as materials based on Balkan models and in various American social and political movements, this home is being constantly remodeled and adapted to suit the needs of its inhabitants. I believe that the warmth and vibrancy of this home is largely dependent upon tender care and timely maintenance that continues to attract new dwellers.

In spite of its name, this home is certainly an American home, with house rules and values that sometimes appear most pronounced to an outsider. It is largely in assigning meaning to repertoire and its sources as well as participants' own involvement in its re-creation, that group boundaries, or house rules, are defined. The relationship between the American women's movement of the 1970s and Balkan female vocal polyphony (see chapter 9) clearly shows how the one uses the other creatively to communicate and express its own values. An even clearer example of this reinscription of meaning can be found in the attitude toward sex and its perceived relationship to circle dancing. Dancing kolo nude in the moonlight and skinny-dipping at Balkan camps certainly has nothing to do with the Balkans. When Acocella (1993: 31) writes about sexual practices of Koleda members, she is clearly describing one segment of American society in the 1970s.

> While some people, both homosexual and heterosexual, went in for the kind of promiscuity popular in those years, others were stable married couples or conservative-minded single people who were just interested in friendship and dancing. This great range of sexual habits led to and was supported by a philosophy of extreme tolerance. "You could do anything you wanted," says Mary Hoagland, "as long as you danced or sang."

Many of the Balkanites' practices and habits are even completely unrelated to music and dance. As one member of the EEFC list observed:

> Folk dancing is a hobby, but to a newcomer it can look like a lifestyle, even a cult! . . . At many events I've been to there's a clique of regulars that sit in the corner often doing something that has nothing to do with folk dancing and probably looks pretty odd to a newcomer, like combing each other's hair. . . . While I loved listening to the music and thought the dancing looked like fun, it also seemed to me since I did comb my hair, I did shave my legs, and I did not squeal during meals, I could never get involved in folk dancing.

While combing each other's hair, squealing during meals, and not shaving your legs are imminently unrelated to Balkan music and dance, they are related to shared values of the American "land of the folk." Combing each other's hair and giving back rubs are expressions of "communal" values shared by the American folk scene in general. These are peaceful, time-consuming, personal interactions that are perceived to be "of the folk." Similarly, dancing nude, not shaving your legs, or not wearing makeup are ways to express "naturalness" and, with it, comfort with your own body and

its natural beauty. As we can see from the above example, the expression of a particular value can be several steps removed from music and dance. The relationship between unshaven legs and Balkan songs is probably understandable only to someone who is inside the Balkan scene, or at least familiar with related subcultural scenes and practices.

Once people get hooked on Balkan music and dance, they tend to start socializing with people from the same folk dance group, organizing their social life around this interest and the people who share it. The intensity of social interaction is even higher for musicians playing together in a band. For 62 percent of questionnaire respondents, the majority of their friends are also Balkanites. This is not surprising, especially considering the fact that many people report that the majority of their free time is devoted to this activity and that even their choice of where to live is largely determined by the presence of an active Balkan scene.

Practically, of course, musicians must get together to rehearse, to play and sing, and dancers get together to dance in folk dance clubs and classes. But reasons for in-group socializing surpass the practical. The scene is hardly completely uniform, yet people who encounter it and do not feel at home there do not become part of it. There is enough similarity between various segments of the scene to make individuals feel surrounded by kindred spirits.

The Balkanites use somewhat derogatory terms to refer to themselves. The existence and frequent usage of such terminology point to a shared awareness of belonging to a group. In this manner, too, individuals identify with other scene members. I was initially surprised to hear people refer to themselves as "weirdoes, nerds, misfits, socially inept, oddballs, square pegs in round holes, people with two left feet, etc." The prevalence of such half-joking celebration of personal foibles was new to me on my arrival in the United States, but I soon became familiar with phrases like "I'm a chocoholic" and "I'm the world's worst driver."[1] The self-perception behind this humor is not a recent phenomenon in folk dance circles. Since at least the 1930s, perhaps earlier, folk dancing has attracted people who have felt ill at ease in many other social circumstances. Folk dance classes were often set up as situations for people to meet people and socialize (see chapter 6).

> I have long believed that the reason that there is an inordinate number of "weird people" at folk dance gatherings is that: One needs few or no social graces to get into a folk dance line and learn a dance. Therefore, if one has few such graces, one may, in keeping one's mouth shut at appropriate times, learn many dances and be welcomed. This takes place where, in other social interactions, one's lack of social grace might get one into trouble and, hence, no return invitation. But, at a folk dance gathering, all you need to know is how to dance, or, even if you can't—how to TRY to dance! (Craig, EEFC list, December 19, 1997)

Folk dancing provides a structure for social interaction that demands a minimum of initiative on the part of the individual while at the same time

giving each individual a feeling of belonging to a social whole, of partaking in a communal, social experience. "We tease it's a nonsocial person's social hour. You can sort of be talking, but music will take you away, dancing will take you away. You don't have to talk for too long and you don't really have to be close to anybody, except you have to hold their hands" (Judith, Interview, 1997).

A member of the EEFC list compared the social situation at folk dance events with dancing in clubs and parties outside of the folk dance world (Andrea, EEFC list, December 18, 1997):

> My impression has always been . . . that loud and dark parties are designed to cover the awkward silences that often occur in new relationships formed based on external appearances rather than some kind of shared mutual interest. Folk dancing provides similar "protection" without the noise—"I need to concentrate to do this dance. Oops, 'scuse me but I want to do this!" etc.—and an instant shared mutual interest.

The appeal of the social scene is multifaceted and varies between participants. For some a major attraction is a "clean" environment that does not involve drinking and smoking. For others it is a "quiet" and "cheap entertainment," an opportunity to be with like-minded people or in a supportive environment. Of course this "environment" is shaped by its members on the basis of values that are shared on a level deeper than many of the scenes' imminent features and the thoughts about them that are most often expressed. Through devotion to an evolving assemblage of repertoire, practices, and ideas, the Balkanites have created a social home in which they are governed primarily by their own rules, and are free to pursue their passion.

Yet, the communal feeling generated through participation in music and dance of the Balkans cannot be underestimated as it certainly accounts for one of the major attractions to the scene in general (see also the conclusion). The very repertoire the Balkanites are drawn to fosters group experience and social enjoyment of music and dance in the ways many other musical styles do not. Songs intended for such social enjoyment tend to have anthemic qualities. The melodies are very singable, sitting comfortably in the average person's register, allowing for easy harmonization and responding well to being sung full voice in a noisy room. The sentiments expressed tend to be general ones of love and longing. The fact that the Balkanites are singing in a foreign language does not detract from, but possibly contributes to, their ability to pour their hearts into the songs without reservation. (Many would surely blush to sing them in translation.) As I was growing up in Sarajevo, a bunch of friends and someone with a guitar was customarily all that was needed for a great communal music experience, and no party was without this feature. As long as someone can lead the song, everyone else participates to the extent and in the way they feel compelled, comfortable or able. Nobody is in the spotlight, yet everyone has the opportunity to contribute to the overall atmosphere. It's more

like a pickup game of soccer than a major league baseball game. By accident and design the Balkanites have put in place many mechanisms that foster such shared repertoires that are so vital to communal musical experience. It is truly amazing that in the midst of the United States one can find a large group of Americans singing a Bosnian[3] song **(CD 2)** knowing, not only the melody and the lyrics, but expressive language and social dynamics of music making akin to those one would find in this music's homeland. Participation in Balkan music and dance does provide for kinds of social intimacy largely absent in American society, physical closeness of musicians and dancers, intensity of social experience, group focus, and bodily behaviors such as draping an arm around a friend or sitting on their lap.

"Sick and Tired of Being American": Difference and Choice

> For me, it was the representation of the times . . . the early sixties was a time of antiwar movement, counterculture. I was interested in anything that was not pure lily-white American. I was sick and tired of being American.
>
> —Larry, Interview, 1994

An important appeal of things Balkan can be found in the various levels on which it is, or is perceived to be, *different*. As seen above, this difference gave an alternative, countercultural status to Balkan music and dance in the context of American culture in the 1960s and 1970s. While part of the distinctiveness of Balkan folk material lies in its obscurity and "difference," part of its attraction too is that it is actively sought after, not "force-fed." The fact that Balkan music was not readily available, that it was not presented for consumption through media advertisement, made it additionally attractive to the 1960s and 1970s counterculture, in which resisting the media was, itself, a valued action. This attitude is part of the legacy inherited by the Balkan scene from earlier movements.

One's *choice* of this type of expression can be a statement that is not only personal but political, particularly in a nation whose self-image and national rhetoric is so tied to ideas of "choice." Such choice constitutes action. Part of the raison d'être for this alternative choice is resentment toward the options available in American society. Of course, Balkan music and dance *is* also one available option and, one could argue, quite a "lily-white American" one. Larry certainly did not escape being American by dancing Balkan dances but, through this activity, chose to identify himself alternatively. One doubts that he was truly sick and tired of *being* American, but dissatisfied and uncomfortable with aspects of mainstream American society.

Involvement in something "different" helps people position themselves outside the American mainstream, providing a sense of personal and group identity through engagement in a unique activity, enabling people to say and feel: "I am John Smith, *the* gaida player," or "we *are* the village, we *are* the community." "Face it, folks," Jim writes (EEFC list, 20 March 1997),

"what we do is ABOUT 'strangeness.' If we hated the alien, we should have stuck with square dancing or disco." One reason they did not is that it was either American, thus too close to home, or popular, thus seen as having little value.

The choice of things Balkan parallels the choice to identify with the most "distinctive" part of one's ethnic background—it adds a "safe color" to one's identity. A sense of personal distinction is only one part of the picture, of course, and something scene members might consider of minor importance in comparison with the genuine difference they see their activities making in their lives and in the world. It is certainly not primarily the *idea* but the *experience* of "newness" and "difference" that most Balkanites are after. What's more, feelings of being "different" or unsuited to American popular culture have been important, pre-existing factors in the creation of the scene and in motivating many to participate. But, whatever the nature of individuals' relationships to the idea, "difference" remains important in scene rhetoric and self-image. "You know, it is a lot easier to form a rock and roll band. . . . Everybody can do rock and roll, but how many people do Macedonian folk music, how many people do Bulgarian folk music?" (David, Interview, 1997). This point is further detailed by an EEFC list member. "If folk music and dancing became a nationwide craze, I suspect that most of the current aficionados would find something else to do, purely because anything the masses like becomes McDonald's food." This brings us to a seeming paradox of the Balkan scene and the folk dance scene in general. On one hand its practitioners talk about the whole world holding hands and dancing in unity, while, on the other hand, they tend to see themselves as part of a select, possibly superior, enlightened minority. This condition and the insider dialogue about it parallels a dynamic found in other countercultural or political arts movements, from Depression era art music to the hardcore punk scene of the 1980s.

People's devotion to Balkan music is such that several I interviewed claimed it was the only music they listened to at home or in the car. Even the few ex-scenesters I interviewed still listen almost exclusively to Balkan music, though they no longer feel part of the scene or attend any organized events. In these cases the aspects of the scene's social appeal we have examined do little to explain the love of the music, even if one can still experience, in private listening, aspects of sociability and experience the music as a comfortable space.

"This Is Real!"

One answer I got to the question "Why Balkan?" was, "What better? I think the American culture is very hollow and we wanted to fill it with richness that we saw in other places"(Carolyn, Interview, 1997). That the United States is a place of cultural poverty is a perception of long standing, voiced famously by such European visitors as Alexis de Tocqueville and Charles Dickens, but also by Americans themselves since before the birth of the nation. The epicenter of this impoverishment is commonly seen to be the

epicenter of all that is new and popular, that is "the media." "Don't listen to what the media is feeding you," said Nada in our 1995 interview. "It's garbage on the radio. This is real!" Balkan folk arts are often perceived in contrast to a media-dominated American culture. But what else is it in these forms that inspires not just enthusiastic interest but the motivation to stick with this choice, often for decades?

In my interviews, I encouraged people to articulate their aesthetic experiences while, as much as possible, separating them from their rationalizations. Although this did not always yield results, it gave me an insight into the ways people hear the music or see the dance. The phrase "it's *real*," spoken with great emphasis, was used repeatedly and is one of the most common threads in answers to "Why Balkan music and dance?" While it is likely that for each of these individuals "real" means something different, we can acknowledge the "reality" of their claim and look at some specifics, with special attention to music. "What do you like about this music? Why is this music real?" I asked.

> It simply is! It is what it is, it does not pretend to be anything else.
>
> I liked the melodies, things in minor keys. That pulled me in and the passionate nature of singing. . . . I liked harmonic singing, I liked close intervals, I sang girlie folk songs and I didn't even know there is another voice.
>
> It is just so wonderful, the seconds, where you have the dissonance just, something goes right through your body . . . right through to the center of your body and it is really hard to say what it is.
>
> It is beautiful. It moves my heart. It's the harmonies, the melodies, the drone, the texture. . . . It's the emotional impact. Balkan music made everything else seem trite and stupid.
>
> Truth, beauty, openness of the heart feelings. . . . Excitement, lots of excitement.
>
> It's because of drone. Drone roots it to the earth; it makes it larger than it is. That's what grabbed me.
>
> I really like monotonous, repetitive stuff. . . .
>
> It is raw power, gives me goose bumps, to be part of that is so exciting.
>
> It is the volume, the focus, the hard edge in the sound. The harmonies too. All those close harmonies, all the seconds, all the harmonies based on drones are very striking.
>
> I liked strong feeling of rhythm and drones. . . .

> There is a different type of tension there. In Macedonian dances, the tension is constant, it is almost like a predator. The passion between a man and a woman can be expressed so beautifully in Balkan music and dance.
>
> It's passionate music, not in a cheesy way. Not sweet but really powerful and direct.
>
> I love when you play and it is right next to your ears, it gets you to a primal state, close to ecstasy, you forget who you are, it transcends you somewhere else. I need that in my world. . . .
>
> It is the intensity. It is driving, compelling music. It sweeps you up.
>
> It spoke to me, it felt ancient to me, it felt natural to me. I don't feel that way when I turn the radio on.

A study in cognitive psychology might yield a more complete picture of the perceived "realness" of Balkan music, but there is much that can be gleaned from ethnomusicological analysis. One important factor in the "realness" of the material is that it appears not to try to be something it is not. In contrast to the formality, commercial aspirations, and image consciousness of popular and classical forms, Balkan music's apparent lack of posturing is part of what is often expressed as its "immediacy." Important musical and extra-musical associations with the ancient, the natural, and the spiritual will be examined below. We have seen the importance of "difference," the beauty and power of the music being experienced in contrast to more familiar forms. But, new to the music or not, for most of the people I interviewed what initially grabbed them and keeps them coming back is something in the "music itself." The attributes most frequently mentioned are modality and drone, vocal and instrumental texture, close harmony and rhythm.

Drone and Modality Functional harmony, in which expressive power and beauty are found in playing with listeners' perception of the music's tonal center, is a characteristic of Western European art music and the genres it has impacted or inspired. Such use of harmony is certainly not unknown in Balkan traditions. But, like much of the world's music, even if it involves harmony, Balkan music often is, or could be, sung or played over a drone. In contrast to a shifting sense of base, drone provides a steady reference point against which to experience changing relationships of pitches and musical movement. Thus, the presence of a drone or steady tonal center in much of Balkan music can suggest a sense of being "grounded" and connected to the rest of the world's music and people; a sense of the universal, transcending time and place. Combined with its "meditative" quality, a nexus of physical experience and cultural expectation, drone enhances the Balkanites' feelings of being one with the sound, with the earth,

and with each other, as in **DVD 8**, sung by Carol Silverman and Ruth Hunter accompanied by a pickup Macedonian izorono ensemble led by Mark Levy. The use of modes, frequently those other than the familiar major and minor, offers expressive possibilities otherwise uncommon or unknown to participants, and an experience that is at once immediate and communal, "earthy" and otherworldly. Furthermore, listeners with a Western musical sensibility often hear unexpected melodic turns and dwelling on scalar degrees other than those commonly used in most Western music as "exotic," "ancient," and "of the folk."

Dissonance and Close Harmony The use of melody against a drone often results in what Western music theory considers "dissonance." In addition, much Balkan polyphony expresses a preference for such dissonances, particularly the close interval of a "second." Traditionally, these seconds are quite variable, and are conceived and experienced not as intervals but as a desired physical effect. On Bosnia's Mount Bjelašnica, for example, tight-knit groups of three or four village girls begin singing together at a young age. Here the older vocal forms rely heavily on these seconds, which vary considerably in character from one group to another, and one song to another. Standing shoulder to shoulder, the singers strive not to create a particular interval, but to create just the right physical and sonic "buzz" between singers **(DVD 9)**. We see, here, a level of convergence between musical values in a Balkan form and the goals of the Balkanites in the desire to experience music physically and interpersonally. The Balkanites' pleasure in close intervals is partly the result of experiencing them not only as musically interesting, novel, and exotic, but as physically satisfying and socially binding.

Timbre and Vocal Production Those I interviewed described instrumental timbre and vocal production in the music they loved using terms like "direct," "strong," and "fearless." Such terms could as easily be applied to the sound of the music as to a perception of the character of the musicians and their culture. And, indeed, even in everyday conversation, how someone uses their voice can often tell us as much about their values, personality, and meaning as we get from their words. Of course, just as music is not a universal language, the significance of qualities of the speaking voice is not culturally universal. Yet in both cases we can imagine something more about meaning than we can based on written text in an unknown script. The clues found in timbre and vocal production are often expanded upon in the imaginations of the Balkanites and are certainly important in their initial and continued interest in the music. For some, these clues are beacons of meaning that lead to the pursuit of deeper understanding of the people and music, while for others they remain largely symbolic.

In Balkan music's general preference for sharp timbres, pragmatic and aesthetic concerns unite. In the case of outdoor music such timbre helps the sound to carry, and in the case of party music, indoors or out, it helps the music cut through the din. At the same time, it has a role in conveying

the "passion" and emotional frankness valued so widely in Balkan cultures. The full-voiced singing that is so common also plays a part in this "wearing your heart on your sleeve." A cultural appreciation, or at least toleration, of the particularities of individual singers' voices should be clear from listening to various Balkan singing styles. This certainly contributes to the perception that the singing is being done by "regular" or "real" people. Thus, the way Balkan singers use their voices can reasonably be heard as expressing strength, emotional openness, and individualism, values cherished in the Balkan scene and illustrated here by the singing of Esma Redžepova **(DVD 10)**.

While there are interesting differences in what these things mean in Balkan cultures, their apparent presence in the music is part of what makes it so compelling to the Balkanites.

Rhythm Throughout the Balkans, tunes in metrical patterns such as those in five and seven beats are common and heard as quite normal, but their novelty to American ears and feet is one of the most mentioned of initial musical attractions to the music. There is even folklore in the scene that such rhythms more closely mimic "the rhythm of the heart" than do more familiar meters. Balkanites themselves have not failed to make an association between the scene's enthusiasm for complex patterns and the overwhelming presence of people employed in mathematic and scientific fields.

In any meter, the successful execution of a newly learned music or dance pattern can be quite satisfying. Whether a particular pattern is novel or familiar, rhythm is perhaps the most social of musical elements, as it is the aspect in which the most people can actively participate simultaneously. Especially in the union of music and dance, rhythm facilitates a kinesthetic enactment of ideas and social ties that bind the "village." This is true even if the rhythm is counted and understood intellectually, as is often the case in the scene, rather than felt and understood throughout the body, as is more generally the case in the music's "natural habitat."

As with instrumental timbre and vocal production, pleasure and depth are found not just in patterns of rhythm but in how they are articulated. In **DVD 11** Michael Ginsburg teaches "Žensko Pušteno horo," a beautiful and complicated dance pattern to equally beautiful recording of Pece Atanasovski.

Associating it with the "primitive," classical music ideals traditionally deemphasize, even denigrate, strong rhythm, relegating it to the realm of popular music. If a survey question asked Americans, "What do white people not have?," "rhythm" would likely be a top response. Balkan music thus fills a void, as an unapologetically rhythmic tradition that is, for the Balkanites, "close to home." It is interesting, of course, that it could be seen as closer to home than thoroughly American traditions like rhythm and blues and hip hop.

Those with more experience, in particular, also find beauty in the subtleties and variety of articulation possible within a single rhythmic pattern. Rhythms, as well as pitches, are stretched or elided in ways impossible to

usefully capture in the shorthand of written music. Free rhythm is one common context for such stretching, as in the following Greek example by the popular Balkan scene band Ziyia **(CD 3)**. Also evident in this example are some of the many parameters of Balkan music in which there is considerable latitude for individual expression, and in which musical choices are as much a matter of social negotiation as personal leadership. Holding true for dance as well, these practices are clearly in line with the ideals of the Balkan scene, and constitute a powerful source of attraction to Balkan forms for scene members.

Authenticity: Peasantry and Preservation

An important aspect of the "real" worthy of further discussion is the association of the Balkans with an imagined peasant/premodern cultural past. The appeal of things peasant and pastoral has remarkable historical precedents in American and European culture. The ideologies of Romanticism germinating in the eighteenth century and of nationalism in the nineteenth century both viewed the "peasant" as the soul of a nation, a sort of mascot of national identity. Marie Antoinette famously played at being a peasant in a garden house especially constructed for the purpose, and eighteenth-century British ballad operas such as "Love in a Village" equally celebrated an idealized pastoral life. Later, such images fed 1960s counterculture ideology on many levels, the peasant standing in opposition to modernity and industrialization and providing an image of peace, harmony, equality, community, friendship, and love. The romantically pastoral is often the "real" to which the "plasticity" of modern life is contrasted. In short, the "peasant" is an image of what, it is believed, America is not.

The perception of the "hollowness" of American culture and "realness" of the Balkans, while it is very common, is not shared by everyone in the scene, nor always felt to be true even by those who sometimes espouse the idea. Some even explicitly disagree with the frequently expressed belief in America's cultural inferiority. "I am not going to think that American culture is bad, and an older culture, like the Balkan culture, is better; I don't believe that" (Craig, Interview, 1997).

But, viewed as culturally superior or not, Balkan music and dance are understood as precious remnants of the past. Like the turn-of-the-century physical educators to be discussed in chapter 4, and the whole line of folk dance lovers to the present day, the Balkanites see this music and dance as something that needs to be preserved. They also share the perception of their own role in this process of preservation as crucial since the Balkan "folk" are unable to see what kind of treasure they possess. This understanding of Balkan music and dance as old, thus valuable, helps makes the time and effort put into learning it feel well invested. "There are more and more Western things in Bulgaria," explained a longtime Balkanite. "We are their nostalgia, we are holding onto their history. We'll hold onto those things maybe we have seen destroyed and taken away in our own history, American history."

Almost every other person I talked to expressed, in one way or another, a belief that the time will come when people from the Balkans, realizing they have lost their precious cultural richness, will come to the United States to learn their songs and dances from Americans who have carefully preserved them. Since traditional music and dance are perceived as precious, valuable, and endangered, many feel compelled to do all they can to preserve them:

> I quickly learned by going to dance workshops in New York and Boston [in the 1970s] that the music is dying out, so I just thought I will go over there and help keep it from dying out. So I was going to go there and record music, and I was going to be a little ethnomusicologist. I didn't really know the first thing what I was doing but I said that's what I was going to do. I was going to collect instruments and dances and when I come back start a folk dance group, folk music group, and do all that stuff. (Anonymous, Interview, 1997)

And why is this music worth preserving?

> This music is, it's hundred of years old, possibly some of the tunes were, and they were still being played. And there was nothing in my culture, in my American culture, where that was going on.
>
> And in peasant culture there is a lot of connection to nature, I think, that we have lost as we have moved to the city. And there is a lot of spiritual knowledge there that is, is being lost.
>
> My fear was that the culture there is . . . just going to get completely overwhelmed by the United States, by American culture.
>
> Popular music, you chew it up and spit it out, but this music has more substance to it.

These thoughts certainly express the perceived value of Balkan music and dance in comparison with the ever-changing popular and mass-mediated art forms which most of these Americans have as points of reference.

If the "realness" of a thing is such a big part of its value, one needs to be able to determine whether or not it is "real," which leads to the scene's great concern for the authenticity of material. This authenticity is often judged on the basis of its source. "We like people that come with 'field-recordings,' as we call them. Bring it from the 'source.' They went to the village, they studied it there, they met those people, and this is what those people sounded like" (Judith, Interview, 1997). The authenticity of the material ensures its value, and what can be labeled authentic can also be labeled good, and worth the effort of preserving. Although authenticity is an invented and ideologically loaded concept, it is largely taken within the group as a qualitative, absolute category. Even when the concept of

authenticity is questioned by Balkanites, its uncertainty often remains in the domain of interpretation, an issue to be resolved by the researcher or student. Some, however, question the very usefulness of the concept. "People here strive to achieve something, what they consider to be authentic," said Craig. "But I hate the word 'authentic.' What is authentic? Authenticity is a joke. It's one person doing one particular thing at one particular time."

Ideas of authenticity play a social and structural role in the scene, contributing to the authority of some members over others, of one interpretation over another, and of some teachers over others. This usually translates to the authority of those from the Balkans or with more Balkan experience over those who have learned only from Americans or Balkan immigrants. Concern with issues of authenticity arises both from concerns for "realness" and from the fact that the group is centered around an interest in music and dance material of another, living culture. "There is a certain amount of rigidity" in interpretation of material, Melinda explained in a 1993 interview: "And that comes from learning it at a remove." Concepts of authenticity and preservationism are used to regulate the scene, to censor and evaluate. Scene members rarely if ever consider that their wrestling with issues of authenticity and preservationism is not particularly about Balkan culture, nor does it occur in the interest of this culture. These issues, rather, help scene members explain and validate their own involvement in Balkan music and dance. While providing a focus for attention, discussion, and action, "preservation and authenticity" help cement Balkanites' commitment to their activity by providing compelling reasons for their devotion.

Serendipity and Attraction: Gut Feeling and Spiritual Calling

Although most people I interviewed initially perceived Balkan music and dance as strikingly and importantly different from anything they knew, instead of feeling it as distant and alienating, they felt it to be something for which they had been already searching, though perhaps unknowingly. The attraction was immediate and powerful.

> STEVE There is no scientific explanation. Spiritual is that wonderful thing that music has that nobody can understand, making you cry, making your spine tingle.
>
> CAROL I did not know I was missing anything in my life until I happened upon this.

Only a handful of people I interviewed at first perceived it as too "weird," "distant," or simply "somebody else's cup of tea."[2] These few required lengthy exposure, usually through a spouse, partner, friends, or family members, before they developed an appreciation for Balkan music and dance and began to participate actively in the scene. Most, however, simply "ran into" it and have held fast ever since.

Such serendipity, as seen above in extracts from first-encounter narratives, must be addressed with seriousness. Before we can apply Finnegan's metaphor of "pathways" (1989) to the Balkanites' experience, we must acknowledge what we might call "run-ins," or "stumble-upons." It is only after a serendipitous encounter with the music and dance that people begin looking for a pathway and perhaps step onto a path traced by fellow Americans who had stumbled upon this material before them. The depth and significance of these encounters is often expressed alternately in terms of bodily compulsion and spiritual inevitability, or a combination of the two.

"A Gut Feeling" In interview subjects' descriptions of their attraction to Balkan music and dance I was, again, struck by the vocabulary people used, the manner in which they used it, and the remarkable consistency between accounts.

> LAUREN There is something about this music that speaks to me on a very primal, deep level that I cannot explain.
>
> CAROL I got totally hooked, addicted.
>
> SONIA It hooked me, it really hooked me. . . . I went folk dancing religiously. Oh, it was a passion. I lived for that. . . . It grabbed me. . . . It was really visceral, it was something at the gut level, the first time I heard *čalgija.* Something just hit me in my soul and I thought I am going to go to Macedonia. I just knew I had to go there.
>
> MARK I just became completely obsessed with it.
>
> NADA This music turned me on and moved me.
>
> RACHEL It touched me somehow. . . . I got really excited. It was great.
>
> CHRISTOS When I hear *zurna* my hair raises. I don't know why. There is an immediacy there.
>
> JUDITH It's beyond reasoning. I just love it. I just loved the sound.
>
> YVES What really hit me was the music. Don't ask me why. It was a gut feeling.

In summary, "I was shocked, hooked, addicted, obsessed, smitten, drawn, I melted, fell in love, it captivated me, touched me, moved me, turned me on, it hit me, I got goose bumps, I got excited, my hair rose. . . . " Their descriptions relate a physical experience, emphasizing irrational, powerful, instinctive, bodily responses to a stimulus, and it is the music and dance which act upon the passive observer. All of these experiences are "on a gut level." In phrases such as "primal" and "visceral" we hear echoes of an association between the instinctive/bodily and the ancient/natural, suggesting that attraction to Balkan music and dance takes place on a plane more "real" than the rational, whether this is the kinesthetic or the spiritual. Without needing to assert a position on the "real" or superstructural nature of the spiritual, we can benefit from a look at the Balkanites' experience of this dimension.

A Calling From even the few examples given above, the reader can see that responses to Balkan music and dance are felt to be beyond the control of the individual. Enchanted by the experience, people decide to "follow" the music/dance, they are pulled into it, drawn to it, hit by it. As Stewart put it in a 1996 interview: "I felt it had power over me. It's a connection to universality, to inner harmony." As the response is immediate and happens on a "primal" or "gut level," it transcends the individual, cultural, and historical and is experienced as metaphysical, magical, or cosmic. Hence, in keeping with contemporary "new age" philosophy, many people view their involvement in Balkan music and dance as a confirmation of reincarnation theory. It is fascinating to note here the persistence of the concept of genetic heritage as the sole explanation for cultural/social distinction. As, in this case, no genetic ties can be made between the Balkanites and the peoples of the Balkans, these ties are "found" in past lives. Some are certain that they were born in one of the Balkan countries in a past life, while others speculate about the possibility. When I asked Steve, "Why Balkan dance?" he replied, "It's a call or something. There is a spiritual connection. . . . Call it Kismet, call it reincarnation. . . . There is something about Macedonia to me . . . it touches me, the music, the strength, the power . . . takes me away from the mundane. I feel I get to a sacred space" (Interview, 1995).

I heard the expression "it is a call," or "it is my calling" many times from different people. Whether in Christianity, new age thought, or other traditions relevant to this study, the idea of a "calling" expresses the finding of one's unique place in the larger scope of life, in this case finding the avenue of expression in which one feels most comfortable, competent, and at home. Part of what makes a calling to learn Balkan dance and music more spiritual than a calling to be a computer specialist is that involvement in this activity cannot be explained through economic necessity, societal expectations, or family tradition and cultural heritage. There is no "reason" to do it.

"I have the impression," Judy writes (EEFC list, Dec. 18, 1997) "that there are a larger number of Pisceans than other signs at both IFD and contra dancing. Maybe it only seems that way because I am one, or maybe because we 'advertise' ourselves more than other signs (the contradancing Pisceans have a group birthday party every year, and the IFD Pisceans used to do a head count every March)." Conventionally, the realm of the rational is considered to be somewhere between the physical and the metaphysical. But, perhaps because reason can find equally impenetrable the kinesthetic and the metaphysical, a conflation of the two is, in effect, "reasonable." In any case, heightened by its inexplicability, the nourishment of body and spirit Balkan music and dance provides for its practitioners elevates the activity from the mundane to the sacred. Finding, among scene members, kindred spirits with strikingly similar stories further enhances this aura of spirituality.

Such concerns hardly occupy the Balkanites' every waking thought, and there is considerable range in the degree of importance given to issues of

spirituality. But whether people articulate their attraction and involvement in terms that are primarily kinesthetic, musical, social, or spiritual, the place of individualism in scene cosmology assures a place for their perspectives.

Taste

Whatever specifics people recognize as important, they find the music and dance resonant with their perception of who they are. As Nada said, "This music, it's me, it is harmonious with who I am." Stewart elaborated on the subject: "I felt like this is my music, it felt natural to me, it did not follow any script in my life but somehow I felt physically and emotionally part of that music. It spoke to me viscerally." Stewart was very articulate and introspective about the place of Balkan music and dance in his life, and I encouraged him to explain further what made him feel this music was his music, what made him feel that he was physically and emotionally part of it. After a short break he exclaimed: "Why do I like a certain person, or certain colors? You are asking me about my taste!"

The work of Pierre Bourdieu (1984), though it focuses rather heavily on class as the dominant factor in the formation of personal taste, decisively shatters the old assumption that taste is "given," thus analytically untouchable. While the first-encounter experiences Balkanites describe may indeed be "love at first sight," Bourdieu points out that such an "act of empathy . . . presupposes an act of cognition, a decoding operation, which implies the implementation of a cognitive acquirement, a cultural code" (Bourdieu 1984: 3). However, his suggestions (1984: 2) that "a work of art has meaning and interest only for someone who possesses the cultural competence, that is, the code, into which it is encoded" and that "a beholder who lacks the specific code feels lost in a chaos of sounds and rhythms, colors and lines, without rhyme or reason" (Bourdieu 1984: 2) are clearly not always the case. People can indeed be powerfully moved by music and dance they had no prior knowledge of, in which case the sense of recognition is not based on knowledge or understanding of the "cultural codes" of the tradition in which the music and dance was created. What makes this experience for some people "familiar" and "close to the heart," or "harmonious with who they are," is partly a resonance between their understanding and perception of what they hear/see with their value system, or a projection of a desired perception of self. Obviously, we are prone to project our *own* codes, particularly when we have no others to rely upon, as illustrated by the case of the nude kolo dancers and others.

What one "recognizes" is certainly in large part a projection of one's own worldview rather than a penetration or adoption of a different worldview. Also, what one recognizes upon first encounter will most likely change over years of exposure to a tradition. What each individual "recognizes" when he/she stumbles upon a folk dance class or a recording of Balkan music not only differs from one individual to another, but is usually unrelated to

Balkan cultural codes. As Stewart mentioned, this music did not follow any script in his life. There were no clear paths to follow in his musical/cultural upbringing that apparently led to his involvement in Balkan music and dance. However, after he felt a bond with the material and the context in which it occurs in the United States, his life pathways changed and were shaped by his desire to continue to deepen his involvement in this adopted tradition.

Whether taste is tied to class, gender, education, or something else, it appears to be largely learned behavior, the idea of "cultural codes" implying traditions of value, perception, and meaning. Through my work in the Balkan music and dance scene, I have been drawn to such traditions of thought and behavior, and our often-unknowing embodiment of them. We are all multiple inheritors. Children of Balkanites, for example, inherit scene involvement as a possible option, but also inherit other ideological and behavioral options from the culture at large that could lead to their becoming involved in the scene. It is interesting that our discussion of music and dance choices beyond the bounds of heritage should lead us back to a discussion of heritage. This is not, of course, a study in ethnic identity but a discussion of historical developments leading to particular options in thought and behavior within a social milieu. Like the "different village" described in one interview, this is a "different heritage." If the primary bearers of this heritage were musicians from the Balkans, our investigation might now turn eastward. But as this is truly a heritage of ideas, practices, and people in the United States, our investigation will keep place as a constant but look back in time.

PART II

Folk Dancing and Turn-of-the-Century America

3

Folk Dancing and the Settlement Movement

Having learned something about the contemporary Balkan scene, we now take a dramatic step back in time to see something of its American ancestry. Examining a variety of historically relevant and interconnected movements, ideas, and uses of folk dance and music outside of their respective ethnic communities, we begin to see templates, or at least precedents, for interests, ideas, and behavior of contemporary Balkanites. Settlement houses not only provided immigrants opportunities to participate in their own dance traditions and those of others. They promoted the idea that crossing boundaries of ethnic heritage through music and dance could help immigrants become truly American. We do not know exactly what dances of the Greeks, Russians, Jews Bulgarians, etc., were done in the settlements, but we do know that they were used to foster values and qualities of life thought to be endangered by industrialization and urbanization. While there are interesting continuities in repertoire and its treatment from past to present, from movement to movement, repertoire will be discussed mostly in passing, as the focus is on providing a broad cultural and historical backdrop for the current scene. As you read, keep in mind the ideas about heritage, peasantry, folk arts, and American culture expressed in earlier chapters.

"Residents" and "Neighbors" in the Fight for the "Common Good"

The first "Americans" to be taught an international folk dance repertoire, including songs and dances from the Balkans, were the children of immigrants. Although folk dance in immigrant communities is not our focus, this early grouping of disparate styles, taught to and performed by immigrants and their families, is critical to an understanding of later movements. The earliest centers of this activity were the settlement houses of the late 1800s, in which the rich and the poor, American social reformers and immigrants, intersected.[1]

Urbanization and industrialization in the United States were accompanied by a heavy influx of immigrants. The second great wave of immigration in the decades immediately before and after 1900 brought over

twenty-seven million people from various parts of the world to the United States, primarily to its urban centers. While northern Europeans constituted the bulk of the 1830s and 1840s immigration wave, most turn of the century immigrants came from Italy, Eastern Europe, and southeastern Europe. These newcomers were generally illiterate, poorly educated, unable to speak English or perform skilled labor, and were therefore subject to exploitation by industrial management. Overworked in industrial sweatshops and overcrowded in the slums of New York, Boston, Chicago, Philadelphia, and most other large cities, these new American citizens often lived in extreme poverty. The tenements in which they lived were poorly maintained and ridden with crime, disease, and pollution. These new Americans, "the dangerous classes," were seen as a potential threat to themselves, each other, and to American society.

American attitudes toward the new immigrants were far from uniform. Gordon (1964:85) distinguishes three main axes around which the "philosophies" of assimilation have grouped themselves: "'Anglo conformity,' . . . 'the melting pot,' and 'cultural pluralism.'" Central to the Anglo-conformity theory was the demand for a "complete renunciation of the immigrant's ancestral culture in favor of the behavior and values of the Anglo-Saxon core group." A vision of America as a melting pot supported "a biological merger of the Anglo-Saxon peoples with other immigrant groups and a blending of their respective culture into a new indigenous American type." The foundation of cultural pluralism is the "preservation of the communal life and significant portions of the culture of the later immigrant groups within the context of American citizenship and political and economic integration into American society." While each of these ideologies had its adherents, many people fluctuated from one to another or adopted positions somewhere in between depending on the specifics of place and time, and especially on the origin of the immigrant group in question. In his assessment of the settlement house movement's view on assimilation, Gordon (1964: 137) points out that "The first manifestations of an ideological counterattack against draconic Americanization came not from the beleaguered newcomers, who were, after all, more concerned with survival than with theories of adjustment, but from those idealistic members of the middle class who . . . 'settled' in the slums to 'learn to sup sorrow with the poor.'"[2] A noteworthy parallel can be drawn with contemporary Balkan people, too busy with surviving, urbanizing, and modernizing to care about the traditions and repertoires the Balkanites have the luxury and time to recognize as valuable and worth maintaining.

Settlement houses built and inhabited by rich, "mainstream" Americans were located in the midst of poor neighborhoods in the hope of educating and Americanizing their inhabitants. The insider terminology used to delineate the two groups of people involved in the settlement movement was not the "rich and the poor," the "American and the immigrant," but the "settlement worker," or "resident," and the "neighbor." This choice of terminology reflects the ideology of the organic unity of mankind that motivated settlement work.[3] Calling the poor and immigrants "neighbors"

emphasized not only physical proximity, but intimacy and interdependence. The idea behind settling among "neighbors" was that this immersion would enable the "residents" to learn more about the needs and the deficiencies of the "neighborhood" settled. At the same time, the "neighbors" would become good American citizens by modeling themselves after the highly educated, upper middle-class "residents." This was true in both urban and rural areas.

The majority of well-to-do Americans were unaware of the living conditions of the American poor and recent immigrants.[4] Some pioneers of the settlement movement in the United States, including Jane Addams, Lillian Wald, and Jacob Riis, literally stumbled upon the poor, and this initial contact motivated them to move into a poor neighborhood to establish a settlement house. The first settlement house in the United States, founded in New York in 1886 by Stanton Coit,[5] was modeled after Toynbee Hall in London. Several other settlements, including Hull House (formed in Chicago in 1889 by Jane Addams), the Nurses Settlement, and later the Henry Street Settlement (formed in New York in 1893 by Lillian Wald), opened shortly thereafter, marking the beginnings of the settlement house movement.

Ideological Background of the Settlement Movement

The pioneers of the settlement movement were inspired by, and closely connected to, influential social and cultural thinkers and reformers of the time from both the United States and abroad. The writings and ideas of Leo Tolstoy, Thomas Carlyle, John Ruskin, and William Morris, as well as Americans Stanley Hall, Felix Adler, and John Dewey had resonance with the settlement pioneers. Carson (1990: 2) points out that "Thomas Carlyle raised the first resounding cry against the materialism and spiritual sterility of modern society. 'Men cannot live isolated,' he exhorted the Victorians; 'we *are* all bound together, for mutual good or else for mutual misery, as living nerves in the same body. No highest man can disunite himself from any lowest.'" This idea of the interconnectedness of all people was the defining premise of the American settlement movement. It was used not only as a basis for bridging the gap between rich and poor, but to blur national and ethnic boundaries and acknowledge immigrants from all over the world as part of the universal humanity embodied by American society.[6] To paraphrase Felix Adler's[7] speech at the University Settlement Society (1911), the goal of this work was not to work for the poor, nor *with* the poor solely for their own benefit, but rather "to work with the poor for the purpose of promoting social progress. The benefits of progress, indeed, are to accrue to the poor, but under the condition that whatever measures are undertaken shall also promote the progress of human society as a whole."[8] The idea of progress was framed by the idea of a universal humanity in which, since all people were connected, the betterment of one caused the betterment of others. Thus the progress of humanity was not progress in terms of modernization and

economic efficiency. This progress was not to be achieved through further industrialization and alienation, but through democracy, cultural pluralism, equality, mutual appreciation; it would be achieved by partaking in one another's lives and cultures, learning through experience and example, finding artistic means of self-expression and returning to manual labor and traditional skills.

The Arts and Crafts movement of John Ruskin and William Morris also had great appeal among settlement workers because of its emphasis on learning through experience. This movement was a response to alienation within urban industrial society and a call for the rejection of mechanically produced goods. It can also be understood as a call for a return to the cultural values of traditional, pre-industrial society.

Another important aspect of settlement ideology is seen in the movement's application of John Dewey's educational theory. As a leading American educational reformer at the beginning of the twentieth century and a close friend of Jane Addams,[9] head of the Hull House settlement in Chicago, Dewey was influential in the settlement movement. He expanded Ruskin and Morris's ideas of learning through experience, emphasizing that through experience and play one learns basic societal and cultural values. The idea of giving importance to play, activity, and education found resonance and wide application in settlement folk dance programs. Particularly relevant to the settlement work was Dewey's belief that children should internalize ideas of democracy, equality, responsibility, and loyalty through directed fun and organized play rather then through books and lectures.

Stanley Hall's theory gave an interesting twist to the understanding of the immigrant/American dichotomy. Hall suffused ideas of the interdependence of body and mind with evolutionary theory, drawing a parallel between individuals "neuromuscular development and their 'race history'."[10] In Hall's (1905) opinion it was true not only that play and dancing developed brain centers but that, through play, children could recapitulate "the activities of our ancestors, back we know not how far, and repeat their life work in summative and adumbrated ways" (figure 3.1).

Figure 3.1. "We Grow Old because We Stop Playing," (Hinman 1937, vol. IV)

Of particular significance is the fact that the link he made between the development of children and the evolutionary stages of human development, particularly the idea that movement recapitulated "race history," was embraced by folk dance advocates, including Hall's friend and contemporary Luther Halsey Gulick. Hall's theory encouraged the perception that immigrant cultures were at a lower evolutionary stage than that of American culture as a whole. As such, these cultures were "childlike" and close to nature. Through folk dancing an individual was not connecting with specific immigrant cultures but with nature and the history of mankind. As embodiments of the neuromuscular history of the human race, folk dances made possible a recapitulation of human history.

Thus, inspired by ideas of universal humanity, backed by the Victorian cult of character, and confronted by the wide gap between the rich and poor, settlement workers saw themselves as attempting, through education and social work, to aid the poor and improve living conditions in their chosen neighborhoods, thereby facilitating the progress of American society as a whole.

Immigrants and the "Evils" of Urban America

The bulk of settlement work was realized through clubs, classes, and services that differed from one settlement to another, depending on the needs of the neighborhood and the ability of the residents to meet those needs. Supervised by the head of the settlement, a number of residents, usually well-to-do college graduates interested in social work, lived in the settlements and provided and organized various kinds of services and activities for the "neighbors." These ranged from distributing milk, arranging visiting-nurse services, giving hygiene and cooking instruction, providing childcare and playground space, to teaching English and citizenship classes, founding music schools, and organizing folk dancing.

The turn of the century saw rapid growth in the settlement movement. In their 1911 *Handbook of Settlements*, Woods and Kennedy (1911: vi) documented the growth in the number of settlements from the seventy-four listed in 1897 to 103 in 1900; 204 in 1905; and, by 1911, 413 settlements in thirty-four states. Broadly speaking, the settlement movement can be viewed as a response to the consequences of rapid urbanization and industrialization, and to that extent it parallels the settlement movement in England. However, when these factors were compounded by the flood of immigration to the United States, the situation for social work changed radically. In an atmosphere of increased awareness of the diversity of the American population, with its many languages, customs, and religious affiliations, much of the emphasis in settlement work was placed on immigrants' education and assimilation into the fabric of American culture and politics.

Alienation, displacement, materialism, utilitarianism, and a lack of cohesive culture, community, and modes of self-expression were seen as

further byproducts of urbanization and industrialization. American settlement workers fought the perceived "evils of urban life"—saloons, dance halls, and prostitution—which reflected a lack of moral laws and traditional values of order and respect. The American cultural elite, to which most leaders of the movement belonged, was generally opposed to commercial forms of entertainment for youth, American and immigrant alike. Dance halls were detrimental in part because they created peer culture and peer entertainment, thus furthering the generation gap between the immigrants and their children that settlement workers desired to bridge. The settlement workers' distaste for the dance hall was certainly shared by the temperance movement[11] and other social reformers of the time.

The dance hall was seen as an embodiment of many ills in contemporary American society. The youth would gather in these establishments to dance popular couple dances of the time to dangerous "syncopated music" without adult supervision.[12] The dances themselves were perceived as racy because of their "loose" body language and physical contact between dancers. In addition, dancers were free to change partners from one dance to the next, creating social promiscuity and threatening even the very institution of couplehood. What happened between dances was just as troubling to social workers as were the dances themselves. Only the more upscale establishments, known as "dance pavilions," provided official supervision to ensure proper behavior between dances. What's more, many working-class dance halls were attached to saloons, with liquor and prostitution as part of the scene.[13]

In discussing the dance hall, Jane Addams (1909: 13) reveals familiar antimodern, anti-industrial sentiments: "Perhaps never before have the pleasures of the young and mature become so definitely separated as in the modern city. . . . The public dance halls filled with frivolous and irresponsible young people in a feverish search for pleasure, are but a sorry substitute for the old dances on the village green in which all of the older people of the village participated." Folk dancing thus needs to be seen as, in part, a substitute and a cure for the dance halls and related activities. "It finally became clear that the question whether or not young people should dance was academic; dance in any case they would. The sole issue was in what surroundings and with what associates they should disport themselves" (Woods and Kennedy [1922] 1990: 102–103).

On settlement folk dancing as experienced by the young, well-to-do "residents," Addams writes (1910: 231) "Many of these young Americans found in these exotic celebrations the brighter side of the urban 'reality' they sought. Here were genuine manifestations of the European folkways they had read about in college, nostalgic survivals of 'simpler,' pre-industrial cultures." This longing for a pre-urban, pre-industrial life style, seen as a possible antidote to the ills of the modern city, was among the motivating factors in the organization of festivals, pageants, and folk dance classes. One Hull House resident, Rita Wallach, explained that these local festivals were a form of experiential education that allowed young people to "reliv[e] those experiences which in former times occupied man's leisure—

when he still was unspoiled by the commercial spirit, and his spontaneous joy in the beauty of life caused him to express himself artistically in poetry, painting, song or dance."[14]

Carson (1990: xi) observes that the settlement movement's "history is a variation on the important theme of the survival of the old at the heart of the new." In this respect the immigrants who were the focus of American settlement work were positioned ambivalently. They were seen, at once, as an embodiment of pastoral, pre-industrial culture and as the main spinners of the industrial wheels, their poverty symbolizing both the failure of modernism and the destruction of traditional values. The immigrants were seen as possessing the "tradition" and "cultural wealth" of the Old World (folklore, close-knit community, and traditional values), a wealth that America needed. But urban industrial America was seen to be destroying the best of the immigrants' possessions while at the same time longing to have those possessions herself. As Lillian Wald (1915: 303) put it, "Great is our loss when a shallow Americanism is accepted by the newly arrived immigrant, and their national traditions and heroes are ruthlessly pushed aside."

It is a measure of the settlement workers' success that a century later folk dance and music could be embraced and perceived to embody the same values they saw in it. The contemporary Balkanites are, in a way, respecting their heritage through rejecting "shallow Americanism," though they are almost universally unaware of the precedents.

Folk Dancing in Settlement Houses

Understanding the complex dynamics between settlement workers' desire to preserve the immigrants' cultural wealth while cultivating and integrating them into American society is the key to understanding this movement's use of folk dance. Folk dancing took place in settlements in at least four contexts: social evenings, pageants, festivals, and folk dance classes.[15] There are small but significant distinctions between these categories, and between the repertoires used in each context. The folk dance material used for pageants and festivals was often highly stylized and quite focused on the nations selected for representation. Festivals often had a specific concentration, at times featuring only one immigrant group. In pageants, folk dances and songs were most often used to support a narrative. Furthermore, pageants and festivals were usually large productions that occurred only a few times a year. Preparations for these events would often last several months. Folk dance classes, on the other hand, were regular, formally organized activities in which a great variety of folk dances were taught in a much less stylized manner.

Folk dance classes were a common aspect of settlement house programs. According to the *Handbook of Settlements* (Woods and Kennedy 1911), folk dance classes were listed in the following settlements: California—Oakland Social Settlement, Neighborhood House in Santa Barbara; Illinois—

Archer Road Settlement in Chicago, Chicago Commons; Louisiana—Kingsley House in New Orleans; Massachusetts—Boston Social Union, Dorchester House, Parker Memorial, Lincoln House, and North Bennet Street Industrial School (Guild of St. Elizabeth, Catholic) all in Boston, and Stearns Neighborhood House in Newton; Michigan—Weinman Settlement (Catholic) in Detroit; Minnesota—Pillsbury Settlement House in Minneapolis; New York—Downtown Ethical Society, Stillman Branch for Colored People, Lenox Hill Settlement, Social Centers of the Political Equality Association (Harlem Club), Richmond Hill House, Riverside House, Warren Goddard House, and Visitation Parochial School in Brooklyn; Ohio—University Settlement in New Richmond; Pennsylvania—Irene Kaufman Settlement in Pittsburgh; and Wisconsin—Wisconsin University Settlement in Milwaukee. These are the settlements that specifically listed folk dancing as one of their activities, but the actual number that offered it is much greater. A number of settlements reported "dancing" or "various kinds of dancing" as an activity, without specifying "folk" dancing, and many settlements included it under "girls and boys clubs," not listing it as a separate category. Archival documentation from the Henry Street settlement and Lincoln House in New York, for example, shows folk dancing to have been a common activity in these institutions, although neither lists it in the Handbook.[16]

Pageants and festivals were organized by most settlements. The core materials for these events were choreographed folk dances and songs. As stated in the Report of the Henry Street Settlement, 1893–1914 (p. 40), probably written by Lillian Wald:

> To the music of the festivals we have given great consideration. The ritual chants and synagogal melodies have been gathered after careful research. For the dances and other musical setting we have incorporated classical compositions that seem to suggest the idea most fittingly. Symbolism has been the keynote of the color schemes in costume and stage-setting, and it is with the utmost regard for the symbol or idea that the dances have been developed. On every hand we attempt to suggest rather than represent, to interpret rather than describe.

This is a good illustration of the treatment of folk material in pageants and festivals where neither the "authenticity" nor the "stylistic purity" of the repertoire was a concern.

The Greeks Are Dancing

The first occurrences of folk dances in settlements appear to have been those in which a single immigrant group engaged in dances of their native land. Overworked and overcrowded, recent immigrants must certainly have relished opportunities to dance familiar dances at social evenings in a settlement gymnasium or dance hall. References to Jews, Greeks, Rus-

sians, Bulgarians, et cetera dancing in the settlements are frequent, though mostly in passing. They are almost never dated and lack detail. We almost never find the names, or even a general description of the dances, the number of participants, or the type of musical accompaniment. But the numerous accounts of folk dancing in the early settlements testify to the fact that settlement leaders encouraged and provided space for this type of activity. Folk dances were often organized for and/or by a particular immigrant group, but they also happened spontaneously. In the University Settlement Society Annual Report for 1910, the following account of folk dancing at the silver anniversary of the wedding of the president of the club is provided:

> What proved to be the most interesting feature of the evening was the folk dancing by the members [of the Mother's Club]. They renewed their girlhood days as they were wont to spend them in the foreign countries. The different dances in which they joined had not been indulged in, as some of them said, since their arrival on these shores. All that was lacking was their "old country" costumes.

Here, folk dancing is taken as a matter of fact, as a natural expression of the immigrants without an apparent agenda. It is seen to signify connection with the past, and its role in the present is one of reminiscence, of "reliving the girlhood days . . . in the foreign countries." The temporal and spatial distance of these dances from the present is emphasized by the perceived lack of "old country costumes." This highlights significant differences between perceptions of the role and meaning of folk dance performed within the boundaries of an immigrant group and situations in which folk dance spans the boundaries of cultural heritage, or in which folk dances of many lands are grouped together.

A 1906 brochure from the Chicago Commons, quoted in Tomko (1999: 169), reports on the Commons auditorium "packed with the men and women of our polyglot people":

> There on the stage were their own representatives to sing and dance in their old-country ways. The graceful delicate dancing of the Italian children, the gay costumes and chivalrous movements of the Norwegians, the plaids and courtesying [*sic*] of the Scotch grand dames, the Greek whirl of men's skirts, all interspersed by the music of the mandolin club, the chorus of the Choral, and the songs of all nations, lifted all up above their little patriotism and blended all hearts in the neighborly spirit of our American international citizenship.

It is through grouping dances from different lands that "little patriotisms" are surpassed even when each group dances its own dances. The "spirit of American international citizenship" was more readily attained through participation in dances of the "other."

Helping the Greeks Dance

In approaching an understanding of the use of folk dances outside of their immigrant group of origin, it is interesting to consider the following account: "The Hull-House residents and club leaders organized Greek clubs of various kinds and Greek dances, when there were so few Greek women that the women residents, young and old, were called in to 'help the Greeks dance'" (Davis and McCree 1969: 114).

Although this account does not help us date occurrences of Greek dancing in Hull House, it is enlightening as an account of residents' participation in the folk dances of an immigrant group to which they did not belong. Whether performed exclusively by the Greeks or by other immigrant "neighbors" and American "residents," the dances were clearly Greek. As noted, the others were "helping the Greeks dance." Participation in Greek dance apparently arose spontaneously as an expression of sympathy with these immigrants, who were unable to perform the dances on their own due to the scarcity of Greek women. This spontaneous interaction and the resulting exchange can be understood as an expression of support, encouragement, and appreciation of the Greeks and their cultural heritage. Placed in the geographical, historical, and cultural context of an American city, "helping the Greeks dance" can be understood as one expression of Americanness. However, it was not preconceived as a confirmation of Americanness.

Dancing Folk Dances of the Greeks

A rather different situation arose when folk dances of various ethnic origins were grouped together and taught to "new" Americans regardless of their ethnic background. Boundaries of cultural heritage were crossed twice; both by the dancers (members of different immigrant groups dancing together) and by the dances performed (folk dances from around the world being grouped together, irrespective of the dancers' backgrounds). In such cases, folk dancing became less a symbol of the dancers' heritage and reminiscence of the past than an active element in defining and shaping their American present. In other words, the purpose of partaking in each other's dances was not "to help the Greeks dance" but rather to help the Greeks become American, to help others see the Greeks as Americans, and to help the dancers see themselves as Americans while dancing Greek and other dances. In this context the power of folk dance to reinforce social cohesion on an ethnic, "in-group" basis, i.e., "among the Greeks," was shifted toward establishing and reinforcing American identity. Under such circumstances, folk dances of a particular immigrant group (Greek, Bulgarian, Italian, etc.) transcended ethnic boundaries and became building blocks of American citizenship and signifiers of democracy, equality, and freedom. Settlement workers hoped to build a sense of community that would provide equally for group cohesion and loyalty to the new country. As seen by Felix Adler (Adler 1906, in Lubove 1974),[17] the unique function

of the settlement was to "rescue for us and to develop a department of ethics which has almost been lost to us, namely, the ethics of neighborhood."

In the Report of the Henry Street Settlement, 1893–1914, its founder, Lillian Wald, states:[18]

> I opened my report with an allusion to the beautiful pageant that was held on the streets last June. That was but one example of the really inspired work that is carried on for the neighborhood and by the neighborhood, as represented in the Settlement membership, under the lofty leadership of Miss Alice and Miss Irene Lewisohn and their coworkers. When the pantomimes and festivals are given, something is passed over to the community that transcends my power to describe. It is not only that, by those less impartial than myself, the performances are judged to be beautiful to the eye and to the ear, but that the note sounded is the deep one of democracy and interpretation, for these have been woven out of the traditions of our neighbors, or have transmitted the conviction of a universal brotherhood that is the inspiration of the authors.

In this context, specific dances clearly transcend their ethnic boundaries and, though chosen to symbolically represent specific immigrant groups, they stand as symbols of "democracy" and "universal brotherhood." Folk dancing made possible a direct expression of these beliefs, and the belief, central to settlement work, that America and American identity comprised multiple ethnic identities. But it was only through recontextualization and integration into a new whole that folk dances of Russians, Eastern European Jews, Norwegians, Bulgarians, or Greeks could transmit "the conviction of universal brotherhood."

Harmony Through Exposure to the Other

Looking at dancing in settlements Linda Tomko (1999: 85) concludes that "a specific conjuncture of people, theories, and events positioned women settlers to develop dance practices as direct forms for engagement with pressing Progressive era problems of immigration, ethnicity and urbanization." Settlement leaders and residents throughout the United States needed to cope with the growing cultural diversity of their neighborhoods. The Report of the Henry Street Settlement, 1893–1918 (p. 71) states: "The total club membership is about seven hundred, and includes people of many races. One club of twelve members represents eight different nationalities whose various characteristics are being harmonized through closer contact and understanding of each other." We have noted the settlement ideology that cultural difference could be bridged through exposure to the cultural wealth of each immigrant group in the interest of the nation and humanity in general. This laid the foundation for widespread use of folk dances and songs of many nations to encourage understanding, appreciation, and harmony

among different immigrant groups, as well as between recent immigrants and more settled Americans.[19] "Bigotry, intolerance or even an unswerving faith in the superiority of one's own religious and political creed are much shaken when individuals are brought face to face with each other, or have the ideas of others continuously and forcibly placed before them" (John Dewey, in Davis and McCree 1969: 96–97). The settlement leaders observed the following:

> It is easy enough to bring together the most antagonistic elements in pageants, mass meetings, and large-scale recreative events in which several nationalities hold solidly together. Exaltation of popular heroes, exhibition of literary, artistic, and musical masterpieces, performance of folk dances, mass singing of national hymns, anthems, and folk songs, promote toleration, a sense of live and let live, and a measure of mutual respect. These events have their greatest usefulness in preparing the minds of individuals for more personal relations across racial lines. . . . Most groups are fortunately quite willing to include a small proportion of the unlike, and even seem to enjoy the flavor of strangeness so introduced. (Woods and Kennedy [1922] 1990: 338)

The authors chose their words carefully. "Toleration" was "promoted," and the minds of individuals were "prepared" for more personal relations across "racial" lines. The activities and events cited were apparently seen as existing in a space separate from the daily lives and attitudes of immigrants toward each other.[20] The authors continue, suggesting a limit to the possibility of crossing "racial" boundaries: "But when inherent differences reach a point that invites struggle for supremacy, the worst passions of each element are unloosed" (Woods and Kennedy [1922] 1990: 338). One of the appeals of folk dancing was that it provided a safe space for "exposure," "toleration," and "integration." Folk dance events did not invite struggle for supremacy, and even if mutual respect and tolerance were largely symbolic, the experiences were nonetheless powerful for many participants.

Integration of Immigrants into American Society

The settlement movement's vision of integration was not unidirectional—the simple assimilation of immigrants—but was conceived more dialectically as a "give and take" between immigrant groups and the country at large. As Miss Follett put it, "All diversity if wisely handled may lead to the something new which neither side possesses, whereas if one side submits to the other or a compromise is made, we have no progress in the end." Integration, seen as a synthesis between the parties involved, occurs according to Follett "in the sphere of activities, of desires, of interests, not in that of mere ideas or of verbal symbols."[21] It becomes clearer why grouping folk dances of various immigrant populations under a common de-

nominator, thus causing each to yield to a larger entity, was encouraged as a "wise handling of diversity." It provided for integration in the sphere of "activities, desires and interests" and imprinted the ideology of the settlement movement in participants' minds, especially in those of the recent immigrants' children who were the main participants in pageants and festivals. An important point in the above quotation is the idea that, in order to achieve social progress, there must be exchange between different groups. This thought is very illustrative of the settlement ideology of democracy and equality, and expresses the importance it placed on ideas of universal humanity and subcultural interdependence. It also expresses a belief in an American identity resulting from the exchange between immigrants and the native-born.

The integration of a deeply multicultural American society was to be facilitated by breaking down isolationist forces within its constituent parts. Affirmation of this belief can be found in the words of Woods and Kennedy:

> The weight of experience shows that under all but most extreme conditions the neighborhood can be in part, and for moments completely, lifted to a plane where barriers of race and tradition begin to lose their isolating power, . . . a common language, charged with rich significance, becomes the means of interchange among different racial groups. ([1922]1990: 340)

We can easily see how folk dancing was to enable "interchange among different racial groups." Immigrants from as many countries as were represented in a neighborhood could unite, at least temporarily, through dancing each other's dances. Thus, any particular tradition would lose its isolating power and the desired "common language" could be established. This common language was both figurative and literal (figure 3.2).

"One thing in particular that arouses my indignation," said Commissioner of Immigration, William Williams, in his address to the University Settlement Society (NYC Annual Report 1915–16, p. 17),[22] "is to find immigrants who have been here for several years and yet do not know our language. . . . The fact is, that there are in our midst colonies of foreigners who do not mix at all with the Americans. This condition is not a wholesome one, and I hope a means can be found to break up those colonies and make these foreigners become a part of the body politic and useful citizens of the country in which they take up their new abode."

While I would not suggest that folk dancing was introduced with the *purpose* of "breaking up" these immigrant colonies, it was clearly employed as a vehicle for Americanization through integration and the establishment of a common culture and, as such, it *did* aid in breaking them up.

Research of settlement folk-dance programs highlights aspects of settlement ideology that are not brought out in most writings about the settlement movement. It is often thought that the settlements' primary goal was to Americanize immigrants. But, while Americanization was among the central goals of the movement, the complexity of the very issue of Ameri-

Figure 3.2. "Dancing around the Tree" (Gulick 1911: 129)

canization and of the settlement workers' opinions about it are often overlooked. Let us briefly investigate the aspects of this issue that are directly connected with folk dancing.

The Settlement Movement, Folk Dancing, and the Americanization of Immigrants

The goal of Americanization had not always been central to settlement work. It achieved tremendous importance during World War I, a time of increased public resentment toward foreigners. In 1928 Gregory Weinstein (1928: 78) defined the "tendency to bait and nag the foreign born" as "recent" and "altogether new to this country." In his opinion, "this peculiar post-war method of 'Americanization' is . . . responsible for the failure of the proverbial 'melting pot' to melt satisfactorily." Interestingly, the opinions of those in the settlement movement did not match public sentiment toward immigrants at the time.[23] As a matter of fact, throughout the war, settlement leaders stood fast against public suspicion, defending foreigners and their loyalty to the United States. But, they believed, this loyalty could only be achieved if immigrants were to realize that America was their country, where they experienced democracy, freedom, tolerance, and equality.[24] "Instead of teaching that America is the great land of unlimited opportunity for wealth . . . we are teaching that this country has been and must continue to be the product of the cultural and racial contributions of many countries. To teach them not that America is the place to get, but that America is the land to serve."[25]

In the foreword to the 29th Annual Report (1915–16) of the University Settlement Society in New York, Robert A. Crosby writes:

> The talk in favor of "Americanization" which has been heard so much during the past two years has been interesting to everyone connected with settlements, not because it was a new thought, but because it was such a fine endorsement of the settlement movement. If there is any one agency whose primary purpose has always been Americanization, it is the settlement. It is now thirty years since the University Settlement ceased to theorize about Americanization and began to teach it. . . .

Teaching Americanization was a common goal of the settlement houses, but it is often misunderstood. Mary Simkhovitch,[26] as quoted in Carson (1990: 158), clearly expresses her view of the role of settlements in the Americanization of foreigners: "To Americanize I do not mean New Englandize or Old Colonialize. . . . We desire indeed to keep the ideals of our forefathers as to liberty, economic opportunity and religious freedom, but there are also . . . [i]deals of culture and association, and . . . [w]e ought to welcome and conserve variety in our newcomers." Again, we see an emphasis on appreciating immigrant culture and the expression of a sincere belief in cultural pluralism.

It may seem paradoxical that institutions whose aim was to shape immigrants into American citizens were among the most vocal about preserving the values of immigrant cultural heritage as expressed in various traditional art forms. But there is no contradiction here if one perceives "American identity" to be pluralistic and the process of assimilation to be an exchange of cultural values between the immigrant and the native-born. What the settlement leaders attempted to achieve was a balance that would make these "two prongs" merge into one. "This feeling of reciprocity, of mutual give and take, between those who belong to the older American citizenship and those who come from the new, is one of the most wholesome phases of the Playhouse work" (Report of the Henry Street Settlement, 1893–1918, p. 56). The goal of showing immigrants they were, themselves, Americans was best accomplished through shared experience and participation in activities that fostered an inclusive, American identity. Folk dancing was thus perceived as something that could enable immigrants to recognize and internalize Americanness through experience.

Folk Dancing in Training for Good Citizenship

> Were the last foreigner to come among us to be Americanized, still there would remain the everlasting problem of making the native born into men.
>
> —Weinstein 1928: 79

The lasting Victorian concept of character building was essential to settlement work. It was believed that character building had to come first, before Americanization could be accomplished. Through example and education one could make "good men and good women." As an outcome of this process they would become good citizens. "The settlement invariably organized play groups, clubs, and classes where the children of the neighborhood received, under a resident's personal guidance and attention, their training for future citizenship" (Lubove 1974: 188–89). Winning a child's loyalty and affection was important, as it helped to influence and mold his or her total personality and aided the "public schools in the transformation of the crude immigration material into real citizens and citizenesses" (College Settlements Association Report 1905–06: 36). Lectures and classes were seen to be much less effective in training for citizenship and molding a child's character than were directed social activities and play. As John Dewey wrote in *Freedom and Culture* (1939: 10), "We are beginning to realize that emotion and imagination are more potent in shaping public sentiment and opinion than information and reason." The sheer sense of belonging and camaraderie established among the children of immigrants through their participation in group activities like folk dancing (figure 3.3) was seen by settlement workers and tenement dwellers as a most precious achievement.

Settlement workers saw a need for various arts programs for immigrants, since creativity and self-expression were seen as prerequisites to progress and true humanity. Lillian Wald thought that the capacity for "play and joy and beauty . . . [were] among the essentials for a successful civilization"[27] (as quoted in Tomko 1990: 277). Involvement in art was meant to enable immigrants to transcend the repetitiveness and ugliness of their

Figure 3.3. Rooftop playground, Pittsburgh (Gulick 1911)

daily lives. "Their ideas and resources are cramped. The desire for higher social pleasure is extinct. They have no share in the traditions and social energy which make for progress."[28] However, the immigrants were not simply encouraged to find for themselves "social pleasure" beyond their cramped neighborhoods and redundant factory work. They were to find "higher" social pleasure in "the traditions, which make for progress."

The settlement leaders wanted immigrants to be engaged in what they saw as valuable, wholesome social activities; activities which would uplift the spirit and create an atmosphere of moral uprightness. "As it is possible to establish a connection between the lack of public recreation and the vicious excitements and trivial amusements which become their substitutes," writes Addams, "so it may be illuminating to trace the connection between the monotony and dullness of factory work and the petty immoralities which are often the youth's protest against them" (1909: 107).

Folk Dancing to Bridge the Generation Gap

Besides keeping youths out of the dance halls, folk dancing was intended to bridge the generation gap between immigrant parents and their children. "One of the problems that confront any social program in a center like this is the fact that the younger generation feels itself to be of a different nationality—almost a different race sometimes from the generation to which its parents belong," concludes the author of the Report of the Union Settlement of New York City. He sees the possibility of overcoming this difficulty by "helping the younger people to appreciate the contributions of their fatherland"[29] and describes a project undertaken by the settlement to address this generation gap:

> The children are being encouraged to bring in the songs of their own country which their parents have taught them. They are to be bound together in a book decorated with designs typical of the country represented. This book will, I hope, be a symbol on the part of the Americans of the Settlement, that their neighbors have a contribution of value to make. The book will be a tangible result, but by no means as important as the less obvious one of creating a feeling of comradeship in the home where these songs of the homeland will take on a new value.

No doubt, similar effects were achieved through organized mass singing of folk songs and national anthems, through folk dances and festivals. As Rita Wallach explains in her 1906 article "Social Value of the Festival," "By placing immigrant traditions in an art context, the festival publicly assigned value to immigrant culture and confirmed adults in their sense of worth."

One might wonder why it was important to settlement leaders and residents to bridge the generation gap between immigrants and their children.

Would it not have been easier to let the children of the immigrants "Americanize" themselves? Wouldn't it be logical to let them accept the "shallow Americanism" and popular, commercial music and dance styles they were drawn to in the first place? Why was it important to teach second-generation immigrants to respect the values and traditions of their parents' native lands? Firstly, the generation gap was seen as the main problem in maintaining respect and orderliness among immigrants. Thus it was seen as an obstacle to making the children of immigrants into respectable citizens. The lack of respect shown, not only to their parents, but to their ancestral value systems was what settlement leaders wanted to correct in children, and harmonizing intergenerational tensions was seen as a precondition for progress. Reestablishing family ties and the traditional family values of the old world was an effort to reduce crime and the "restless search for pleasure" among the youth. This brings us to a familiar point: the gap that settlement workers wanted to bridge was not simply a gap between one generation of immigrants and their children, but between the values associated with pastoral, pre-industrial societies, and those of the "modern world." Settlement workers sought more than an alternative to commercial forms of dancing. They also wanted to instill or impose a particular set of values. Jane Addams wrote, in her 1909 book *Spirit of Youth and the City Streets*, "These old forms of dancing which have been worked out in many lands and through long experiences, safeguard unwary and dangerous expression and yet afford a vehicle through which the gaiety of youth may flow. Their forms are indeed those which lie at the basis of all good breeding, forms which at once express and restrain, urge forward and set limits."

Settlement Houses and Public Schools

This kind of "good breeding" was necessary for immigrants but also for "American" youth. The use of folk dance in the transmission of the set of values described above was not limited to the settlements, but was widely accepted in public schools and physical recreation programs in colleges, parks, and even in industry. "School as a social center," write Davis and McCree (1969: 98), "must provide means for bringing people and their ideas and beliefs together, in such ways as will lessen friction and instability, and introduce deeper sympathy and wider understanding. . . . What we want is to see the school, every public school, doing something of the same sort of work that is now done by a settlement or two scattered at wide distances through the city."

The connection and interchange between the settlements and other social and educational institutions at the turn of the century was both ideological and practical. Settlement workers, educational reformers, and physical educators were well aware of each other's work. They exchanged ideas, personnel, and teaching materials, and organized many collaborative projects between various institutions. Mary Wood Hinman, for ex-

ample, brought members of her class at the Dewey School in Chicago to the Chicago settlement houses. Her students would perform the folk dances they had learned at school for the "neighbors." In Hinman's opinion (Gulick 1911: 85–86), "this whole situation would have been made impossible if these boys had not gained through our training [folk dancing] this idea of social life, the appreciation of these people through a knowledge of their national dances, and the feeling that they actually possessed something that would give pleasure." Through learning the folk dances of an immigrant group the students were able not only to communicate with the immigrants but, through the experience, to learn about the social interconnectedness of all people. This was seen as democracy at work. The "idea of social life" that Hinman's students gained through folk dancing was that of the social unity of all Americans, immigrants and native-born alike.

The experimental and pioneering work of the settlements was used as a model for teaching democracy and citizenship in other segments of American society. Let us now turn our attention to some of these other segments and the appeal of folk dance programs to institutions whose work was focused not on immigrants, but on the native-born—"the Americans."

4

Folk Dancing and the Physical Education and Recreation Movements

Continuing our look at the early ancestry of the Balkan scene, we turn our attention to movements in which the importance of folk dancing and music are more clearly in focus. In parks and playgrounds, public schools and pageants, the effects of folk dance and music on the physiological, intellectual, and social development of Americans was highly touted as important to the national interest. What's more, the dissemination of folklore was prescribed as a noble endeavor, even a vital counterbalance to the perceived newness and shallowness of American culture. Although repertoire is still not our central focus, we will discuss some of the early twentieth-century folk music and dance material itself, and the importance of criteria various movements used to select it. Here we encounter some of the earliest known examples of Balkan music and dance published for use in folk dancing, at least one of which (Seljančica) is still popular in the Balkan scene.

Getting the Nation into Shape

The introduction of folk dance programs into colleges, public schools, YMCAs and YWCAs, Normal schools for dance or physical education and commercial dance schools, as well as into recreation programs in parks, playgrounds, factories, churches and old people's homes, sprang from an ideological impulse closely related to that examined in the previous chapter. Though participants in folk dance programs outside of the settlements were less likely to be as ethnically diverse as the "neighbors," the idea of grouping folk dances from various parts of the world together for the ultimate benefit of the American nation as a whole was the same. Folk dance was to shape up the bodies of the nation, foreign and native-born alike, to straighten them, correct their deformities, and (re)construct them into fit citizens: "The loss in physical vigor in the United States, through lack of adequate provision for health care and physical training is incalculable. There is tremendous need today for better training for citizenship" (Williams 1922: 34–35).

The task of getting American bodies into shape became a concern in the mid to late 1800s, particularly after the Civil War. The consecutive wars in the twentieth century also sparked public awareness of the importance of the nation's physical fitness. The Provost Marshal General reported in 1918 that about 30 percent to 53 percent of men called up in the Selective Service Draft were rejected (Williams 1922: 34–35).[1] These reported numbers represent only a statistical confirmation of a concern shared widely by physicians, anthropometrists, and physical educators that American urban youth (male and female) were physically underdeveloped and deformed due to insufficient vigorous physical activity and systematic exercise. Urban living conditions were seen as the main cause of this sloth. Working youths spent their days sitting in offices or doing repetitive movements in factories. Even children, cramped in crowded neighborhoods without space for play, were physically inactive. The dirt and traffic on city streets kept children from playing and socializing in the only available outdoor space. While physicians and physical educators were aware of the negative consequences of urban life on the fitness of the nation, their solution to the problem did not involve restructuring the society and eliminating the causes of unhealthy living. Rather, they attempted to work on the other end of the problem, developing ways to correct the consequences of this situation, to bring up a healthy nation in unhealthy living and working conditions.

The idea of building a strong nation through making the bodies of its citizens strong and healthy[2] is at least as old as Horace's saying, *Mens sana in corpore sano* (healthy mind, healthy body), and even the choice of folk dancing for the accomplishment of this goal has its predecessors. Folk dance programs that aimed to maintain physical fitness, particularly in urban youth, as well as to strengthen national unity and build citizenship, were firmly established in many European countries well before the end of the nineteenth century. As a part of physical education in school curricula and various recreational organizations, folk dancing was taught in Germany, Finland, Sweden, Denmark, Italy, England, and probably other European countries. It was an important part of the Czech Sokol[3] movement and, most likely, the pan-Slavic movement at the end of the nineteenth century. A focus on the lore of the peasants was certainly part of the national awakening in Russia and other eastern and southern European territories as well. It is reasonable to suspect that folk dance programs were part of many national movements across Europe as an outcome of Romanticism, with its emphasis on the peasantry and folklore as the embodiment of national character.[4]

Even within the United States the use of folk dancing to achieve physical fitness and social cohesion was not new. The German Turner societies (or Turnverein)[5] that spread across the United States in the mid-nineteenth century included folk dancing as an activity in their programs, although it was strictly *German* folk dancing. The Turnvereins found folk dancing useful particularly in promoting physical fitness among girls. The Czech Sokol groups similarly embraced shaping up the bodies of the nation,

teaching youth patriotism and loyalty through organized mass exercises and taking pride in national folklore. Both Turner and Sokol societies were focused on their own national folklore, but clear ideological and methodological parallels can be drawn between these societies and the American physical education movement. Understanding American national folklore to comprise folk traditions from many of the country's immigrant groups, for example, makes clear how comparable international folk dancing's role in strengthening American national identity is to German folk dancing's role within the Turnverein.

Folk dancing was certainly not the first, nor the only method of promoting the physical fitness of American youth. Although educators agreed on the necessity of establishing physical education programs in colleges and schools, there was no unified opinion as to what system of physical training to use. The two most influential systems were the German, as practiced and taught by the Turners, and Swedish, or so called "Ling system" of gymnastics.[6] Each system had its advocates, while there were equally strong advocates for devising a specifically American system of physical education, designed to suit American needs. The report (Barrows 1890) of the papers and discussions of the national conference of physical educators held in Boston, in 1889, reveals all the tensions and differences in opinion on the matter. While the German system was criticized for being too focused on the development of muscular strength alone, the Swedish system was criticized for requiring too much mental attention, and both systems were criticized for being "dictatorial" rather then "democratic." Advocating the invention of a new, American program of physical education, Jay W. Seaver of Yale University insisted (Barrows 1890: 53–54) that "here in America (it may be wrong, but it is true) we do not care a snap for any man's say so. We do not like to be ordered around to do anything. It always made me mad, as a boy, and it does still, to have any one talk to me in a dictatorial way. I believe it is contrary to the American spirit and custom." While this remark might appear marginal to our discussion, the belief that American physical education needed in its essence to be democratic, inclusive, and reflective of the "American spirit" was very important to the inclusion of folk dancing in physical education programs.

Folk dancing took priority over other forms of group exercise for a number of practical reasons. The cost of establishing a folk dance program was extremely low in comparison with building properly furnished gymnasia. Folk dance required very little room and could be done in existing spaces such as school roofs or classrooms, playgrounds, church basements, community rooms, parks, and even streets. The activity was suitable for all ages and both sexes, whether they were dancing together or independently. A single teacher could simultaneously instruct large numbers of students. The time allotted for physical education was used to its maximum—there was no waiting time since everybody danced together. It is due, in part, to these practical advantages that folk dancing became so popular in recreation and physical education.

Folk dancing provided for much more then just the physical education of children. Its advocates saw it as a fundamental part of "education for life" and "training for humanity." Through folk dancing children would "develop knowledge of folk lore and folk life, skill and body control, and certain social values in working harmoniously with other people, as an outgrowth, as a result flowing out of the dance, which in itself was an end, and satisfying to the child" (Williams 1922: 11). Among athletics, gymnastics, and folk dancing, the latter was determined to be the most interesting activity of the Girls' Athletic League because, among other things, "the folk dances afforded opportunity for cooperation with other activities of school and home in a way not afforded by either of the other activities" (Gulick 1911: 37).

Beginnings of Folk Dance Programs in Schools and Colleges

It is difficult to determine when and where the first folk dance classes were offered in school and college physical education programs. Folk dancing was introduced independently at several schools and colleges around the country at approximately the same time. The ideological and cultural atmosphere of the time laid the groundwork for the practice to arise in many places at approximately the same time through isolated individual efforts. Folk dances were being learned, taught, or published as early as 1884 and much more frequently in the first years of the twentieth century.[7] The generic term *dancing* was often the only term used in course descriptions before the turn of the century. Physical educators/dance instructors of the time did not use unified terminology to clearly define their dance material, and it is likely that the "dancing" taught in some physical education programs was "folk dancing." Even if the dance programs *were* labeled folk, we cannot say with certainty what that label meant at the time, or what material was presented. For example, Mary Wood Hinman defines her classes as "a combination of ball-room and folk dancing" (quoted in Gulick 1911: 75). Most of the teachers do not offer us even that much information about their dance material. The titles of dance instructors are not much more helpful, as they varied from one institution to another. When *dancing* was introduced into the Boston Normal School of Gymnastics (BNSG) in 1897–98, the title of the appointed instructor Ethel Perrin, herself a graduate of the BNSG, was "Instructor in Applied Anthropometry, Dancing, and Games." In the following school year (1898–99), Melvin Ballou Gilbert was appointed as "instructor in aesthetic dancing" at the same institution, and so on.[8] Luther Halsey Gulick, one of the strongest advocates of the folk dance movement, received his degree from the YMCA School in Springfield, Massachusetts,[9] but I have seen no evidence of Gulick receiving folk dance instruction there. Two of the most prominent folk dance teachers, Mary Wood Hinman and Elizabeth Burchenal, studied dance with Melvin Ballou Gilbert, although there is no evidence that

he gave instruction in folk dancing. While institutions such as BNSG, Wellesley College, NYU, the YMCA school in Springfield and many others would become known for their folk dance programs, it is difficult to determine what was taught at these institutions and where the repertoire came from.

Still, similarity in repertoire is suggested not only by ideological similarities between the settlement and physical education movements but by a substantial crossover in personnel. The energies of a rather small circle of people converged in this sphere of activity, creating a network of folk dance advocates, teachers, and social reformers. The teaching careers of three individuals in particular, Mary Wood Hinman, Louis Chalif, and Elizabeth Burchenal, stand out for their importance to the folk dance developments at the beginning of the twentieth century.

The Pioneers: Hinman, Burchenal, and Chalif

Mary Wood Hinman

Mary Wood Hinman was one of the first professional folk dance teachers in the United States—an inspiration for many women who were trying to make a living in dance.[10] Her teaching career began circa 1894 in Chicago (figure 4.1).

Although she was not a resident at Hull House, she offered classes there regularly beginning in 1898 and taught at other settlements around Chicago, providing a direct link between the settlement house and physical education movements. Hinman also taught in John Dewey's schools (University of Chicago Elementary School, later Francis Parker School, and

Figure 4.1. Private class of Mary Wood Hinman in Chicago (Gulick 1911)

University of Chicago High School) and later provided summer school instruction at Columbia University in New York. In 1904 she opened Hinman School of Gymnastic and Folk Dancing and Hinman Normal School. She achieved considerable national influence both through her own instruction and that of her students.[11] Her entrepreneurial skills led her to even offer long-distance courses to teachers outside the Chicago area. Hinman's life and work illustrate clearly the ideology of many turn-of-the-century social reformers. Doris Humphrey, one of her most celebrated students, viewed her teacher as a "humanist" rather than an "artist." Hinman perceived folk dance as the ultimate communal expression and participatory activity. "Her continual interest lies in people, and whatever concerns giving them more of everything they want" (Humphrey, in Tomko 1999: 163). This populist view of the role of the arts as a vehicle for uplifting humanity motivated Hinman to take every opportunity to both teach and learn a new dance; at times she held numerous teaching positions and she acquired a wide repertoire of dances.

Perhaps Hinman's most far-reaching influence came through her numerous publications of folkdance instruction and music accompaniment that were used by teachers across the country. Hinman's five volumes of *Gymnastic and Folk Dancing* (*Solo Dances*, *Couple Dances*, *Ring Dances*, *Group Dances*, and *Tap Dances, Clogs and Jigs*, in order of publication) offer valuable information on the pioneers of folk dance. In some cases, along with the usual piano arrangement of the music and sketchy step description, Hinman left us brief and somewhat enigmatic references to the sources of her material.[12] According to historian Selma Odom (in Tomko 1999: 153), "Hinman studied various kinds of dance with Chicago dance teachers, dance callers, and perhaps even people in Chicago's ethnic communities." She also "visited Sweden to study folk dances and games at the College of Nääs, and traveled in northern Sweden learning dances. At other times she journeyed to Denmark, Russia, and Ireland, in each case studying and collecting traditional dance material firsthand." Some of Hinman's material, such as examples of African American dance, was obviously not gathered during these trips abroad. It is quite possible that Hinman learned dances from neighbors she worked with in settlements.

Of particular relevance to the later Balkan music and dance scene, it is interesting to point out the illustration of a circle dance on the cover of her 1937 *Gymnastic and Folk Dances*, volume IV (figure 4.2).

Elizabeth Burchenal

The beginning of the folk dance movement is sometimes taken to be 1905, the date when Elizabeth Burchenal established folk dancing in public schools in New York. She formed the Girls Branch of the Public School Athletic League (also known as Girls Athletic League, or GAL)[13] and introduced folk dancing as its main activity (figure 4.3).

The Public School Athletic League (PSAL) was incorporated in New York City, for boys only, two years before the Girls' Branch was established.

Figure 4.2. Cover of the 1937 edition of Hinman's *Gymnastic and Folk Dances*, volume IV

As the director of physical training in New York Public Schools, Luther Halsey Gulick was one of the founders of PSAL in 1903.[14] Though he did not introduce folk dancing into the PSAL, he was highly supportive of folk dance programs in public schools and collaborated closely with Elizabeth Burchenal. He was apparently familiar with Burchenal's work at the Teachers College (1902–1905) in New York and, according to Tomko (1999: 161), he "recruited" her from that position to direct the Girls' Branch of the PSAL.

References to how dancing was actually taught in the early history of folk dancing in physical education are rare. For this reason a brief descrip-

Figure 4.3. "Swedish Klapdans" performed by girls at Public School 23, Manhattan, New York (Gulick 1911)

tion of Burchenal teaching the Hungarian Czardas to the group of forty girls at the East Side Public School in New York (figure 4.4) is a valuable contribution to our understanding of her method of instruction:

> At the close of the program Miss Burchenal inquired if there were any Hungarian girls present who knew the Czardas. The hands of two went up. In a twinkling she had seized the bigger girl by the waist and was whirling her around the room. Immediately the children scrambled for partners and with eyes on the Inspector they began to imitate her steps. Falteringly at first, then more surely and finally with complete confidence, couple after couple made the movement their own until nearly the whole roomful was successfully tripping the intricate steps of the Hungarian national dance. (Perry 1910: 30–31)

Burchenal "traveled frequently to Europe, possibly even annually from 1906 to 1913, walking and living in rural communities in Spain, France, Germany, Denmark, Sweden, and Ireland" (Tomko 1999: 193). Betty Spears writes that "in order to provide suitable dances for recreational activity, she [Burchenal] learned the dances first hand from the immigrant groups in the United States and she also studied in Europe." Although Spears does not provide the source of this information, it would make sense for Burchenal to have learned the dances from immigrants. Perry (1910: 30) suggests that Elizabeth Burchenal collaborated closely with her sister on her European collecting trips. They were "visiting the festivals of the country-folk, and while she [Elizabeth] had learned their dances her companion had jotted down the music." It appears that each of her research trips to

Figure 4.4. Hungarian solo or "czardas" (Gulick 1911)

Europe resulted in a publication of dances learned. The long list of Burchenal's folk dance publications includes several hundred dances. However, Burchenal's most significant achievement was the institutionalization of folk dancing in schools across the country. Even to this day, American children learn folk dances as part of their physical education curricula.

Louis Chalif

In 1905, the very same year Burchenal established folk dancing in public schools, Louis Chalif taught a class at the annual convention of the American Society of Professors of Dancing. Chalif (1876–1948) was a renowned Russian ballet dancer (figure 4.5)[15] who, in 1904, danced at the Metropolitan Opera in New York.

On that occasion Luther Gulick, appointed in 1903 as director of physical training in the public schools of New York City, invited Louis Chalif to stay in New York and start a normal school of dance. Chalif's Normal School of Dancing, sometimes called the Russian Normal School of Dancing, was founded a year later, in 1905, in New York.[16] Chalif most likely arrived in the United States with a repertoire of international folk dances, and presumably Gulick had reason to believe Chalif had experience teaching folk dances when he encouraged him to establish the Normal School.[17] Gulick himself organized the folk dance class for physical education teachers that Chalif taught in August 1905 and was responsible for Chalif being hired to teach folk dances at the Second Annual Convention of the Playground Congress of America in 1908.

Figure 4.5. Louis Chalif in a Russian dance (Gulick 1911)

Though Chalif's work before he immigrated to the United States remains obscure for lack of data, his work in America is well documented. Chalif was a prolific author and excellent businessman.[18] The first instruction in his published dances reads, "In public performance credit must be given for the arrangement of this dance," and only then does he provide the dance instruction. Chalif appears to have published most of the dances he taught. Once he realized that there was a wide market for folk dances he began to target that market, constantly supplying it with useful publications of both individual dances and larger compilations. He arranged over a thousand dances, and five of his textbooks have been translated into a number of foreign languages and distributed throughout the United States and abroad. The dances were compiled according to their level of difficulty within the categories of "folk," "national," "character," "historical," "aesthetic," "pantomime," "ballroom," and, of course "ballet."

To the best of my knowledge the first "Balkan" folk dances published in the United States are in Chalif's "Folk dances of Different Nations" (1914).

Volume I contains a Croatian dance (figures 4.6a, b) among twenty-three "very easy dances." The Serbian dance (figures 4.7a, b) titled "Cola Serbianka,"[19] later known as "Seljančica" ("A Village Girl") is among the twenty "rather easy dances" in volume II and remains popular in folk dance circles **(CD 4)**. The skeletal nature of Chalif's musical notation is amply illustrated by a quick comparison with the lively 1950's recording of "Seljančica" by the Banat Tamburitza Orchestra. Interestingly, the tune was also recycled as the patriotic song "Little Pioneers" (Pioniri maleni) during the socialist period in the former Yugoslavia. The "Bulgarian Folk dance" (figures 4.8a, b) set to a "Hungarian Folk Melody" is among twenty "slightly difficult dances." This example clearly shows the extent of the interpretive liberties of the era.

The dance steps and the music were obviously treated as separate units. The fact that Bulgarians never danced to Hungarian tunes was not a concern for Chalif. This symbiosis was probably a matter of convenience. Most likely, Chalif learned the dance steps and in the absence of the appropriate tune he found a tune that "matched" the steps. In the light of this attitude, it is even more interesting that Chalif noted the different "national" origins of the tune and dance steps.

Chalif's work was present and influential in all the institutions and organizations that supported folk dance programs.[20] Chalif was also active as a teacher in settlement houses in New York City. The head of the Henry Street Settlement, Lillian Wald, said, "Mr. Chalif makes a very important and valuable contribution to our knowledge of people who come to America through his wonderful folk dancing. . . . Mr. Chalif's intelligence as teacher is as marked as performer, and the settlement has valued the assistance and the instruction it has received from him."[21]

Keeping in mind that it is an "in house" publication, through the general catalog of the Chalif Normal School of Dancing for the season 1915–1916 we get a picture of the extent of Chalif's influence: "The favorite form of art in the gymnasiums of America is Chalif Dancing. This is taught now in practically all the normal schools of physical education . . . : Wesley, Sergeant, Columbia, New Haven, Savage, Chicago, Battle Creek, Wisconsin, Utah and California Universities, Kalamazoo and the summer schools of Harvard, N.B., Hot Springs, NC, and Dartmouth." Not only were Chalif's dance instruction manuals being widely distributed, but he himself was giving workshops throughout the country teaching various types of dancing and organizing festivals and "pantomimes" for schools, colleges, playgrounds, YMCAs, and the like. Every year several hundred students passed through his normal school.[22] Chalif advertised his classes as beneficial to four groups of people: dancing teachers, physical culture teachers, recreation leaders, and exhibition dancers. With such a wide sphere of activity, Chalif clearly had considerable influence on the folk dance movement, as well as on the development of dance in the United States in general.

While Elizabeth Burchenal is widely remembered and acknowledged for her contribution to the development of folk dance programs in physical education, Chalif's influence is often overlooked. Chalif has always

Croatian Folk Dance

For any number of couples, very easy, arranged by

LOUIS H. CHALIF

¶ In public performance credit must be given for the arrangement of this dance.

¶ A decided rhythm and much enthusiasm should be expressed in the dance.

¶ The girl's costume is a light brown, very full skirt, rather long, a sleeveless bolero of the same material, a white waist with round neck & very full long sleeves gathered in at the wrist where there are turned back cuffs. This waist is cut with very long shoulders, so that the fullness of the sleeve begins about 3 in. below the shoulder. There is a voluminous white apron coming almost to the bottom of the skirt, trimmed with 2 bands of orange material near its lower edge, tied around the waist & tied again about 6 in. below that. A large, bright flowered handkerchief of cerise & blue is tied around the head with ends hanging down the back. White stockings, pumps with straps, beads & large earrings complete the costume.

¶ The boy's costume is full white trousers coming to just below the knee, a heavy white shirt that is circular in cut & comes about 6 in. below the tops of the trousers, where it flares free, & has a turn-over Peter Pan collar & sleeves like the girl's. There is an Alice blue sleeveless slightly flaring coat of the length of the shirt, fastened at the neck with one hook & flaring open below that, its front edges trimmed with blue & white embroidery. He also wears a yellowish brown hat with a rather wide rolled brim, a yellow flower in his coat & high boots.

¶ The music has 2 counts to a measure; mention of more implies a 2nd measure.

FIGURE I.

Join hands in a single circle.

All step Rf to R (count 1), close Lf to Rf striking it against Rf (ct 2), & repeat starting Lf (ct 3, 4). On ct 2 & ct 4 bend both knees very slightly to give rhythm & accent. 2 meas.

Step Rf to R (ct 1), step on Lf beside Rf (ct 2) & repeat starting Rf again (ct 3, 4). 2 meas.

To give characteristic flavor to the steps of the above 2 meas., bend the L knee slightly & lift the Rf with knee straight just before stepping on Rf, then step with both knees straight.

Repeat all 4 times more, always starting Rf, so that the circle revolves to the R. 16 meas.

20 meas.

FIGURE II.

Repeat the first 2 meas. of Fig. I, starting Rf. . . . . 2 meas.

4 steps toward center of circle, starting Rf & keeping hands joined. . . 2 meas.

Repeat the 1st 2 meas. of Fig. I again. . . . . 2 meas.

4 steps backward, toward circumference, starting Rf. . . . . 2 meas.

Repeat all. . . . . 8 meas.

Join both hands with partner & repeat the 1st 4 meas. of Fig. I, dancing once around each other to R. . . . . 4 meas.

20 meas.

Repeat the whole dance as many times as desirable, with the same partner always.

Figure 4.6a. Chalif's directions for a Croatian folk dance

Figure 4.6b. Music for Croatian folk dance

occupied a space separate from other dance teachers who were primarily physical educators. Unlike other physical education teachers, Chalif's emphasis in folk dance was more on the *dance* than the *folk* aspect of it. Since the dances he taught were more often folk based, or folk inspired, than "authentically folk," they were not completely congruent with the ideology of the folk dance movement in which the value of folk dance lay primarily in the fact that it was folk, i.e. not an individual artistic creation but a communal expression of humanity. Perhaps in part for this reason, Chalif's dance material gradually faded from folk dance programs in schools after his death in 1948.

Cola Serbianka

SERBIAN FOLK DANCE.

Very simple, arranged by

LOUIS H. CHALIF

¶ In public performance credit must be given for the arrangement of this dance.

¶ There are no couples in the above dance, & any number of people may take part. The formation is a single circle, all facing inward with joined hands.

¶ The name means Serbian Village. The dance should be done rhythmically & with enthusiasm.

¶ The girl's costume is a full skirt & blouse of white material, bright embroidery around the lower edge of the skirt, long full sleeves with several rows of embroidery radiating downward from the round neck both in front & behind, an apron of bright striped material, the stripes going lengthwise, many beads, a flower in the hair, white stockings & red pumps.

¶ The boy's costume is short grey trousers slightly full & coming to just below the knee, a bright blue shirt, blousing over the belt, with a soft turn-over collar & red butterfly bow tie, a gray coat that is short enough to show the shirt at the waist, with revers & pockets embroidered in yellow, a red sash whose tied ends show at one side, a round gray hat with rolled up brim, black low shoes & the legs bound spirally with gray to the knees.

¶ The music is counted 1, 2 to a meas: when 4 counts are referred to a 2nd meas. is meant.

FIGURE I.

All step Rf to side (ct 1), step Lf beside Rf (ct 2), step Rf to side again (ct 3), & brush L heel on the floor in front of Rf, finishing with Lf lifted a few inches from floor & R knee bent slightly ct 4). . . . . 2 meas.

Repeat 3 times more, starting to L, R & L alternately. . . . . . . 6 meas.

8 meas.

FIGURE II.

All move sideways to the R with: Step Rf to side (ct 1), step Lf behind Rf bending both knees slightly (ct 2), & repeat for 12 times in all. . . . . 12 meas.

Repeat Fig. I. . . . . 8 meas.

FIGURE III.

All turn to face R, still with hands joined.

Step Rf forward (ct 1), & brush L heel forward (touching the floor) & bending the supporting R knee slightly. Repeat 12 times in all . . . . 12 meas.

Repeat Fig. I. . . . . 8 meas.

FIGURE IV.

Take 24 running steps (1 step to 1 ct) sideways to R, starting Rf, each time stepping Lf behind Rf. . . . . 12 meas.

Figure 4.7a. "Seljančica"

Figure 4.7b. Music for "Seljančica"

The Spread of the Folk Dance Movement

Although Elizabeth Burchenal is often remembered as having started the folk dance movement, the establishment of folk dancing as a part of public school curricula was the result of an organized and coordinated effort. Before folk dance could be introduced in the public school system, there had to be a substantial number of teachers capable of leading these classes.[23] When Burchenal instructed public school teachers in 1909–1910, "eleven

Bulgarian Folk Dance

For any number of couples, rather easy, arranged by

LOUIS H. CHALIF

¶ In public performance credit must be given for the arrangement of this dance.

¶ The dance should be quick and spirited.

¶ The music has 2 counts to a measure; when more cts are named more meas. are implied.

¶ The boy's costume is tan colored trousers, semi-fitting, reaching to the ankles & bound around half-way up to the knee with strips of brown cloth, a white shirt with a soft stand-up collar that is open at the neck, no tie, shirt sleeves that are plain at the top & flaring widely at the wrist, a sleeveless gray coat, cut circular & coming to about 1 in. below the belt & failing to meet in front by 6 ins. or so, a very wide brick-red sash with a band of bright blue embroidery at its center, a tight-fitting brimless hat of brown cloth consisting of a wide band around the head & a flat top, shoes that are like moccasins with very bright embroidery on the instep.

¶ The girl's costume is a gray somewhat circular skirt to the shoe tops, trimmed with 2 narrow bands of red near the lower edge & occasional (4) red stripes coming down from the belt, a gray, tight-fitting sleeveless waist cut rather high in the neck & heavily embroidered, a red belt with 2 large round ornaments near the front, a white waist with long flaring sleeves like the boy's, but heavily embroidered in red, green & yellow, a little of this waist showing at the base of the neck, a white petticoat embroidered in colors showing below the skirt, shoes like the boy's & legs bound up with brown cloth, a little round red cap on the very top of the head.

FIGURE I.

All join hands in a single circle, facing in.

In this figure the circle will move very slowly around to R. The steps are: Make a short step on Rf to R & hop while raising Lf backward a little from the knee (ct 1, and), repeat with Lf, stepping close beside Rf so as to continue moving to R (ct 2, and). 1 meas.

Repeat twice more, starting Rf. . . . . 2 meas.

Make a little jump to a crossed pos. with Rf behind (ct 1), jump to separate the feet sideward a little way (ct and), bring the heels together with a click (ct 2). . 1 meas.

Repeat all 3 times more, starting Rf always & continuing to move around the circle to the R. . . . . 12 meas.

16 meas.

FIGURE II.

Keeping hands joined repeat the same steps, all moving for'd toward the center of the circle. . . . . 4 meas.

Repeat, moving backwards to circumference. . . . . 4 meas.

Repeat all. . . . . 8 meas.

16 meas.

FIGURE III.

Face partners in a single circle. Each one clasp his arms behind his own back, the fore-arms being horizontally at the waist line. Keeping this pos. of the arms throughout this figure, partners change places with each other as follows:

Each dance sidewise to his own R, moving ina semi-circle to his partner's place. The steps are those of the 1st 4 meas. of Fig. I. . . . . 4 meas.

Repeat the steps again, continuing to move to R, while returning to original places. 4 meas.

Repeat all, this time moving to L, starting Lf. . . . . 8 meas.

16 meas.

The dance may be repeated as often as desirable.

Figure 4.8a. Bulgarian folk dance

Figure 4.8b. Bulgarian folk dance set to Hungarian folk melody (Chalif, volume 3)

hundred teachers, representing 178 schools, attended the eleven classes in folk dancing and athletics conducted by Miss Burchenal and her six assistants in the gymnasiums of several high schools. The number of school girls instructed in turn by these teachers was over 13,000" (Perry 1910: 31). Once the folk dance movement caught on, it continued to generate hundreds of folk dance teachers throughout the country. Some were more

influential than others. Their individual level of expertise, range of repertoire taught, and means of acquiring repertoire varied greatly. Among folk dance instructors there were both professionals and amateurs, some making their livelihood solely by teaching dance, others working primarily as schoolteachers, physical educators, or social workers.

Much has been published on instructors in the folk dance movement, and a comprehensive survey of these individuals and their contributions might be of interest. Of greater significance to this work, however, is an investigation of folk dance sources and the overlapping spheres of activity among the teachers and institutions for which they worked.

The YWCA and YMCA organizations provided for situations of "exposure" of their workers to the folk dances of the country in which they were located.[24] Elizabeth Dickerson, an alumna of Wellesley College, was sent to Russia by the YWCA in October 1917 to help establish physical education there. In a letter she wrote from Petrograd she declared she was "wild to take the Russian folk dances" (Dickerson, in *Bulletin of the Mary Hemenway Alumnae Association,* 1918–1919, YWCA). YMCA members were often sent to foreign countries to organize physical education and recreation programs for the military, and it is possible that they were interested in learning folk dances of their host countries. As part of the physical education and recreation programs they established in the host country they taught native children the same dance repertoire they taught in the United States. A fellow ethnomusicologist from Wesleyan University, Su Zheng, showed me a photograph of her grandmother teaching an unidentified circle dance at a YWCA in China ca. 1920 to Chinese children.

The most desired method of acquiring new folk dance material was to travel to various European countries seeking dances at folk festivals and in traditional contexts. But as early as the first decade of the twentieth century, instructors traveling in Europe wrote disappointedly about these traditions dying out even in their native rural areas. "The advertisement of a kermess [festival] in a little, out-of-the-way village in Germany was promising, but in actual fact it was nothing but an all-day dance-hall waltz with heavy beer-drinking accompaniment. The old quaint costumes peculiar to the locality would have been as out of place as in any other ballroom," complains Gulick (1911: 188). The desire to collect dances efficiently and without such risk led teachers hungry for folk dance material to consult with physical education teachers from the country in question.

As mentioned, in parts of Europe, folk dancing was already established in school curricula and seminars, and workshops and summer schools of folk dance were available to those interested in learning the national folklore of a particular country. Elizabeth Burchenal, Mary Wood Hinman, and many other physical education teachers attended such schools of folk dance, including those organized by Cecil Sharp in England. Effie Shambaugh writes (1927: 15) that she devoted two years "to research work in folk dancing (one year of travel, conferences with those interested in folklore, reading in national libraries, dancing with folk societies, studying under private teachers: one year of 'exposure' to folk dances in the countries in which

they originated)." Accounts of such research trips are not rare, but as we see from Shambaugh's testimony, the trips were generally focused on "approved" sources of material, that is, those provided by urban intellectuals, national folk dance societies, and "credible," educated dance instructors.

While it might have been much simpler to learn folk dances from immigrants in the United States, such an approach required a mental leap most educators were not ready to make. Besides, immigrants were typically only capable of teaching dances from their native locality. I have not encountered a single account from this period of an immigrant being invited to teach a folk dance from his/her tradition to schoolchildren. On the contrary, there was concern expressed about learning dances from uneducated immigrants. This attests to a feeling that it was foreign lands themselves, more than people, who were the cradles of tradition. Material gathered abroad was treated as the most authentic, though it might have been much more stylized than a dance enjoyed in an immigrant community at home.

Interestingly, this sentiment is prevalent in the Balkan scene nearly a century later. What Tomko (1999: 213) says for Hinman and Burchenal is just as applicable to many participants in the Balkan music and dance scene. They "keenly felt the absence of comparable traditions and roots for modern America, and creatively tried to fashion a past from other (European) traditions. This fashioning was in every way re-constitutive; it selected, arranged, and appropriated for its own ends rather than attempting to reinstall European 'originals.'" The movement pursued its own kind of "authenticity," however. By accessing European traditions, middle-class American cultural workers believed they tapped into "racially old," primal ways of being in the world that were saturated with capacities for feeling, spontaneity, and imagination.

If travels to foreign countries facilitated the acquisition of new material, the Normal schools of dance and physical education, such as BNSG, Hinman School of Gymnastic and Folk Dancing, Wellesley College, Springfield YMCA, Columbia University, and many others were the centers of dissemination of this material. Graduates taught the repertoire they had learned at these institutions in folk dance classes throughout the country. Intensive courses in folk dance were offered to schoolteachers by Normal schools of dance, including Chalif's in New York and Hinman's in Chicago, and by organizations such as the Girls' Athletic League. "The Girl's Branch offers a course in dancing and athletics, free of expense, to public school teachers who will in return give one lesson per week after school to athletic clubs organized in their own schools. It will be necessary to have at least two teachers from each of the schools represented—one who can play the piano and one who can demonstrate—and not more than four" (Perry 1910: 31). In this manner the wide reach of the folk dance programs was ensured.

The percentage of teachers who traveled abroad was fairly small in comparison with the number of those generated yearly by Normal schools, summer schools, courses, and seminars. In many cases the "teachers" of

folk dance took only a few classes to be familiarized with a limited repertoire before they began teaching it in schools, not only to the students but to other physical education teachers who were unable to attend a course. This practice seems to have set a precedent for later folk dance teachers' insensitivity to the complexities of cross-cultural representation. Through this teaching chain, folk dances were passed on and disseminated throughout the country, becoming progressively further removed from their original forms and styles. Along with this increasing distance from original sources and traditional contexts of folk dancing, we begin to see the processes of canonization of international folk dance through the establishment of a limited set of folk dance favorites. The most popular dances/tunes leaped from one book to another, perhaps to help ensure the interest of teachers in newly published collections.

Soon after folk dance publications became easily accessible they became the primary source of material for schools and recreation programs. In a *Syllabus of Work*, 1915–1916, Wellesley College, it is stated that "beginning December 10, 1915, a certain number of students (5), taught half the members of the class dances which had previously been assigned. These dances were chosen from books upon Folk Dancing and from manuscripts and were new material to the class." Manuscript notes were another written source of folk dance material. They were often taken by teachers themselves after learning the dance at a course and were used as personal reminders of the dance steps.

Beneficiaries of Folk Dance Programs

Whatever the ideological background and goals of folk dance programs, participants in these programs seemed to be very enthusiastic about them. Gulick and Smith (1907: 9447) believed that the appeal of folk dancing lay in the fact that "the emotional life of the child would seek to embody itself in some of the same forms that are normal and instinctive to uncivilized peoples." Children, yet unspoiled by the undesirable consequences of western civilization, intuitively recognize folk dance as a natural expression of humanity. The parallel drawn here between children and uncivilized people again places folk dance closer to nature on a line of civilizational progress.

Such ideological subtleties were of little concern to the children, of course, and folk dance activities were very meaningful to many. What must have been especially savored by children in poor, urban communities, was that folk dance provided opportunities for play, challenging but entertaining learning accomplishments, and something in which they could participate with their peers. There are numerous accounts of children being eager to stay after school for folk dance lessons.

> One teacher went to the piano and the other marshaled the children into an alcove at the farther end of the room. Not a sound was heard

> in the whole vast building above. The roar of wagons and jangle of trolley cars, softened and filtered as it were by walls and shutters, seemed to come from a far-away city. There were no lessons to get, no errands to run, no babies to mind. Tomorrow was a myth; the past never had been; only this blood-bounding moment existed. A chord was struck and then forty little forms, light as fairies and sprightly as imps, came running down the long room. . . . (Perry 1910: 26)

This poetic description of a folk dance class in an East Side public school captures an important aspect of the folk dance programs. For young urban girls in particular it provided an escape from daily life and a rare opportunity for self-expression.

A folk dance class offered, among other things, imaginary travels to distant pastoral lands. I was stunned to discover that when public school girls participated in an annual spring festival in Van Cortlandt Park, New York, in 1908, many of them had never before seen grass! This provides a fascinating little glimpse into the lives of children in congested American cities and insight into the girls' genuine enthusiasm for folk dance. In many schools, folk dance classes would culminate in a festival or pageant often realized through the joined forces of several schools. These special events, in which hundreds of students would participate, were often the high point of the school year.

The popularity of folk dance programs in public schools contributed greatly to their growth or establishment in other organizations and institutions such as YMCAs and YWCAs, playgrounds, commercial dancing schools, colleges, and even factories and business organizations. The physical education program in the Young Men's Christian Associations of North America (YMCA of USA 1914: 14) included folk dancing for the "hygienic" purpose of "gaining and maintaining health and organic vigor, through exercise, and instruction in all matters pertaining to healthful living." Both YMCA and YWCA organizations provided recreational programs in their local communities. As mentioned, such work was also carried abroad in association with missionary work and the establishment of YWCAs in other parts of the world.

Although not limited to girls and women, folk dancing as a means of achieving physical strength and vigor was seen as particularly suitable for them. Gymnastics and other physical fitness programs, when applied to women, met with considerable resentment from the general public and from within academia itself at the time.[25] Attempts were made to prove "scientifically" that women were "naturally" incapable of performing physically demanding tasks and that subjecting them to exercise would lead to health problems and the destruction of their womanhood. Vigorous physical exercise was considered destructive to woman's grace, elegance, and poise—desired expressions of true femininity. Furthermore, it was believed that in puberty women needed to put their energy into developing the reproductive abilities, and the waste of this energy on exercise was thought to endanger women's very ability to bear children. While it was considered

inappropriate to see women in a gymnasium, climbing the ropes and exercising on the apparatus, dancing was perceived as a natural and proper feminine activity.

Folk dancing was seen as particularly well suited to women employed by industry. "In social forms of physical education our ideal must be not only to increase the personal efficiency of each girl through good posture, well trained muscles and improved personal hygiene, but especially to divert and tranquilize her mind. The sheer fatigue of a simple task performed amid the nerve wearing thunder of machinery, the hectic stimulation of selling goods at a bargain sale or serving at the noon hour mob, and the benumbing of brain and finger after a trying day with 'the boss' alike are benefited by wholesome recreation in which large muscle-group predominates: (1) gymnastics (setting up exercises), (2) folk dancing, . . ."[26]

Folk dancing found a place in the recreation of factory workers as well as wealthy businessman (figure 4.9). It became a popular way of socializing and exercising for the young and old and, as noted, was widely accepted not only by school systems but by various religious and social organizations as well.

Despite their popularity, however, folk dance programs were criticized as early as 1908. In a report on folk dance in public schools by the Public Schools of Providence, RI 1908–09 (in *Bulletin of the Mary Hemenway Alumnae Association*, Department of Hygiene, Wellesley College), the complaint was expressed that "where the folk dancing has been gone into with a burst of enthusiasm because something new, without careful forethought, it has been a source of burden to teachers and an overstepping upon the hours of legitimate school work . . . to place folk dances, purely rhythmi-

Figure 4.9. Rhode Island businessmen dancing the "Highland Fling" (Gulick 1911)

cal exercises with music, above all others but defeats their purpose just as college gymnasium instructors maintain that athletics without floor work are of little worth. It is the purpose of the director to encourage the folk rhythmical work to be taken as has been established the dramatization of stories in primary schools."

After completing her research study of folk dancing, Effie Shambaugh, an alumna of Wellesley college, came to the conclusion that since "all folklore is so closely interwoven with peasant song, art and drama that they, too, must be presented for intelligent understanding of the dances. We have made the mistake, in teaching steps, of discarding the songs as childish and in failing to catch the dramatic expression of national character in the folk dances." Shambaugh suggests that "no folk dancing course is justified unless accompanied by an attempt to have the student understand the nationality of the dances—through the singing of folk songs, reading of descriptions (both travel and fiction) of the country, and lectures on folklore which will stimulate breadth of interest." In a critical evaluation of "The Place of Folk Dancing in the Program of Physical Education for Elementary and Secondary Schools" Shambaugh (1929: 13–15) concluded that folk dance instruction was weak on context, that teachers were poorly prepared and failed to make connections with the rest of the curriculum. The lack of instrumental accompaniment, the limited number of Victrola records and their ineffectiveness in work with large groups, as well as the lack of illustrations for costume and setting were some of the other shortcomings of folk dance programs in schools that Shambaugh noted.

Folk Dance Books

A brief overview of early folk dance books provides a clearer sense of the material presented and the manner of its presentation. My intention here is not to provide a comprehensive list of folk dance literature available at this time, but to discuss the importance of folk dance books as sources of repertoire. The records of new library acquisition at colleges with strong physical education programs show that folk dance books were typically added to the library the very year they were published. They were important sources of new material for physical education teachers.

Some of the first folk dance books were, with their descriptive dance notation and music arranged for piano accompaniment, modeled after European publications of this kind, particularly that of Cecil Sharp in England. This format is typical of most folk dance books even to the present day (with the exception of the later inclusion of lists of recordings to which dances could be taught). Dance instructions usually precede or follow a piano arrangement of the tune, although in some cases directions are found interspersed at appropriate moments in the score. The amount and type of information provided in these instructions differs not only from one book to another, but from one dance to another within the same book. Some instructions are quite sketchy and are apparently intended as reminders

for teachers who already knew the dance. Her "Russian Flax Dance" (figure 4.10) is an example of this kind of "notation" (Hinman 1916: volume IV, p. 28). More often, however, the descriptive notation is divided into several parts, such as the general formation of the dance (circle, line, square), the number of dancers needed, and a description of dance figures with the measure count usually provided on the right-hand side of the bottom of the figure description. For an example, see figure 4.8, the Bulgarian folk dance published in Chalif's volume III, page 38.

Diagrams, stick figures and, more rarely, photographs were sometimes added to dance descriptions. See "Egyptian Dance" (figures 4.11a, b), examples of descriptive dance directions placed throughout the score and accompanied by photographs.

It was not uncommon to include a brief description of the "national character" of the people whose dance was being described. Here are two brief examples from the second edition (1919) of Kimmins's *Peasant Dances of Many Lands*. The tone of these blurbs and the ideological background from which they stem should be self-explanatory:

> The folk dances of Serbia are true mirrors of the splendid independence of this brave people. Some dances were truly elegant, others gymnastic feats, accompanied by much snapping of the fingers, clapping of hands, and slapping of knees. Sword dances have their place, and, in this land, where rivers and streams and trees and forests were held sacred, many country dances find a natural place as an outlet for pent-up feelings. (Kimmins 1919: 19)

> A ROUMANIAN PEASANT DANCE, based upon real Roumanian music and folk lore. The Roumanian dances were frequently danced to instruments, but also to songs, and many of these were extemporised, making it extremely difficult to trace the actual dance. Both folk songs and folk dances typify the independence and sturdiness of the peoples concerned. Many of the names of the songs and dances are very humorous—some are called after birds; in some the piper or musician himself dances in the middle, and in many large jumping movements are to be found. The high leaps typify the noon-day elevation of the sun; also, high leaps will be found in the harvest dances, where the reapers rejoiced over the good ears of corn, or the fine length of the flax. (Kimmins 1919: 31)

Compilers of folk dance books for schools tended to include instructions for making "appropriate" costumes for dance performances. These ranged from descriptions of what the author saw as the representative folk costume of the particular nation to what I call "cheesecloth" costumes (figures 4.12a, b and 4.13).

Cheesecloth was often the material of choice because it was inexpensive and because children could dye it, paint "embroidery," and glue or tape the pieces together, thus making the costumes themselves. Photo-

Figure 4.10. "Russian Flax Dance" (Hinman 1916, volume I)

graphs of children in quasi-folk costumes were sometimes used as models so these peculiar garments could be recreated. In case the reader is unfamiliar with folk costumes of these ethnic groups and thus unable to judge how these garments relate to the folk costumes of the respective groups, I have included a photograph of "American polka" dancers in their "native" costumes (figure 4.14).

Figure 4.11a. "Egyptian Dance" (Hinman 1916, volume 1)

Music Accompaniment to the Dances

Specific references to musical accompaniment in folk dance events are rare. But regardless of where a dance came from, musical accompaniment was most often provided on a piano, an instrument that was more or less omnipresent at the turn of the century in settlements, public, private, and dance schools, colleges, and church basements. When weather permitted, pianos were rolled out into the schoolyard or playground for outdoor dancing. In regular folk dance classes most dance teachers, including Hinman, Chalif, Burchenal, and many others, worked with a pianist. Almost every

Figure 4.11b. Music for "Egyptian Dance" (Hinman 1916, volume 1)

folk dance book includes piano arrangements of appropriate tunes along with the step patterns. In these arrangements the tunes are somewhat skeletal, being effectively free of ornamentation, and descriptive terms such as "with feeling," "with dignity," and "very slowly," were often the only indicators of style. The essence of "a people's" musical heritage was seen to lie in tunes rather than style. Many composers and collectors of traditional music have approached folk materials with the same great respect

INSTRUCTIONS For four children.	BARS
Three children dance in a row, and one child dances in front of them, holding a large star.	
All jump with feet placed in 5th position (hands placed on hips).	1
Run quickly and obliquely to right (extending arms to side, right arm higher than left).	
Repeat to left.	2
Repeat I.	4
Place hands on hips. Turn swiftly round to right stepping on right, then left foot.	1
Stamp right and left foot alternately three times.	
Turn swiftly round to left stepping on left then right foot.	1
Stamp left and right foot alternately three times. Repeat II.	4
All dance to right in the following manner, moving obliquely forward :—	
Stamp to right with right foot, turn left foot inwards 2nd position (on toes), then turn left foot outwards and stand on it. This is done three times to the right (3 bars).	
Spring on right, and left foot alternately three times (clapping hands above head three times) (1 bar).	4
Repeat III., moving to left.	4
The child holding the star kneels on her left knee, and the other children dance round.	
Turn round to right with three steps beginning with right foot (crossing arms and waving them across chest). Step on left foot; point right foot (extending both hands towards star).	
This is done eight times.	16
Repeat I. to right and left alternately six times.	12
All turn swiftly round and round to right.	2
The three children stand on their right foot, left foot pointed behind, bending body and head forward, arms extended at side. Child in front holds star high above her head.	

Figure 4.12a. “Serbian Star Dance” (Kimmins 1919:20)

for melody and little or no attention to elements of style. This is a manifestation of the reductionism so present in European Romantic models, and echoed in Cecil Sharp's arrangements of British tunes. Interestingly, this tradition of privileging melody over style and conceiving of the two as separate issues has carried over into the contemporary Balkan scene and aspects of contemporary American culture in general.[27]

From the graphics and photographs in Hinman's “Gymnastic and Folk Dancing,” we can conclude that she worked with a violin player, at least

SERBIAN STAR DANCE

SERBIAN STAR DANCE.—This is one of the most beautiful on record. The Stella Carol is world-renowned, and the stars consist of cardboard, borne by boys known as "Star Youths," and the dance is usually performed round some central figure, or group of figures, or house belonging to some important person. When danced in full it is a very complicated movement with much interchange of hand clapping and stamping of the feet, and quite suddenly changes from robust movements of this kind to singularly dreamy music and movement. Much of the dance suggests clanking of spurs, the drawing of swords, and other parts are suggestive of the open country and the wild hill-sides. (See also picture and further notes on page 19.)

21

Figure 4.12b. Music for "Serbian Star Dance" (Kimmins 1919:20)

Figure 4.13. "Roumanian Dance" (Kimmins 1919:31)

for some outdoor dances. This is a sensible choice because of the instrument's portability. It is likely that the violinist was educated in Western classical music and rendered the written tunes with the same sensibility regardless of their origin. For festivals, graduation ceremonies at colleges, and other special occasions that involved the performance of folk dance, music would sometimes be provided by a small orchestra, usually made up of music students. For example, during a May Day Festival at Wellesley College, held in 1924, "five musicians dressed in peasant costume were providing music for the dances. The two violinists, one flautist, one fife, and one drummer played *Pomp and Circumstance* by Elgar, *Bluff King Hall* as used by Burchenal for *May Pole Dance*, and *Sellenger's Round* from Kimmins."[28] Music for the New York folk dance festivals was provided by brass bands.[29] In the absence of amplification, this type of ensemble was

Figure 4.14. American polka (Kimmins 1919: 44)

well suited to the occasion. Accompaniment for folk dances at outdoor festivals in parks or city streets was often supplied by a much more mobile and inexpensive instrument—the hurdy-gurdy, or "street organ."[30] In the winter of 1909–1910 the first hurdy-gurdy was set to play folk dance tunes. The incentive for using the hurdy-gurdy came from Gulick, or rather from the children of New York City whom he witnessed spontaneously inventing "folk dances" to the music of street organs (figure 4.15) Gulick writes that when the hurdy-gurdy man came into a neighborhood, children would gather and start dancing around him.

I have been unable, so far, to determine the street-organ folk dance repertoire, though it would be fascinating to hear how these tunes sounded on this instrument, and to see what tunes and how many were reproduced on street-organs. The only evidence I have seen of the hurdy-gurdy repertoire comes from photographs (figure 4.16) of girls dancing "Kamarno," "Highland Fling," and "Reap the Flax" to hurdy-gurdy accompaniment (Gulick, 1911).

Folk dances were sometimes set to Western classical music, either well-known "classics" or music by contemporary composers. "The use of good music for both classroom exercises and dances was no small part of the attractiveness of Chalif's work," writes Ann Barzel.[31] She concludes that all of Chalif's one thousand dances were "set to first-rate music." We can only imagine what is implied by the qualifying term "good music" or "first-rate music." Among Chalif's transcriptions of folk tunes there are certainly

Figure 4.15. Children devising dances to hurdy-gurdy music (Gulick 1911)

arrangements of existing folk tunes, but in some cases the dances were clearly made up to fit a piece of classical music. If, in some cases, it is hard to determine whether or not there is any relationship to a folk tune, in the case of the "Chinese Serenade set to a delightful tinkle by Poldini," there is little doubt. Clearly this is a dance invented by Chalif, set to music that was meant to sound Chinese. Likewise, the so-called national dances in Chalif's repertoire are generally accompanied by music composed in Western classical style. Examples of his musical choices for "national" dances include[32]:

Gipsy Rose, 2/4 music by Behr.

Pliaska (Russian) to the Russian airs.

Modjeska (Polish) delightful music by Scharwenka.

Figure 4.16. Children in New York dancing "Kamarno" to a hurdy-gurdy equipped to play music for folk dances taught in school

Lubka (Hungarian) music: Hungarian airs.

Water Carriers (Oriental), music by Moussorgsky.

Druschba (Polish) Mazurka by Scharwenka.

Otchi Tchernia, Compellingly romantic gypsy music.

Raz, Dva, Tri, Russian folk. Your classes will surely enjoy this dance with its stirring music to spur them on and their own singing to make them happy.

While Chalif, as a professional teacher and choreographer, often treated both folk dance and music as building blocks for his own creations, other physical education teachers were less experimental with the material. Folk tunes were stylized, harmonized, and arranged for the piano but it was important that they were still "folk tunes." Gulick and Smith (1907: 9451) declared that traditional folk dance music "is always appropriate. It is the music that has grown up with the dance and belongs to it—the strange harmonies and peculiar rhythm of a Slavic *chardos*; the spirited, sharply accented air, with the bagpipe drone imitated in the bass, of 'The Highland Fling.'" Needless to say, these dances did not "grow up" with pianos, but traditional instrumentation was not considered an integral part of the music.

According to Ed Kramer (in Casey 1981: 89), even half a century later, when there were no appropriate folk dance records, dances were set to any available record that the teacher found suitable to the steps:

A teacher would learn of a dance either in a discussion with elderly dancers about dances of their youth or by finding dance descriptions in old books or manuscripts; the teacher would first analyze the dance in terms of structure (measures, bars, counts, figures, repeats) and then look for a record that was fairly close to the dance in structure and in timing (polka, schottische, waltz, mazurka) and proceed to adapt the dance to the record. If the dance was, say, Russian, the teacher would attempt to find a Russian record—but if that was not possible, the dance would often be done to a record of another nationality—Scandinavian or whatever was available and fit the dance!

Music and dance were not treated as inseparable elements of an artistic whole, and stylistic authenticity of music and dance was sought primarily on a symbolic level.

As recording technology developed, so did the importance of records as musical accompaniment for folk dance classes. The Victor Talking Machine Co. recorded folk melodies, nursery rhymes, and play-songs for educational use as early as 1911. By 1915 Victrolas were sold to schools in 3,019 cities, and by 1923 to 12,313 cities (Dunham, in Pearlman 1996: 3). By 1916, the Victor Phonograph Company issued recordings of dance tunes Burchenal had published and used in her classes. These recordings were characteristically devoid of traditional stylistic elements and instrumentation and were performed by the Victor military band. The growing prominence of recorded music might be viewed as the triumph of convenience and efficient technology over the "back to the basics" and "do it yourself" ideology that figured so prominently in the folk dance movement's birth. Although recordings could have provided culturally appropriate music for the dances, the folk dance movement apparently did not take advantage of this opportunity. Later in the century, recorded music was to play a critical role in the rising popularity of international folk dance and the consequent formation of specialized music and dance movements, including the Balkan scene.

Selection of the Repertoire

Not all folk dances were considered suitable for school curricula. If this activity was employed to transmit and reiterate a very specific set of values, the dances selected had to be those that embodied these values. Only the learning of the "proper" kind of dances could yield the desired results. Needless to say, individual interpretations of the meaning of folk dances from different parts of the world were crucial to their inclusion or exclusion from the folk dance repertoire in the United States. These interpretations were often based on commonly shared stereotypes, but sometimes varied from one individual to another.

"The folk dances of *civilized nations* [italics mine] which are suitable to our modern social conditions provide very valuable and delightful forms

of activity, highly acceptable to a naturalized program of physical education. These folk dances, if intelligently selected and adapted to different ages and to different racial and social types, provide splendid, wholesome contributions to programs of educational activities for children and to recreational programs for adults" (Wood and Cassidy 1927: 346–347). According to Wood and Cassidy only the folk dances of "civilized nations" were desirable. We might ask which nations were "civilized," and how their dances, once chosen to be a part of the folk dance repertoire in physical education programs, could come to be viewed as uncivilized or, rather, "precivilized," natural expressions of humanity. This double positioning of the chosen folk dances is based on comparison. In relationship to American culture and its popular music and dance forms, folk music and dance of the Old World were perceived as more communal, more natural, less civilized and thus more human. However, in comparison to folk dances from Native American, Asian, or African sources, the Old World dances were seen as more civilized.

Gulick elaborates for us in detail his guiding principles for the selection of folk dance materials. He suggests that dances which do not take too much space and in which most of the students can be active most of the time should get priority. Since the aim of the activity is, among others, physical fitness, the chosen dances should involve large movement of the trunk, arms, and limbs. In his opinion this consideration disqualifies dances from Java as being too focused on small movements. "The Indian dances with body bent forward and bent knees are also excluded," on the account of "forming of habits of movement or posture that are disadvantageous from the standpoint of health." "The dances from the East" he finds unsuitable "because of their emotional content and their relation to the morals of our civilization." He also suggests that dances need to be simple enough for children to learn them without an undue amount of training (Gulick 1911: 38–40). He finally concludes (1911: 41) that "the range of available folk dances meeting the various conditions is comparatively small. While the Girls' Branch does teach folk dancing, it does not by any means advocate an indiscriminate teaching of all the folk dances of all the peoples. The work consists only in teaching those folk dances meeting the physiological, moral, and social requirements that have been mentioned."

This remark is crucial to understanding the folk dance repertoire approved for wide use by Americans. Folk dance programs were not established for the purpose of studying folk dances themselves. Rather, these programs were vehicles for achieving a specific set of goals, such as physical fitness, nationalism, patriotism, social cohesion, character building, and racial superiority.

When Gulick (1911: 135–140) states that there are four categories of criteria for selection of folk dance repertoire—the physiological, neurological, psychological, and aesthetic—he obviously excludes the category which precedes and preconditions all four of these: his own cultural, educational, and ideological background. Gulick and his colleagues shared ideas about individual and common good, health, beauty, and propriety.

On the basis of these shared ideas they agreed upon the particular type of folk dancing that was valuable and useful for the American nation. Specific dances within this approved repertoire were left to be chosen by the folk dancers themselves. Thus, Gulick writes that "it is not yet certain what dances will prove the best suited for our American conditions. Some of the spirited and characteristic folk dances of Sweden and Russia have so far seemed to make the very greatest appeal to the children." Of course, the children (and adults as well) were in a position to choose only from the selected and approved repertoire.

The selection of repertoire for physical education programs, especially in schools, occurred mostly from the top down. This repertoire was determined by the availability of folk dance material only within the specific boundaries described above. The greatest portion of the repertoire was comprised of folk dances of Western Europe, particularly England, Sweden, Denmark, Norway, Germany, Italy, and France. Among the Central European nations, Polish dances were widespread, although Hungarian and Czech dances were often included as well. Russian folk dances were the most prominent part of the repertoire from Eastern Europe, and only occasionally does one find dances from Serbia, Croatia, Rumania, and Bulgaria. For a long time, the emphasis on Greece as "the cradle of Western civilization" disqualified Greek folk dances from inclusion in the folk dance repertoire, although Hinman's teaching of Greek dances may be a notable exception. This was probably the case because "Greek dances" were a separate dance genre, based on an imagined ancient Greek civilization, rather than contact with Greek immigrants, or research in modern Greece (figure 4.17). In some folk dance collections one can find folk dances attributed to Japanese, Chinese, or Indian sources, as well as African American and Native American cultures. However, the bulk of the repertoire, especially in schools, consisted of European folk dances. The repertoire taught in private dance schools like Chalif's was much more wide ranging.

The Folk, the Old, and the American

> While our American nation includes in it representatives from most of the peoples under the sun, we possess less of the folk music, the folk dances, folk lore, folk games, folk festivals of the world than do any of the peoples of which we are made . . . whatever be the cause of our poverty in these directions, our need of social customs is great, and the growing movement toward a restoration of them in forms suited to the present day is promising. (Gulick 1911: 5–6)

One of the most persistent beliefs articulated in the American national discourse is the newness, thus the shallowness, of American culture. In an excellent analysis of Alexis de Tocqueville and the American national identity, Karin Amos (1995: 84) has noted that "the qualifier 'young' is a part of American national perception. Like the term 'experiment' it indi-

Figure 4.17. "Greek Dance" (Gulick 1911)

cates potential, but also insecurity." A large number of Americans currently involved in Balkan music and dance have recognized in this activity a depth and stability that they felt was lacking in American culture. This perception was certainly shared by the settlement leaders and physical educators at the beginning of the century.

If the common perception was that there was, on one side, American culture whose values are determined by commercialism and, thus, are ever-changing and shallow and, on the other side, Old World folk cultures that were stable, tried and true, historically proven, rich and deep, it was obvious that the latter needed to be saved and embraced in order to give depth and stability to American culture. The folk dances "should be preserved,

not only to keep alive the charm and grace of the people themselves, but because America needs—and needs greatly—just this contribution" (Gulick 1909: 4). The new American nation needed to learn from old examples. The failure to do so might be not just culturally impoverishing but deadly:

> The national and folk dances, while interesting as a spectacle, have not been prepared and are not given primarily because of the immediate interest or beauty that may attach to them. Behind it all there lies the conviction that we in America have so far largely failed to appreciate the significance of the fete, or festival. For example, the few holidays that we already have are celebrated in ways which not only largely fail to accomplish the objects for which they were set aside, but which are in themselves a menace, and, as in the case of the Fourth of July, a positive evil from many standpoints. It is reported from apparently trustworthy sources that more persons have been sacrificed in celebrating the Fourth of July than were fatally injured in the War of independence itself. [The table taken from the *Chicago Tribune* on dead and injured on 4th of July (Gulick 1909: 13)]

This citation expresses clearly, perhaps somewhat humorously from our perspective, a great remorse over America's shortage of appropriate and worthwhile cultural expression. Gulick's choice of example emphasizes his view that the lack of cultural wealth in the country not only affected American lives, but was destroying them. In this light, teaching and transmitting the folklore of other world cultures to American youth becomes an urgent and noble task.

The folk dances "must be resurrected and given again to the children as part of their birthright," writes Gulick (1911: 185). That the folk dances *must* be resurrected points to the urgency, necessity, and even inevitability of the work. But if the folk dances were never *given* to the American children how can they be *given again*? And what is it that is being *resurrected*, we might ask? Gulick's choice of words here is deliberate and revealing. The fact that the dances are *given again* rather than *taught* or simply *given* to American children underlines the belief that they ultimately *belong* to the children as part of their *birthright,* their inheritance. The children are seen to be receiving not just folk dances of *other* cultures, but the folk dances of *their* culture. American children are the descendants of "the other," and as such they have a birthright to "get back" what is essentially theirs. Furthermore, as embodiments of universal humanity, the national origin of the music and dance is perceived, in this case, as almost irrelevant. Part of this "universal humanity" is a relationship with nature. "These folk dances express in extraordinarily complete form man's history—the sowing of grain in the spring, the reaping in the fall. . . . In fact, all of man's life has been portrayed and crystallized in these art forms" (Gulick 1911: 185). Here, the influence of Stanley Hall's racial theory is quite clear. Of all the world's dance traditions to depict only a particular idea of European folk dance as a "crystallized" expression of man's his-

tory is another outgrowth of Romanticism, and is a part of the discourse on the newness of American culture.[33] The value of the "old," surviving in the "folk," had been historically proven. In its universality and connection with nature it was transcendent. Thus, folk embodiments of the "old" were not bound to the cultures that created them, but fundamentally human and natural.

It is through the reenactment of the peasant world that American children and adults alike were to connect with nature and true human character. Along with the "old," the "peasant" is an inseparable aspect of the "folk." Peasants knew the real values and joys of life. Replication of the movements peasants made in their dances was supposed to enable one to find the peasant within and get in touch with one's true nature. Things peasant in this context are idealized as "spiritually enlightened," if simplistic. Thus, through engaging in "peasant" activities, it was expected that youth would be encouraged to turn away from materialistic and commercial aspects of American culture. Even the attractiveness of the dance hall was supposed to be lessened "for those who can have in school the beautiful old-world folk dances" (Gulick 1911: 42). Only through this enlightenment could the youth resist the lustful temptations of modern, urban life and its materialism. "There is now going on a great revolt against materialism, and the folk-dancing movement is part of that reaction. Folk dancing means the pursuit of that thing which is ideal—the joy of living—that which is more real than the drudgery of everyday life, that which makes human life interesting and significant" (Gulick 1911: 214). This citation could have been written at any point from the turn of the century to the present day. The belief is persistent that, through industrialization and mechanization, American society has lost touch not only with nature and community, but the joy, even wisdom, of living. This belief is almost always accompanied by the belief that life's secret, or truth, or real experience can be achieved, or "regained" through involvement in folk dance. Thus, dancing folk dances from around the world was not conceptualized simply as appropriation or exploration of the "other," but as a bridge to one's own "forgotten" past. This is not a cultural past, but the "natural," "truly human" past at the heart of one's being.

PART III

International Folk Dancing from the 1930s to the 1950s

5

Dance and Be Merry

In the middle of the twentieth century, the American people went in search of fun. Looking at what led up to the explosion of international folk dancing as a pop phenomenon, this chapter traces some of the components that fed its popularity: the dark days of the Great Depression and subsequent flood of WPA funding for all things folkloric, a new sense of internationalism, a renewed emphasis on participatory over passive enjoyments, and a "growing hunger" for novel cultural experiences. What's more, being "ethnic" became, for some people and some purposes, cool.

> For the good are always merry
> Save by an evil chance,
> And the merry love the fiddle
> And the merry love to dance.
> —Keats

These lines of Keats quoted in Hinman appear on the inside cover of Mary Wood Hinman's *Gymnastic and Folk Dancing*, volume II (1930).[1] Nothing characterizes the second phase in the development of the international folk dance movement better than the titles of the most popular folk dance books published in this period. Titles such as *Merrily Dance*, *Dance and Be Merry*, *Folk Dances for Fun*, and *Folk Dances for All* summarize a basic premise and intention of the movement—the production and democratization of fun. The serious, educational, even scientific approach to folk dancing of the turn of the century gave way to a lighter, more entertainment-oriented view of the role of folk dancing in American society. This is not to say that the strong emphasis on the educational role of IFD disappeared. The divisions between different periods in IFD history are not clear, nor does a particular usage of folk dance vanish when new uses and places for the activity emerge. The seeds of new ideas are planted long before they flourish, just as older plants keep living for decades after they have reached their first bloom.

Still, in response to the shifting tasks and challenges of the times, new attitudes toward international folk dance and new perceptions of its role in American society arose. With this in mind, the 1930s and the mid-1950s form rough borders of what is here considered to be the second phase in the history of ideas and developments in the IFD movement.[2] Resonating with the social, political, and cultural climate of the times, international folk dancing groups increased tremendously in popularity and membership during the 1930s and 1940s. John Martin, the dance critic for the *New York Times*, reported: "The rapid growth in the number of folk-dance events in the concert calendar has taken on all the characteristics of a 'trend'" (*New York Times*, May 8, 1932). Likewise, on the West Coast, folk dancing was acknowledged in 1941 as "the reigning sensation of the nation."[3]

In the following chapters we will examine how and why folk dance acquired characteristics of a national trend, and what kinds of changes took place during this period. While Serbian, Croatian, Macedonian, Bulgarian, Romanian, and Greek dances were frequently danced as a part of the IFD repertoire, they were not grouped together as "Balkan" dances. Throughout this period dances from the Balkans remained only one ingredient in the international mix.

Internationalism in America During the Great Depression and New Deal Era

While the "internationalism" of the settlement house, physical education, and recreation movements was essentially national, that is, focused on multiculturalism within the United States, internationalism in this later period was rhetorically expanded abroad and was essentially transnational. While in the first period folk dancing was used to promote tolerance among various American immigrant groups, in the second period it was also seen as an activity that symbolically promoted peace among the peoples of the world. The internationalism of the second period is also wider in its scope, including a greater diversity of repertoire. With the huge wave of immigration slowing in the 1920s, the focus shifted away from the assimilation and education of immigrants. Although the rhetoric of "immigrant gifts to American people" persisted within the IFD movement, definitions of Americanness were placed in a transnational perspective.

A new type of international awareness arose in the United States during World War I. One need only glance at the major newspapers of the period to notice an upsurge in reports of international entertainment, international balls, and international folk dance events. Benefit dance parties to aid the Allies in World War I were organized and advertised in many American cities.[4] The *San Francisco Bulletin* (January 11, 1917) expected "the international entertainment and dance . . . for the benefit of the allies' war relief fund" to be "one of the most brilliant affairs of the season." This program, which included "French, Russian, Irish, Italian, Scottish, Serbian, and Polish dances and drills," was followed by a grand march in

which representatives of "Ireland, Wales, Isle of Man, the British colonies, France, Italy, Belgium, Serbia, Poland, Russia and Japan" were "led by prominent San Franciscans bearing the Stars and Stripes." As one of the many international events organized during the war this was, in both form and content, very similar to folk festivals organized earlier by settlement houses and recreation departments. However, its context and message to participants and spectators were essentially different. In these events, folk dances and songs were used as the best representatives of different *nations*, rather than different *immigrant groups*.[5] The earlier narrow national perspective was broadened, and along with the idea of various immigrant groups comprising the American nation, the united American nation was celebrated for its leadership of the other nations of the world.

It is beyond the scope of this work to discuss various types of American internationalism, Jewish, Old Left, liberal, conservative, or simply populist. What is most relevant is an acknowledgment of the formation of organizations and institutions that would work not only to organize immigrant groups but help create a new vision of American identity. "International institutes," "international homes," and "international folk festivals" mushroomed in the United States after World War I and particularly during the Depression and New Deal era.

Folk festivals were a transitional step in the history of IFD.[6] There were basically two kinds of folk festivals in the United States, national and international. Both were concerned with defining Americanness, but their ideological premises were different. Music, dances, and crafts of groups that had been present on American soil for a comparatively long time (Native Americans, African Americans, Latinos) were presented at national festivals. At international festivals, various local immigrant groups were included as part of the American fabric, but "older" settler groups were generally excluded. English, German, French, and sometimes Irish and Dutch groups were included in both national and international programs.

Differences between the two types of festivals went far beyond the selection of participants. For example, the two folk festivals organized in St. Louis in 1934, the "Festival of Nations" (April 18, 1934) and the "National Folk Festival" (April 29–May 3, 1934), happened within the same month but were organized by completely different personnel and organizations and aimed at different audiences. Commenting on the divisions within the folk dance world of New York, John Martin reported that "Folk dance affairs . . . have grown to such proportions and in such different directions that the mere enthusiast who is not fortunate enough to be an expert is likely to tread on somebody's very sensitive toes unless he confines himself to a policy of non commitment" (Martin, *New York Times*, April 16, 1933). Ironic though it may be, many organizations and leaders whose primary theme was promoting tolerance and diversity were sensitive, territorial, and uncompromising when it came to determining what "diversity" was to include and what kind of folk dancing was to serve as an appropriate expression of this diversity. In the same article Martin somewhat naively brushes over the conflicting politics, ideologies, and

personal interests of the people involved in the three folk dance organizations in New York (the English Folk Dance Society, the American Folk Dance Society, and the Folk Festival Council),[7] concluding that "The fundamental purpose that underlies all three of them is substantially one." While at one time organizational and ideological unification might have been seen as a possibility, the movement, in fact, became more and more factionalized, largely due to competing and sometimes radically different ideas about folk dancing. This segmentation speaks to the fact that folk dance material can be infused with different ideologies. Not only was new meaning assigned to a particular dance or group of dances, but particular dances were chosen to accompany particular ideological rhetoric.

Getting Together to Folk Dance

While earlier in the century "international folk dance" was used by existing institutions for particular purposes and existing groups of people, a new twist was the formation of organizations and interest groups whose primary goal was to further the "genre" and the practices surrounding it. At this point in its history IFD experienced a grass-roots movement. People got together to folk dance, they organized themselves, incorporated their groups, supported their newsletters and magazines, and created whole infrastructures of the folk dance world from the bottom up. At the same time, however, top-down models of the teaching and presentation of dance material, as well as rhetoric on the importance of folk dancing to American society at large, were inherited or adopted by this grass-roots movement. The movement's practices of drawing from both the "top" and the "bottom" helped its growth in popularity.

Mary Wood Hinman, then active in New York, attributed changes she observed as folk dancing developed to changes in American society at large. In a paper presented in 1933 at the Mid-West Physical Education Association Convention, she observed a "shifting in one or two of the old channels of thought, not thoughts on dancing, but opinions on life, and because of this, something is happening to the dance and to the average person's reaction to it."[8] Hinman identified two major changes: the first was "a shift away from vicarious recreation and an awakening to the joy found in participation," and the second "a growing hunger for broader cultural backgrounds, which leads to a wish to understand people as they are, and a desire to be freed from opinion handed down from Mid-Victorian times."[9] Both of these points require elaboration.

One can argue that "vicarious recreation" is a type of active participation, but in Hinman's statement these two stand in opposition to each other. What Hinman was implying was a shift from bodily exercise to the creation of fun, from folk dancing as a drill, a means of achieving physical vigor, to folk dancing as an engaging social activity. In its then new incarnation, folk dancing was used not to discipline, not to shape the bodies and educate the foreign and the poor, but to entertain, to enable and teach

people to have fun, interact with each other, and develop interest in others (figure 5.1). Here, the agency is in the hands of participants. Hinman concluded that any existing resentment toward the folk dance programs in school curricula was to be blamed on the fact that the fun of mutual interaction between the sexes had been robbed from folk dancing when the dances were introduced separately to girls and boys. For this reason the activity became "worthless as an expression of joy."[10] The sheer imitation of the physical movement involved in folk dances of various cultures was no longer seen as a sufficient aid to the physical and moral fitness of the American people. The trend shifted away from viewing people as bodies to be acted upon toward an emphasis on the interactive and expressive experience of individuals. "It is in an atmosphere of mutual respect and understanding, of confidence and 'belonging,' of shared leadership and spontaneous interplay, of full participation and achievement that 'something' happens to the attitudes and feelings of people, that the heart as well as the mind becomes involved" (Allen n.d.: 1).

In order to be successful, a folk dance program had to enable people to have fun, but the terms under which participants were to experience fun were preset. Catherine Allen's *Pocket Full of Fun* provides this "Simple Recipe for Fun":

> To familiar activities add variety and the spice of humor and color. To this mixture, add the surprise of new types of activities. Stir well. Throughout the blending, pour in generous amounts of YOU, THE LEADER—the sincerity and contagion of your friendly smile, your effective voice, and your well-poised, graceful, easily-moving body.

Obviously, "fun" was perceived as a state of being that could be produced and reproduced, and thus controlled. "Fun" could be triggered when the right circumstances were created.

Teaching people to have fun is quite a different task from teaching them folk dance steps. Folk dance books and instruction manuals could perhaps capture the steps, but not the fun of executing them. In order to be able to transmit the excitement of doing folk dances, teachers had to have first-hand experience of the joy that could be found in participation. This joy in social interaction was again seen to be the strongest within traditional contexts. For this reason, Hinman began to feel the need to provide background and color to the dances that were taught. "The growing hunger for broader cultural backgrounds" was to be fulfilled by ["real natives" prominent community leaders (1933: n.p.)]. While previous folk dance teachers had turned to foreign lands for authentic material, being "ethnic" was now, for the first time, perceived as advantageous, and ethnic teachers were not to be questioned about the sources of their material and information.

This attitude soon resulted in a reversal of roles between the students/teachers and immigrants/Americans. Instead of educated Americans of Anglo-Saxon or Jewish[11] origin teaching illiterate, poor immigrants in

Figure 5.1. The pursuit of happiness (Hinman 1937, volume IV)

settlement houses, or immigrant and native-born children in public schools, it became the norm for acculturated immigrant teachers to lead folk dance groups comprised mostly of mainstream Americans of Anglo-Saxon or Jewish origin. While the first group of students primarily needed to be educated and "set on the right path," the second group was already on the right path and needed only to be engaged in the production of fun through participation in a social activity regarded as having cultural merit.[12]

Henry Glass, a long-time folk dancer and the first president of the Folk Dance Federation of California, founded in 1942, attributed the national interest in folk dance to the Depression. "Early folk dancers were products of the great depression," Glass writes (1972: 68). "They knew want and deprivation and found in friendly dancers a chance to live brotherhood." An "awakening to the joy found in participation" was one of the basic premises of folk dance programs in the Great Depression era. The concerted effort made to create fun for the American people reflected the social and economic circumstances of the time.

Folk dance programs and festivals got an especially big boost from the Works Progress Administration (WPA), the governmental program created in 1935 to provide economic relief and create jobs during the Depression. These events had not only a populist appeal, but also perceived artistic merit, which ensured funding through the Federal Art Project, one of the divisions of the WPA. Interestingly, the construction of the Mendocino Woodlands Camp, home of the West Coast Balkan camps, was a WPA project. The capacity of folk dancing to engage large groups of people in a

social exchange and to mobilize whole communities was congruent with the tasks of the Project. The national director of the Federal Art Project, Holger Cahill, reported: "the organization of the Project has proceeded on the principle that it is not the solitary genius but a sound general movement which maintains art as a vital, functioning part of any cultural scheme." Folk dancing was understood to be a communal project not only in its realization, but in its conception as well.

We can ascribe the appeal of international folk dance to its unique position in the American high art/popular art dichotomy. Like other forms of mass culture popular at the time, folk dancing was enjoyable without previous training and was a fun, manageable activity. But unlike other forms of popular culture that were denigrated by the cultural elite as unworthy, decadent, immoral, and unsophisticated, folk dancing was perceived as simple but nonetheless artistically valid, authentic, and true human expression.

Folk dancing came to be viewed as an activity that could counteract, at least to some degree, the personal isolation and individualism of advanced capitalism. Folk dance groups provided their members with the opportunity to participate simultaneously in the acts of creation and consumption of what they had collectively produced. Folk dancing brought people the joy of social interaction while "awakening" them, through participation, to the elimination of the boundaries between performers and audience, between the personal and communal, between creation and consumption. Similar efforts in the domain of literature at that time have been discussed by Walter Kalaidjian in *American Culture Between the Wars*. Kalaidjian's interesting reading of this period of American cultural history points to the privileging of the social over the literary, popular culture over formalism, and global multiculturalism over domestic nationalism: "The conjuncture of popular culture and left politics, as you find it in America's little magazines between the wars, fostered an alternative discourse of racial, sexual, class, and transnational experience" (Kalaidjian 1993: 3). While international folk dance had clearly provided, and continued to provide, an alternative discourse of racial, sexual, class, and transnational experience, its position within American culture and society between the wars differs in several respects from the position of Kalaidjian's "little magazines." What is extraordinary about the place of international folk dance is that it embodied both sides of the binary oppositions listed above. And, most interestingly of all, international folk dance simultaneously advocated, implicitly or explicitly, both global multiculturalism and domestic nationalism while remaining essentially apolitical. This apolitical position allowed for flirtation with both political left and right. Being wedged between these categories, international folk dance was able to mobilize membership and, more important, support from both liberals and conservatives, immigrants and the old American elite. I believe it is, in part, this multiple positioning that helped folk dancing, constantly adapting to the demands of different cultural, political, and social climates, remain a vital presence in American society.

Mary Wood Hinman and the Folk Festival Council of New York

International folk festivals were events in which physical education and recreation leaders were joined by leaders of the immigrant performing groups; where the "top-down" and "grass-roots" aspects of the movement intersected. It was through participation in various folk festivals that most of the next generation of folk dance leaders came into the scene. These festivals also enabled "ethnic" teachers to learn dances and songs of other local immigrant groups.

Mary Wood Hinman and the FFC of New York embodied an important point of connection between turn of the century folk dance and the next generation of "ethnic" folk dance leaders such as Michael Herman, Tashamira, Elba Farabegoli Gurzay, and many others.[13] As head of the FFC of New York, an organization sponsored by the Foreign Language Information Service, Hinman attempted to break through the existing model of folk dance classes organized in settlements, public schools, factories, and YMCA and YWCA organizations. The very statement of purpose of the FFC (as quoted by John Martin in the *New York Times*, January 8, 1932) suggests a change in the justification for, and intended beneficiaries of, the folk dance programs. "The purposes of the FFC are twofold: 'to give *the people of New York* an opportunity to enjoy the contributions of foreign-born groups to the folk arts,' and 'to keep these arts alive as a vital part of *our* community life by providing *foreign-born people themselves* with fine and dignified opportunities for artistic expression [emphasis mine]." It is for the people of New York—for "us"—that the dances of the foreign-born need to be preserved. The distinction between "us" (the people of New York) and "them" (the foreign-born), although clearly emphasized, was not to be understood as a black and white division. The FFC membership comprised dozens of ethnic groups that would present their folklore at the festivals.[14]

In 1933 Hinman organized folk dance groups at both the NYU Music Department and the Graduate Music School of Columbia University. A series of folk dance evenings titled "Dances of Many Peoples" was inaugurated in 1932 under the auspices of the FFC of New York. Each session, held at the New School for Social Research, was devoted to learning dances of a different nationality. The idea of these classes was to invite "a couple from one of the foreign groups to come to them in their own folk costumes" and share their folk dances. Talks and lecture demonstrations were held on these occasions and folk dancing would follow "until the lights were put out" (Hinman 1933: n.p.). Arthur Leon Moore, executive chairman of the FFC, said that hundreds of people who belonged to the organizations which it comprised, knew not only the folk dances of their countries of origin, but the dances of other nations as well, due to extensive visiting between various dancing clubs.

John Martin of the *New York Times* followed the activities of the FFC and the sessions at the New School closely. "At these sessions there is no

audience," he reported (October 8, 1933), "everybody participates, and apparently has to be forced to quit when the hour grows late. Men and women of all ages and sizes and interests work like Trojans to master the intricacies of the figures and to obey the prompter's calls." Tashamira, of the Chalif School, and Miss Geraldine Smith, head of social service work at the Bellevue Nurses Home, were in charge of encouraging the audience to join in the dancing.

The festivals organized by the FFC were well attended. It was not uncommon for one hundred to two hundred people to attend the classes at the New School, with three times as many participating in festivals. For example, seven hundred people in folk costumes formed the nucleus for dancing at the Folk Festival Ball in September 1932. The participatory nature of the program was advertised, as can be seen in the press statement given by Mary Wood Hinman: "First a group, say of Bulgarians, will give an example of one of the simplest dances. . . . Then they will take partners from the audience and demonstrate just how the Horo is done. Every one may dance, and, according to comments at the festival last Spring almost everyone will" (*New York Times*, September 25, 1932).

But these folk festivals were not always accepted with enthusiasm. As Michael Herman recalls, some members of ethnic groups were not pleased to see their dances done by people of other nationalities and races.[15] Also, John Martin (*New York Times*, April 16, 1933) indicates ideological conflict between the society at large and the programs organized by the FFC. "Undoubtedly its programs have violated, at times, the high theory of the American society. It is not necessary, however, that they should do so, and it seems reasonable that they will not do so when the huge enterprise has fully found itself."

Folk dance programs such as Hinman's encountered other difficulties as well. The biggest problem the FFC encountered resulted from its attempt to preserve the existing model of folk dance instruction, i.e., the provision of a written description of dance steps with musical transcription for piano accompaniment, while using "authentic" dancers as instructors. Community leaders, though they may have been beautiful and skilled dancers in their own immigrant communities, were neither physical education leaders nor dance educators per se. As Dick Crum pointed out (Interview, 1997), "the leaders of these ethnic performing ensembles were accountants, bakers, housewives, etc. These people did not know how to introduce their folk dances to Americans." Consequently this teaching model did not work as expected. One way to address the problem was to hire educated dance instructors who had immigrated to the United States. For example, Tashamira, a ballerina who came from Zagreb, Croatia and joined Chalif's school in the early 1930s, worked closely with Mary Wood Hinman in the FFC. Another option was to hire ethnic teachers and a mediator to work alongside them, someone who could not only translate during classes, but also provide a dance syllabus and piano transcription of the relevant dance tunes. One of these mediators in the FFC was Michael Herman, a man who was musically literate, who was of Ukrainian descent but spoke perfect

English, and who was an able dancer. It is through the activities of this new breed of folk dance teachers, particularly Michael Herman, Vyts Beliajus, and Song Chang, that international folk dance found a new shape and role in American society, ultimately giving birth to the American Balkan scene.

6

Emergence of the New Folk Dance Leaders
Vytautas Beliajus, Song Chang, and Michael Herman

Through the folk dance activities of three "ethnic" teachers, Vyts Beliajus, Song Chang, and Michael Herman, we explore regional developments on the East Coast, West Coast, and in the Midwest beginning in the 1930s. These three men, along with others of their generation, may be considered the grandparents of the Balkan scene. While the 1930s and '40s saw the emergence of significant and enduring regional differences in approach, repertoire, and organization, there were remarkable similarities as well. The national attention folk dance received from its inclusion, beginning in 1933, in the World's Fair, for example, contributed to its growing popularity, and this attention contributed to the birth of a host of publications and organizations serving folk dancers both regionally and nationally/internationally. A survey of some of them is followed by a brief analysis and summary of regional differences in the scene during this period.

Although the personal contributions of Michael Herman, Song Chang, and Vytautas Beliajus differed greatly in both scope and nature, they are, to the present day, widely revered as among those who contributed most to the development of the modern international folk dance scene. There were others: Lucile Czarnowsky, Madelynne Greene, Jane Farewell, Ralph Page, Sarah Gertrude Knott, to name only a few. These leaders contributed substantial bodies of folk dance material and, more important, personal initiative and enthusiasm to the movement, but their influence was not as comprehensive or relevant to the emergence of the Balkan scene.[1]

It is perhaps because Herman, Chang, and Beliajus were each associated with a different geographical area—the East Coast (New York), the West Coast (San Francisco), and the Midwest (Chicago) respectively—that in the overall history of the movement one cannot avoid talking about each of them. Undoubtedly, each was a folk dance giant in his own area, but on a national level their contributions differ in scale as well as character.

Like the synchronicity of the establishment of settlement houses with their folk dance programs, the synchronicity of the emergence of three major "ethnic" folk dance leaders must be understood in the context of developments within the folk dance movement as well as in American

culture and society. Each man was either a first- or second-generation American who found folk dancing to be an expression of internationalism. Working independently of each other, they each commanded a large following composed predominantly of more established, mainstream Americans. Chang, Beliajus, and Herman each had experienced discrimination on the basis of their ethnic backgrounds. "Sensitive to the discrimination he had to undergo as a Chinese, he [Chang] decided that the folk dance would prove a solution in bringing the various people together" (Norton, 1962). The inclusiveness espoused by the IFD world provided these men a degree of shelter, and helped them find a valued place in American culture.

IFD in the Central United States—Vytautas Finadar Beliajus

Vytautas Finadar Beliajus, commonly known as Vyts, emerged as a folk dance leader in the early 1930s in the Midwest. As a fifteen-year-old boy, Beliajus immigrated from the village of Pakumprys, Lithuania with his grandmother. In September 1923 they settled with relatives in a Lithuanian neighborhood in Chicago. It was here that Vyts's folk dance career began. Vyts liked to give the impression that the majority of his international folk dance repertoire was acquired in Lithuania, learned firsthand:

> In Prienai, every weekend, either Friday or Saturday night, I and a few other school mates our age, met at the home of two sisters who lived in the last house of the main street, near the Nemunas River. There we danced the Lithuanian dances to our singing of the words, or the current popular folk dances of all the countries in the Russian sphere—*Noriu Miego, Suktinis, Aguonele, Kokiekta, Anelkute Kaire Koja. Vengierka, Padespan, Karapiet, Aleksandrovska, Korobushka* and a ballroom-style of *Krakoviak* were danced through the entire countries of pre-WWI, ruled by Tsarist Russia: Ukraine, Belarus, Poland, Lithuania, Latvia, Estonia and Finland.[2] (*Viltis* Jan.–Feb. 1993/51, 5)

Apparently Vyts was dancing "polkas, a rare waltz and the current ballroom dances of the era" at weddings in his village and learned German dances while standing behind the fence of the German School in Prienai watching German schoolchildren dance. Although not impossible, it is hard to imagine that Vyts was indeed able to memorize all the dances, songs, and steps as a schoolboy. It is possible that he had seen these dances performed in Lithuania, but that he also used instruction booklets and songbooks to recreate them for teaching purposes. Dick Crum suggested that a number of dances published by Vyts are probably translations from folk dance books published in Russian or Lithuanian.[3]

Trying to trace Vyts's path in the folk dance world is complicated by the large amount of undocumented and uncritical information on his life

and work floating around in numerous articles in folk dance books and magazines. These sources usually tell more about the author's enthusiasm and fascination with Beliajus than about the man himself.[4] Vyts's own writing is problematic for the researcher, as conflicting information appears not only from one magazine issue to another, but sometimes even within the same article.

Whatever the status of Vyts's knowledge of folk dance before settling in United States, there is no doubt that his repertoire expanded in Chicago. "Some of my first acts," writes Vyts, "were to attend dances either at St. George's Parish Hall or the Lithuanian Auditorium. That was more like what I was yearning for. Folk dancing predominated" (*Viltis* March–April 1949/6). Vyts was directly associated with Chicago settlements, which may be where he was first introduced to the idea of international folk dance, possibly even where he got his first folk dance training.[5] The following excerpt from *Viltis* is illustrative of the depth of Vyts's involvement with the Chicago settlements:

> After 1937 I instructed Croatian Kolos at Chicago's Howell House, a settlement house on Racine near 18th St., in the heart of a Croatian and Czech Settlement. I also had a Czech group, where the Beseda and Czech couples dances were taught. We organized a small Kolo group, probably the first in the United States, whose purpose was to demonstrate the Jugoslav dances, mostly done at presentations connected with the Howell House. . . . I have been instrumental in introducing Kolos for the first time to many non-Jugoslav groups throughout the country, from coast to coast and from border to border. My Lithuanian group, LYS (Lithuanian Youth Society), even danced a group of Kolos at a National Folk Festival (about 1939 or 1940) to the playing of the presently famous Duquesne University Tamburitzans when that year they didn't bring a kolo group with them. (*Viltis* Oct.–Nov. 1954/13: 6, "Lithuanian 'Hrvats' in 38")

Through his friend Michele Gamboni, Beliajus was also introduced "to the Hull House and the highly loved and revered Jane Addams." It was also at the Hull House, Vyts writes in "Jane Addams and Hull House" (*Viltis* May 1960/19,1: 15), that he was first exposed to folk dance festivals:

> Eventually even I and my group danced and presented programs at the Hull House. Later I myself become involved in Settlement House work. I had a wonderful group of Polish kids at Northwestern University Settlement House where Harriet Vittum, second only to Jane Addams, was head resident. I worked with Mexican kids at the Henry Booth House, at Howell House with Croatian and Czech young people, and with Lithuanian kids at the Fellowship House, where Alice Mauck was head resident. Mrs. Mauck was also my "godmother" who sponsored me when I took out my citizenship papers.

Although his work with Lithuanians at Fellowship House is last on Vyts's list, I do not believe this should be understood chronologically as the last settlement with which he became involved. The fact that the head resident of Fellowship House supported Vyts in acquiring citizenship suggests, rather, that he was involved with this settlement for a longer period of time.

Many articles on Vyts include a story about his childhood fascination with Jules Verne's book *Around the World in Eighty Days* and his desire to make friends with the inhabitants of a multitude of exotic countries. "I had read about the Hindus and India in the book 'A Trip Around the World in Eighty Days' . . . while still in Lithuania," writes Vyts (June–August 1991/50, 2: 16) in an article titled "My Hindu Cycle" (figure 6.1) "I attribute to this book my interest in nations previously not met." Indeed, Vyts was involved with different societies, religious organizations, dancing styles,

Figure 6.1. Vytautas Finadar Beliajus, "My Hindu Cycle," c. 1930 (*Viltis*, June–August 1991)

and ethnic groups at different times in his imaginative globe-trotting,[6] explorations of the "other" he referred to as "cycles."

Mary Bee Jensen explains how, in Chicago, Vyts "had an exciting opportunity to meet others from many nations. He first became interested in Mexican culture and folk dances, then soon began to include Italian and Hindu dances in his repertoire." He then "became deeply involved in Hasidic dancing" (in Casey 1981: 11). "The first I sought out in my second year in Chicago were the Moslem Arabs, then the Italians, Sephardic Jews, Croatians and others" writes Vyts in *Viltis* (1991/50, 2: 16). This was not a usual route for a folk dancer. Dick Crum saw Vyts as a follower of Ruth St. Denis and Ted Shawn, pioneers of modern American dance who, with their Denishawn dance company, experimented with movement based on ethnic and tribal dance. Judging from Vyts's approach to dance, typified by exoticism more than a "back to nature and cultural roots" philosophy, as well as from his interests, biographical details, and pictures of him in costumes emulating those of Denishawn, their influence is quite apparent.[7]

Beginnings of Beliajus's Teaching Career

Vyts's teaching career probably began in the early 1930s and was focused at first on Lithuanian dances. He organized the Lithuanian Youth Society[8] in Chicago, and with this group participated at the Chicago World's Fair *A Century of Progress International Exposition* in 1933.[9] Although the appearance at the World's Fair gave Vyts tremendous visibility in the field and boosted his folk dance career, his group was still limited to representing Lithuania with Lithuanian dances on the Lithuanian day. As we shall see, this is quite different from the experiences of Song Chang and Michael Herman, who presented international folk dances as representative of Americans at the San Francisco and New York fairs respectively.

Beliajus was also hired by the Chicago Park District to teach folk dancing, beginning in 1936. "I taught various native dances varying with the ethnic population living around the parks. Turkish 'Havassi' dances to a Ladino group, the then current Palestinian dances to Jewish groups, Polish, Russian, Latvian, Lithuanian, German and Ukrainian" (Beliajus in Casey 1981: 91). Like other prominent folk dance teachers during the New Deal, Beliajus worked for the WPA. In fact, between 1936 and 1938 Vyts was the editor of the first folk dance magazine, *Lore*, published by the Chicago Park District under a WPA project.[10]

By the late 1960s Vyts claimed to have taught "in every state except Hawaii and . . . in Canada and Mexico" (Beliajus, in Casey 1981: 99). Between 1937, when he started teaching outside of Chicago, and 1940, "he'd taught at over two hundred universities, colleges, and institutions and had sparked nationwide interest in folk dancing" (Jensen 1981: 12). Touring would become much more common in the next phase of folk dance development, when teachers began to specialize in dances of a particular area of the world. Soon it would become common practice for teachers to travel from one folk dance club to another. This development demanded of teach-

ers that they come up with new material to teach from one tour to the next. Under these circumstances teachers found their own ways to feed the growing folk dance market. "Vyts taught dance after dance after dance, and would never say where they were coming from, and nobody ever asked him" Dick Crum commented (Interview, 1997). "He would never tell his sources. He enjoyed the impression that everyone had, that he somehow came to the U.S. with all this knowledge. . . . He was often forced into situations where he was called on for expertise that he did not have."

Viltis

Beliajus's unique and possibly largest contribution to the folk dance world is his folk dance magazine *Viltis* ("Hope" in Lithuanian). It started as a mimeographed letter for servicemen in May of 1943 in Fairhope, Alabama, where Vyts was teaching at the time.[11] He described its original purpose as "to keep up with the activities of our friends in the Armed Forces scattered throughout the world, and to exchange news" (*Viltis* 1974/33, 1: 3). In the mimeographed form, *Viltis* was at its peak reaching "350 boys in the service all over the world." These were the folk dancers Vyts knew before the war. It was not until 1944, when *Viltis* first appeared in printed form, that it became a folk dance magazine, an amateur publication created to suit the needs of international folk dancers. *Viltis* remained in print six times a year and gained a national and even international readership over the years.

One could argue that the feeling of community Michael Herman endeavored to create through an emphasis on sociability in folk dancing Vyts realized through his magazine. Readers were encouraged to send news and announcements to the regular column "Among Friends," which included information and trivia from the private lives of folk dancers. This helped the readership keep up with each others' lives and the folk dance world in general, engendering a feeling of community, continuity, and cohesion among people who were not regularly in touch or may never even have met. In this manner *Viltis* presaged the Internet chat rooms and list serves that were to develop a half century later.

In another regular column, "As For Myself," Vyts offered reports on his teaching tours, travels, and visits with various folk dancers, as well as very personal news about his frequent ill health, which gave readers the sense that they knew him. In the eyes of many of his "followers" he became an embodiment of American unity in diversity. "I think of Vyts," William Rotch wrote in a tribute called " '*Viltis*: The Spirit of a Man and 50 Years of Hope,' when I read the stories of horror in the newspapers, when I glimpse scenes of death and destruction on television. Here was a man who devoted his life to demonstrating that there is a better way. He showed through folk dancing that Native Americans, Asians, Africans, Europeans, Hispanics, North Americans, can find common interests, can work and play together" (*Viltis* Sept./Oct. 1995).

The magazine also carried folk dance news and articles on related subjects, including costumes, customs, and recipes. Vyts's editing was uneven,

or, rather, the quality of the articles varied considerably between authors. Many articles were full of errors, misinformation, and speculation. Vyts proudly called this *Viltis'* "original personal journalism." This type of personal writing, with its feeling of in-group camaraderie, is characteristic of many other folk dance publications, including Herman's *Folk Dancer, Northwest Folkdancer,* and *Folk Dance Scene in Baton Rouge,* and is a manifestation of the general attitude of democracy and supportiveness.

Since Vyts's death in September 1994, *Viltis* has been issued by the International Institute of Wisconsin. An extensive collection of folk dance and folklore materials was donated to the Special Collections and Archives of the Carson-Brierly Dance Library of the University of Denver's Penrose Library.

IFD on the West Coast—Song Chang and Chang's International Folk Dancers

Song Chang

Perhaps the most puzzling of the three leaders is Song Chang, a Chinese American who spent only a short period of his life actively involved in IFD. However, due to the intensity and timing of his involvement, as well as the geographic region in which he was active, he became known as the "West Coast father" of the movement. His name is still well known in IFD circles, and the group he started, *Chang's International Folk Dancers* (later changed to *Changs International Folk Dancers*), is still active in San Francisco.[12]

Chang's name appears frequently in regional press of the day, but we know little about his personal life or his motivation for becoming involved in IFD.[13] As is true today, in the 1930s and 1940s people of Asian descent constituted a tiny minority of those active in the American IFD movement, which lends even more interest to Chang's story. I have been able to piece together only a sketchy biography, and the information available often fluctuates between fact and folklore. Much of what is in print is, if not contradictory, at least clearly a variation on previously published material.

Various accounts trace Song Chang's exposure to international folk dance to his work on a ship. As he traveled to various European countries he reputedly learned folk dances when on shore leave and from other sailors. The most detailed account is provided by Grace Tener Frye in her master's thesis titled "The Revival of the Folk Dance as Social Recreation in Northern California."[14] Frye writes (1947: 28) that Chang "started folk dancing on a German boat bound for France, in 1930. From 1933 to 1937, this leader spent considerable time among the Scandinavian groups learning dances from them."[15] According to Frye, "While en route to China, aboard a Japanese boat, in 1937, the people who were going to the Portuguese colony in southern China, taught him the Portuguese national dance, the 'Vira.'"[16] While Chang may have learned folk dances on these trips, one wonders if it wasn't a pre-existing interest. San Francisco was certainly full of opportunities to encounter folk dance, ranging from folk festivals

and the city's many "ethnic clubs" that welcomed outsiders to their dance parties,[17] to school physical education classes and dance classes organized by the San Francisco recreation departments.[18]

Beginnings of International Folk Dancing in California

It is often repeated in folk dance circles[19] that folk dancing in California germinated in San Francisco at the Swedish Applied Arts, a school of weaving and folk arts that was organized and led by Valborg ("Mama") and Axel Gravander.[20] The couple had a small restaurant in the basement of the school where, two nights a week, people in Swedish costume served a smorgasbord dinner followed by Scandinavian dancing and singing. According to Morton (1962) [21] "It was to one of these dinner and dance evenings that Song Chang was brought by one of the members of the 'family,'" Vivika Timirasieff. The "family" was made up of students who "either lived at the school/house or attended regular classes." Another member, Patricia Lamont Holmberg, also knew Mr. Chang, and "Vivika, Patsy and I," Morton writes, "gladly assisted him in learning some of the dances."

Chang was not a regular at "Mama" Gravander's, but he was "intensely interested in the folk dancing" (Morton 1962). The fact that soon after his appearance at Gravanders' Chang organized a performing international folk dance group suggests that this visit was more likely a chance to acquire repertoire than a first step in becoming involved.

The first meetings of Chang's International Folk Dancers were held in late 1937.[22] The group was comprised almost exclusively of artists, painters, sculptors, and actors.[23] This circle of artists included Song's wife, Harriet Roudebush Chang, who may even have introduced him to the other group members.[24] The social stratum of this group was very different from that of people involved in the earlier period of folk dancing and in other locations. In Chang's group we see a group of equals; artists/intellectuals gathering for mutual enjoyment in an activity of their choice. It may be true that Chang's group "afforded an outlet for idealism and romanticism," as is stated by Henry Glass (1972: 68), one of the early Californian folk dancers and first president of the Folk Dance Federation of California. However, this does not seem to be a group of people to whom his statement "where life was hard, there was the magic of peasant dance and music" especially applied.[25]

In early 1938, Chang's group moved to the Green Lantern Cafe, a restaurant/bar located at 704 Kearny Street in San Francisco. Morton recollects that the clientele of the Green Lantern consisted of "young artists, writers, models, etc., who lived in the Telegraph Hill and North Beach areas" many of whom were employed through the WPA. The Green Lantern was one of the first folk dance venues to resemble ethnic social clubs in which folk dancing took place over the course of an evening along with dinner and drinks. Chang's group was somewhat unique among IFD groups in that they were a group of friends who started folk dancing and decided to form an exhibition group rather than a group of folk dancers who be-

came friends. They gathered, not to help establish social ties and a sense of community, but to learn and perform dances (figures 6.2a, b). Dick Crum posited (Interview, 1997) that Chang treated IFD as an art, not as a vehicle for getting people together and socializing. "The product was more important than the producer. All the dances are more showy, more for spectacle . . . you are all there to achieve perfection in this dance that he was presenting that evening." Although Crum never met Chang, his impression that Chang's group was more performance-oriented than either Herman's or Beliajus's is well supported. Judging by the record of the group's activities, public presentation was clearly an important part of its raison d'être. Interestingly, folk dance continues to be more performance-oriented on the West Coast than in other regions.

Song Chang did most of the folk dance teaching at the Green Lantern. As Virgil Morton recalls in his notes, the music for the dances came from records provided by Song and Harriet Roudebush Chang. Interestingly enough, at this time folk dance classes were free, and only occasionally would a hat be passed for donations toward the purchase of new records. The Green Lantern expanded and redecorated in order to suit the folk dancers, but Chang decided to move the classes to a spacious studio on 415 Broadway, creating some friction within the group. At that point Virgil Morton began teaching the classes at the Green Lantern and many in the group began frequenting both places. The large dance hall at 415 Broadway was leased to Chang by the North Beach Workers Center, and Morton writes that the hall "proved to be a boon when we started attracting notice at the Golden Gate International Exposition, in 1939."

The Growth of International Folk Dancing in California

Participation in the World's Fair on Treasure Island was a turning point not only for Chang's International Folk Dancers, but for the development of folk dance in California and in the United States in general. The Golden Gate International Exposition opened in May of 1939, and Chang's IFD had a standing engagement during the fair season. Virgil Morton (1962: 4) recalls:

> Song and Harriet Chang had made arrangements for the group to participate in folk dance activities at the Federal Recreation Building. Later, through arrangements with Dr. Moses, the group was invited to dance at the Estonian Village on every week-end and on holidays. We also expanded our dance activities to the plaza of the Guatemala exhibit where the Hurtado Brothers Marimba Orchestra played exciting Latin rhythms to which some of us danced. The "Beer Barrel Polka" had been introduced that year, and it became an unofficial theme song for the folk dance group. Wherever it was played on Treasure Island you would find some members of the group improvising a lively polka.

Figures 6.2a, b. Folk dancing with Chang, c. 1938. (Photos by Jay Risling, courtesy of the San Francisco Performing Arts Library and Museum)

The tremendous public exposure they got at Treasure Island is most clearly seen in the subsequent growth in group membership. "Our appearances at the fair," Morton recalls (1962: 4), "attracted new members from all over the Bay area, including members from the many ethnic folk dance groups that were active with their own dances. (We had previously made unsuccessful attempts to form a 'Union' with these ethnic groups.) Our membership list grew at an explosive rate."

Indeed, in 1939–1940 folk dance groups mushroomed throughout the Bay Area, and Chang, Morton, and many other folk dance instructors stemming from Chang's group had their hands full organizing and teaching classes. In the early 1940s, membership in Chang's group grew to the point where, according to Morton, it was not unusual to have a hundred people in a class. Apparently Chang's membership was unhurt by the formation of other groups. In 1940 the group moved to Maple Hall, where meetings were held five nights a week,[26] as local groups proliferated. "Song Chang has been so energetic in building folk-dance groups that it is now possible to dance seven nights a week, from San Anselmo to San Mateo, with a group of Chang's," the *Folk Dancer* bulletin reported in November of 1941.

In the fall of 1939, after the World's Fair at Treasure Island closed for the year, the group formally organized themselves, incorporating under the name "Changs International Folk Dancers" and establishing a membership list and dues.[27] In early 1940, Song Chang resigned from teaching and gave up his presidential duties because of a personal conflict with a member of the group who, according to Morton (1969, in a letter to Robert Chevalier) had been trying to oust Chang ever since he joined the group at the Green Lantern. Although the group continued to bear his name, Chang himself seldom participated.

Virgil Morton took charge of the instruction of new members as the first official teacher. His class was the first to charge students a regular fee. At this time the group met in a hall that was shared with the Poppy Social Club, a group of white Russian intellectuals who taught the group some of their dances. "Striving to keep folk dancing in its pure ethnic form," Virgil Morton urged "members to visit the various ethnic groups in San Francisco to witness at first-hand the various dances" he was teaching (Morton 1962: 6, and 1969).

Under Morton's leadership, Changs IFD was concerned "that deviations did not creep into the dances that had been learned from various ethnic sources. To help ensure that this 'purity' of form and character would be maintained by the new groups that were forming, as well as with our own members . . . we wrote down the dances that were used by Changs Intl. Folk Dancers." What Morton describes was an attempt to gain control over the growing number of groups that branched out of Changs IFD. Writing down the dance instructions was meant both to prevent deviations and variations from one group to another and to accumulate an authoritative core repertoire. This was the first step toward the formation of the Folk Dance Federation of California.

Morton perceived a metamorphosis in the club over the years. In a letter written to Robert Chevalier he expresses grief over leaders who "turned the organization into a greedy, self-centered group which refused to let any of their dance material be used by others." These leaders, according to Morton, "turned the trend toward theatrical character dances with the emphasis on 'advanced' exhibition dancing." The "refuge for romanticism and idealism" that Henry Glass described was threatened by the unexpected marketability of IFD. The demand for teachers, dances, and performing groups grew with the increasing visibility of the activity.

Changs International Folk Dancers became primarily an exhibition group, preparing their repertoire for performances. "The exhibition group emerged from the type of demonstrations in which all the membership took part." Thus, from a gathering of artist friends, the club became hierarchically segmented into beginning and advanced classes and an exhibition group. At the same time group members were teaching IFD throughout California, forming new clubs and contributing to the growth of the IFD market.

As clubs grew in number and membership, more attention was given to the "authenticity" and "purity" of sources, as well as to accuracy in performance. The meaning of such terms is generally tailored to their use. As is often the case, here "authenticity" was to be established first in the visual domain through the use of folk costumes. This was particularly true for the exhibition group. Morton points out that "national costumes corresponding with the nationality of the dance to be exhibited were required, and special teachers were employed to teach exhibition material."

> In a group interested in performing accurately the dances of various nationalities it is important to know as much as possible about the wearing apparel of those nationalities, as well as other facets of their native culture. To provide easy reference material for new members, and also to eliminate to some extent the necessity of verbally lecturing on these points in the classes, it was decided to form a Research Committee. . . . From National Geographic Magazines and similar sources we compiled several books of folk lore and costume references which were to be used for study by the members. (Morton 1962)

While folk dance teachers wanted to avoid teaching classes that could be perceived as lectures, they saw the lack of background information on the dances they were teaching as problematic. The format of the classes, with their emphasis on practice and participation, did not allow for much passive reception of information. One way of getting around this problem was to create reading material for people to study outside of class. These written resources were, generally speaking, not ethnographic studies but compilations of easily digestible "facts."

The explosion of folk dance in the Bay Area complicated communication between groups and made it harder to maintain a sense of unity and consistency throughout the increasingly vast membership. The establish-

ment of a monthly bulletin called *The Folk Dancer* in February of 1941 was one step toward addressing the situation.[28] According to Virgil Morton, the bulletin, later to be named *Changs*, was established in large part due to his insistence.

> My purpose in having this bulletin was to inform the rapidly expanding membership about the ethnic backgrounds of the dances and to attempt to break down some of the hackneyed opinions people so frequently form in regard to nationality and religious backgrounds other than their own. The bulletin was also to be used as a news source regarding meetings and items of general interest. (Morton 1962: 8)

Unwittingly, *Changs* magazine and others like it often did more to create new stereotypes and affirm old ones than they did to help deepen dancers' understanding. The format and scope of *The Folk Dancer* was certainly not conducive to breaking down stereotypes, as what few short paragraphs there were about each dance were often full of sweeping generalizations. In order to make the information more colorful, dances that somehow incorporated a story were favored. "Americans want a bedtime story with every dance," said Dick Crum about the persistence of this practice (Interview, 1997). "Those stories are always around, and they are made up by anybody. This is an antiquated idea that probably came from ballet, where the dance tells a story."

Despite the shortcomings of the bulletin, *The Folk Dancer* did accomplish its primary goals, helping to inform and unite folk dancers and to establish some degree of control over repertoire and its presentation by approving a particular version and interpretation of a dance.

The Folk Dance Federation of California The second, and much larger, step toward the unification of Californian folk dancers was the establishment of the Folk Dance Federation of California in 1942. This organization is active to the present day along with other state folk dance federations.[29] The impetus to form a federation of all the Californian folk dance groups came from Henry Buzz Glass, a member of Changs International Folk Dancers since 1940. He became the organization's first president on June 14, 1942, at a big folk dance picnic in Golden Gate Park.[30] Echoing the goals of *The Folk Dancer*, "the objective of the organization was not only to promote folk dancing but to exercise control over the many versions of dances that were being introduced to different groups" (Morton 1964, letter).

The Federation grew out of the increasing popularity of IFD, but the IFD movement also grew with the Federation.[31] As its first president notes (Glass 1972: 68), it began to involve "Y's, churches, ethnic and recreation centers, ski and hiking clubs and a host of private groups." In short, the Federation not only united the many groups that grew out of Chang's club, but became an umbrella group for many other organizations in which folk dancing took place. The federation enabled the institutionalization of international folk dancing in California, and with its increasing membership

and duties, the infrastructure of the organization grew. "The formation of the Federation encouraged the development of exhibition groups, folk dance camps, teacher training sessions, workshops, publications and monthly festivals" (Glass 1972: n.p.). This organization became the heart of the folk dance movement in California and had a significant impact on the development of folk dance in the United States in general.

The most important contribution of the Federation on a national level is the work of its Research Committee. Lucille Czarnowski of the University of California, Berkeley, was its first chairman. The committee not only published numerous volumes of folk dance books but, as Glass points out (1972: n.p.), "a format for writing dances was established that was later to furnish a working structure for other writers." Many teachers and folk dance groups across the country used the folk dance books published by the FDF of California as a source of new material.

The control the Federation established over the numerous folk dance clubs enabled it to approve dances and dance instructors alike. The organization intended, ultimately, to establish a unified folk dance repertoire that would make it possible for folk dance enthusiasts across the country to dance in exactly the same way. This would prevent dance teachers from inventing dances or creating a repertoire that would be particular to a specific club or instructor.

The fact that Changs International Folk Dancers still exists under the same name perhaps speaks to folk dancers' love of history and heritage. Chang himself danced with the group for less than a decade, but after he withdrew from the folk dance scene his name remained as a legacy. The Folk Dance Federation of California, North and South, has exerted tremendous influence on international folk dancing in the United States over the decades. Currently FDF of California, North, consists of over sixty clubs and two thousand members; FDF of California, South, is comprised of about half as many clubs and members. *Let's Dance* and *Folk Dance Scene* are their official newsletters.[32]

International Folk Dancing on the East Coast—Michael Herman

Beginnings of Michael Herman's Career

Michael Herman is often acknowledged as the father of international folk dance in the United States. As Dick Crum commented, "Nobody contributed to the overall development of recreational folk dancing as much as Michael Herman" (Crum, Interview, 1997). Herman stands out from the other folk dance giants because he was not only a dancer but a musician, competent organizer, publisher, writer, and record producer.[33]

Michael Herman was born in 1910 in Cleveland, Ohio to Ukrainian parents. His family apparently moved frequently when he was young, so he lived in many different ethnic neighborhoods: Polish, Ukrainian, Czech, Serbian, and Romanian. "I lived in all those places," Michael told me (In-

terview, 1994), "making friends with all those people. Music was all mine." This living environment was formative in Herman's interest in folk music and dance. It is certainly unusual for a young Ukrainian-American man to have attended many social affairs of different ethnic groups where he "listened to their music, and often danced with them." It is likely that this attraction to the music and dance of various immigrant groups was influenced by settlement house ideology.[34] If Herman was exposed to folk dances of various ethnic groups in the ethnic neighborhoods of Cleveland, it was only within the Ukrainian community that he was active as a performer, as both a dancer and violinist. At the age of twelve he performed a solo Ukrainian dance at the Edgewater Park Festival of Nations.

The first crucial event in Herman's folk dance career was joining the Ukrainian Folk Dance Group of Cleveland under the direction of Vasile Avramenko.[35] With Avramenko, Herman not only acquired his first professional dance training but learned how to teach and notate dance instructions, skills that would be in extreme demand in his later career. As an able young dancer Herman became Avramenko's assistant at the school and, when he decided several years later to move to New York, he came to Avramenko's studio in Manhattan. "I was invited to be a teacher for him in New York. I was his assistant teacher. He taught Ukrainian and Russian dances. We danced at the opera house in 1930" (Interview, 1994).

Both Michael Herman and his future wife and teaching partner Mary Ann Bodnar, a member of Avramenko's folk dance group in New York, participated in Ukrainian festivals at the Metropolitan Opera House and Carnegie Hall. "Mary Ann," Michael writes (Herman, Notes), "born in Manhattan's ghetto also full of ethnic groups was exposed at an early age to songs and dances of many lands." Both Michael and Mary Ann were very involved in the affairs of the Ukrainian community in New York. Mary Ann worked for the Ukrainian newspaper *Svoboda* and conducted an English language Ukrainian radio program under the sponsorship of the Surma Book and Music Company. Michael was a part of the music division of the WPA, giving music teachers workshops in folk songs and dances.

It was in Avramenko's school that Michael and Mary Ann learned most of their Ukrainian and Russian repertoire. The Hermans adopted Avramenko's normative and prescriptive way of teaching, but used it only when they taught the Ukrainian repertoire in their future international folk dance programs.

> When Mary Ann or Michael would teach Ukrainian dance, it would differ from any other kind of dance they taught. There was only one way to position your arms or legs in Hopak . . . "The hand of the woman in Hopak goes like this, under a certain angle, six inches apart," etc. . . . And there would be a reason for it: "The women in Hopak would hold their arm like this so they can hold their beads." When the Hermans would get up to teach Hopak they were two different people. Mary Ann would drop the needle of the record and say: "This dance does not belong to you, it belongs to the Ukrainian people, and you need to return it to them in the same form." But I wondered, how can she say

that and the next day put on a dance from somewhere else with no style, no detail, where whatever you did was okay. (Crum, Interview, 1997)

Crum's vivid account is significant in many respects. First of all it tells something about the style of teaching folk dance that folk ballet masters like Avramenko adopted. The Hermans, as Avramenko's successors, seemingly treated Ukrainian folk dance with the rigidity, precision, and discipline of movement found in ballet. One aspect of this normative and "scientific" approach to interpreting folk dance was the rationalization of, and attribution of meaning to, dance movement, turning the dance into a narrative. This created narrative contributed to the value of folk dance as a cultural signifier. The Hermans learned their other dances under different circumstances and without this embedded narrative. Hence, these other dances were transmitted with more freedom of movement and interpretation. Another factor in this double standard is the fact that teachers, the Hermans included, are often the most prescriptive and normative about the material they know best. Disconnectedness from the material and the culture in which it was created tends to result in teaching without attention to style and detail.

In the 1930s Herman attended various ethnic events around New York City and partook in festivals organized in New York parks by the Folk Festival Council. There he joined various ethnic bands and learned their melodies on the violin (Interview, 1994). "They [FFC] would invite me to come to their parties and I would dance with them. That's how I learned the dances," Herman recalls. Because of his ability to dance their dances, Herman believed, many ethnic groups adopted him as one of their own.[36] "I did Balkan dances before the forties. There was a place called the Balkan Cafe on 24th Street and 8th Avenue . . . and Banat Orchestra played there. They had one dance called Veliko Kolo that they said nobody can do it unless they are from their country. I saw them do it and then I did it and nobody said that anymore" (Interview, 1994).

Mary Wood Hinman was "one of the truly influential people" in Michael Herman's life (Interview, 1994). When the classes at the New School for Social Research began, Herman was asked to teach, as well as to help various ethnic groups in their presentations. "Ethnic groups were not used to teaching Americans their dances, and often asked Michael Herman to help them" (Herman, Notes). He also wrote down the music and directions for many of the dances. This work was, in many ways, preparation for the years to come.

Michael Herman's skills were in high demand in the 1930s in New York. Unlike other ethnic dancers he had the advantage of being fluent in English and professionally trained in both music and dance. During his first few years teaching in New York he primarily taught Ukrainian dance to various folk dance groups in schools, Y's, churches, and classes organized by the FFC. At this time he also started his nineteen-year teaching engagement at the International House on Riverside Drive.[37]

The New York World's Fair

Throughout the 1930s Michael Herman was very active in New York folk dance circles, but more as a facilitator than a leader. The moment of transformation in his personal career, and in the history of international folk dance on the East Coast, was the New York World's Fair. Pat Parmalee, active in the FFC, was responsible for suggesting that Michael Herman do the teaching at the "American Common" in 1940. As happened in San Francisco in 1939, folk dancing took off after the fair in New York.

In addition to the "nationality days," in which ethnic performing groups were showcased, general folk dancing took place at the Common. While at the Golden Gate Exposition a year earlier Chang's group presented international folk dances as an exhibition, Michael Herman taught such dances to fair visitors. "It is estimated that over 5,000 people took part in the program of Folk Dances held at the Common of the World's Fair in 1940" (Herman, *Folk Dancer* March 1941/1: 1). Herman attributes the success of the program to the fact that "it was based on the realization that folk dances, one of the most colorful contributions by immigrants to this American culture, are NOT to be watched as just colorful entertainment, but should be PARTICIPATED in" (Herman, ibid., emphasis in the original).

Michael Herman proved to be an excellent choice for the job of directing Folk Dance Evenings at the Common. Music for the dances was provided by Mary Ann Herman on the piano, Walter Ericksson on accordion, and, occasionally, Michael himself on the violin, when he wasn't running back and forth cajoling casual fair-goers to join the dance (Herman, Notes).

> Before they quite knew what was happening, they were dancing a folk dance together with several hundred other folks. There were tall ones, and short ones, some thin, some plump, and some just average. They ranged in ages from 8 to 80 and came from all walks of life . . . students, teachers, professionals, laborers, fathers and sons, mothers and daughters. Every nationality and race was represented on the Common platform, and all were dancing away together in harmony and fun. (*Folk Dancer* March 1941/1: 1)

This vision of humanity, joyful and harmonious, was very attractive and many were eager to participate in its creation. The interest in Folk Dance Evenings at the Fair "grew so rapidly that the crowd would number over 1,000 at times. In fact people began to come to the Fair just to dance" (Herman, Notes). As the fair drew to a close, Herman saw a need to continue the program in New York. In response to interest in the establishment of a folk dance center, he began compiling a mailing list that, by the end of the fair, included approximately 1,500 people from the New York City area (Herman, Interview).

The beginnings of the Community Folk Dance Center, in a rented Ukrainian National Room on East 6th Street, were less than spectacular. After

sending out 1,500 mailers, only sixteen people showed up for the first meeting on October 15, 1940. But Michael persisted and, as he recalled, "every week the crowd doubled." Because the Ukrainian Hall was in a reputedly bad neighborhood and Herman found the management unreliable, he moved the center two blocks north to the Polish National House, also called Arlington Hall (19 St. Marks Place), where folk dancing would be held for the next seven years. "At Arlington Hall, folk dancing really took hold, without advertising, just word of mouth, the group grew and grew, until instead of just one night a week, Friday, they were meeting three nights, Tuesday, Wednesday and Friday" (Herman, Notes). With the move to Arlington Hall, the first issue of *The Folk Dancer* was published in March 1941. Note that only a month earlier, in February, Changs International Folk Dancers in San Francisco published the first issue of their periodical, also called *The Folk Dancer*. Michael Herman edited and published his magazine monthly from 1941 to 1947, when the publication was discontinued for financial reasons.[38]

Folk Dance Records

One of Michael Herman's most enduring and unique contributions to the folk dance world is the series of records that, in many places, are still used in dance classes.[39] "I was saying that if this thing is to get big you have to have music. Unless you have records that are cheap to buy, this movement won't grow" (Herman, Interview, 1994). Herman realized that music for the dances had to be readily available, as hiring musicians for dance classes was not only costly but also difficult. Ethnic musicians were accustomed to playing their own dances but not to traveling the world, so to speak, from one dance style to another.

Herman's proposal to make records of the most popular international folk dance repertoire was initially rejected by large record companies, including RCA and Columbia who had extensive releases of foreign music. It was a Yugoslav record producer, Mr. Marsich of Sonart Records, who finally responded to the idea and released the first album tailor-made for international folk dancers. The album contained Mexican, Lithuanian, Danish, Czech, Swiss, Estonian, and Polish dances. Performed by Michael Herman's Orchestra, a group assembled with the help of Walter Ericksson who had played with Herman since the 1930s,[40] the recording was met with considerable enthusiasm. The response was such that, after Marsich's death, Herman went on to produce a series of some 300 recordings on his own "Folk Dancer" label, including releases by ethnic orchestras such as Kostya Polyansky's Balalaika Orchestra for Russian dances, Banat Tamburitza Orchestra for Yugoslav kolos **(CD 4)**, Tom Senior's Irish Orchestra, the Ralph Page Orchestra for American squares and contras, and many others.[41] These recordings were a huge step forward from the old days of skeletal piano notation such as Chalif's (figure 4.7). The recordings of "ethnic" orchestras in particular exposed dancers to elements of style that must have been revelatory.

One of Michael Herman's first recording projects was for the Methodist Church. He was contracted by the General Board of Education of the Methodist Church to produce a series of what was initially to be six records for their recreational program. Titled "World of Fun" (1947), the records were accompanied by a twenty-five-page booklet of dance directions most of which were written by Herman himself.

The booklet assured the reader that the records "can go a long way toward helping your group to appreciate what other peoples have contributed to the fun of the world. . . . In their own right they are fun—these folk treasures from other countries. Wise ministers, counselors, and youth leaders of recreation will of course recognize this." Distanced from their cultures of origin, folk dances were reduced to the single category "fun." As "contributions" to the "world of fun," folk dances did not belong to the people that created them or danced them, but to everyone. Responsibility to original sources, or even interest in them, was not an issue here. The details of a particular style were of little interest to the musicians and folk dancers alike, and the significance of the dances as "international" was primarily symbolic. The records were, above all, utilitarian. It was important to make the rhythm straight and the tempos comfortable for dancers so the records could do their job. The "World of Fun" booklet says of the recording process: "Rehearsals and recording were all done in the studio. We ran through each selection for style and tempo, timing it carefully with a sweep-second-hand clock. . . . Mary Ann Herman and Larry Eisenberg, in the studio, went through the action to help keep the records at the right tempo (Harbin, Eisenberg 1947: 2).

As it was commissioned by the Methodist Church, the music was "toned down" and dances were called "folk games" to discourage an association with popular dancing. Michael reminisces that "Only three pieces were used in the orchestra, and they were admonished to play the music 'straight' . . . not too frivolous. Can you imagine playing Irish Washerwoman for five minutes without changing keys or varying the tune?" (Herman, Interview, 1994). Contemporary listeners, with the benefit of virtually unlimited access to the world's music, might find even the liveliest of Michael Herman's Orchestra recordings equally pallid **(CD 5)**. Most featured the same instrumentation and more or less the same style, regardless of the genre. However, in their day these records provided an exciting opportunity to hear dance tunes from many cultures in one place and, perhaps more important, provided a steady rhythm that contributed to the growth of the folk dance movement.

Folk Dance Camps

The well-known recreational leader Jane Farwell approached the Hermans in 1938–39 with the idea of having a camp for adults in which folk dance, costumes, crafts, and cuisine would be integrated into the daily programs. Michael recalls that "It was Jane Farewell who had the idea. . . . We helped her organize the first folk dance camp in the country in 1940 in Oglebay

Park, West Virginia" (Herman, Interview, 1994). The premise of this and similar folk dance camps was that they would enable attendees to have fun, to socialize and live for a week or two the values of humanity, community, and friendship.

Summer camps were hardly a new phenomenon. Beginning in the early 1880s as summer getaways for children of wealthy New England parents, the popularity and reach of summer camps mushroomed during the early twentieth century. By 1925 there were more than one thousand to choose from. There had even been summer camps emphasizing ethnic heritage, identity, and folk arts since at least the turn of the century, including Camp Cobbossee, which in 1902, was started as the nation's first Jewish camp. Luther Halsey Gulick started a Girls Campfire Camp with his wife in 1910 and offered folk dancing as one of the camp activities, although the purpose of this camp differed greatly from that of Oglebay Park and the other folk dance camps that were to come.[42]

Jane Farewell also initiated the Maine Folk Dance Camp, which Mary Ann and Michael Herman went on to take over and run for more than four decades. Over the years, the Hermans collected numerous folk costumes to be exhibited at a camp. Campers would "travel" from one country to another, dancing the dances, eating ethnic foods, and viewing appropriate folk costumes, and each day a different nationality would be featured. "At one time we had people dressing up in costume and people explaining what these costumes are" (Herman, Interview, 1994). In later years the costumes were shown every day after lunch. When I interviewed Michael in 1994 he said with some bitterness, "now they are all so busy dancing that they do not have time for costumes." This remark reflects a shift in interest from general socializing and communal work to the learning and acquisition of new repertoire.

The Folk Dance House

The opening of Folk Dance House in 1951 was a milestone in the history of folk dance on the East Coast. There Michael Herman, more than ten years after the end of the World's Fair, was finally able to create his own schedule and have a place to call his own.

Renovating the former Humphrey-Weidman Dance Theater, adapting it to its new purpose, took six months and a lot of volunteer work, work that evidences the level of enthusiasm and communal spirit felt among the folk dancers. Throughout his career, Michael Herman had strongly emphasized the social aspect of folk dancing. The very choice of words in the titles of his folk dance venues, such as "*Community* Folk Dance Evenings" or "Folk Dance *House*," highlights his commitment to the idea that folk dance could bring people together.

"Michael had this idea of the dance being specifically designed to make friendships happen, and to make relationships happen and to make people happy . . . Michael Herman would say style was important, but looking people in the eye and having fun is more important" (Crum, Interview,

1997). Later in life Michael grew bitter about folk dance groups and leaders who were hungry for new dances. Seeing this development as evidence of the degradation of the IFD movement's founding principles, he observed to me, "now they are making up so many dances that nobody is smiling anymore, they won't even hold your hands, or look at you in the eye."

Folk Dance House was an establishment unique in the folk dance world. "It was a very large space . . . the legal occupancy limit was 280 people. . . . There were big colorful posters on the walls, a raised platform with a phonograph on it" (Crum, Interview,1997). Having an actual physical place that belonged to the folk dancers enabled them not only to decorate it and transform it into a folk world oasis, but also to deepen their feeling of being a community. Folk Dance House in many ways promoted social interactions among its members and served as a community center.

The schedule at the Folk Dance House grew to include various age groups and levels of experience. "There were classes of all kinds, every day of the week, family day programs for children, parents, grandparents on Sunday afternoons" (Herman, Notes).[43] There was even a type of daycare with "'arts and crafts' stuff to do" for children while parents were dancing. "Schools were bringing bus loads of students to learn the dances and finger the costumes. There was a teenage program on Saturday afternoons," Michael Herman remarked with excitement and pride, "with high school boys folk-dancing for five hours straight." One of those teenage boys dancing at the Folk Dance House in 1961 was Michael Ginsburg, who remembers his early days at the Hermans':

> At first there was a small group of teenagers who danced from 6:00 to 8:00 on Saturday evening. As the group began to grow, some of the kids got more into it and Herman started a session from 5:00 to 6:00 for an advanced group for teenagers. And then, about seven or eight of us got so well into it that the advanced session was not enough for us so that we came at 3:00 and danced until 8:00. (Ginsburg, Interview, 1994)

The Hermans were tireless advocates of the movement, responding swiftly to any expressed interest in folk dancing, whether it came from teenagers or seniors. Those who knew them attest to the fact that the Hermans' primary interests were not financial. Many stories of Michael's impulsive generosity show him as "no crass, conniving businessman" (Crum, Interview, 1997). According to Michael Ginsburg the teenage group was allowed to use the dance studio free of charge.

The two decades of the Folk Dance House were certainly the height of the Hermans' careers. "Michael ruled the roost in the folk dance world. There was nobody else there. . . . He was the principal figure" (Crum, Interview, 1997). The loss of Folk Dance House was, in the opinion of many old-time folk dancers, the beginning of the decline of Herman's influence in the movement. Many elements contributed to the demise of the establishment. One important factor was that, with the growth of the movement,

Figure 6.3. Michael Herman's Orchestra playing at the Waldorf Astoria Hotel for the Annual Folk Festival, c. 1950 (photo courtesy of Sally Ray)

folk dancing became lucrative for new teachers who wanted to start their own classes. "Everybody wanted their own loft folk dance group," Crum recalls. Commenting on the popularity of folk dance parties in New York City, Elizabeth Bernstein (*Viltis* Summer 1957/16) humorously remarked, "The landlords have not as yet reached the stage of 'No folk dancers allowed.'" However, she said:

> Private groups in homes are sprouting all over. It is not unusual to be invited to a home folk party, here where space is at a premium, and when arriving at the building see arrows pointing the way to the laundry room in the basement. There you will see the ghosts—bendix washers and dryers covered with sheets—the whole place transformed into a folk dance hall. The colors of the girl's costumes, the vivid imaginations of the dancers and the music make all oblivious of the bare walls.

Dick Crum suggested that the perceived danger of night rides on the subway, as well as heavy tolls on the bridges into Manhattan, contributed to the dispersion of folk dancers from Folk Dance House to their own neighborhoods. The new generation of folk dance teachers offering different material and a different approach also had an impact. As the folk

Figure 6.4. Michael Herman and his wife and teaching partner, Mary Ann Herman.

dance infrastructure grew, a constant influx of new dances became a necessity. Michael Herman was greatly disappointed by these developments:

> We started teaching everybody in 1940 and all those years it's spread to every city. New people, like my teenagers, started to teach. They want to become famous too. When there are three teachers in the same city . . . everybody will go to the one that would teach new dances. Then the other teacher says: "Gee! I have to have somebody teach me new dances." They assumed that all the new dances will be of the same qualities. And you get to the point where it is stupid. (Herman, Interview, 1994)

These words imply much about problems the movement encountered as a result of its growth. With the increased number of teachers there came competition for class membership, and teachers began to fight for their share of the market. The demand for new dances often led teachers to make up new dances and stories to accompany them. Providing new material, dances never before presented to Americans, became not simply a fashion but a demand. Groups came to rely on this constant influx of new material to keep them going. Herman's comments both criticize these new teachers with their dances of untried quality and justify his own repertoire. At a time when many younger teachers had begun traveling abroad, doing some ethnographic research and learning new dances, particularly in Balkan villages, Herman was unwilling or unable to alter his approach.

Although he went on teaching tours, most notably to Japan in 1956, when he taught international folk dancing to thousands of Japanese participants, he never did go abroad on a research trip and stuck with his tried and true method of teaching and acquiring repertoire. Michael Herman remained active as a teacher until the end of his life, but with the end of Folk Dance House his place in the IFD world came to be seen as largely historical.

Regional Differences

The regional differences we have seen in the IFD movement arose from circumstances of culture and geography and from the individual legacies of Beliajus, Chang, and Herman. Along with the awareness among folk dancers that they were part of a national trend came an awareness of the different goals and aesthetics that became attached, not only to the leading teachers, but to the regions with which they were most closely associated. There was considerable variety, even fiery disagreement, locally and nationally, as to personal and collective goals and the role of folk dancing in people's lives. Many of these differences developed during the period from the 1930s through the 1950s and, interestingly, many hold true to the present day. The most noticeable split in the folk dance movement is between the East and West Coast scenes, the Midwest being much closer in spirit and practice to folk dancing in the East.

Although the distinction is by no means categorical, East Coast folk dance has tended to emphasize community building and West Coast dance tended toward performance. When folk dance camps were organized on the East Coast their primary goal was not to enable people to learn a lot of material in a short time period, but to help create an oasis of community. Dancing was just one aspect of a "folk" lifestyle to explore and indulge in at the camps, which also offered a range of social activities and arts and crafts. In an effort to encourage and support every prospective folk dancer, East Coast leaders favored easier dances that were more interesting to do than to watch. West Coast Camps like Stockton, however, placed a much greater emphasis on formalized instruction and the acquisition of new material. Competition between West Coast exhibition groups impelled them to seek dances and choreographies that were better suited to stage presentation. When Chang's group took part in the World's Fair in San Francisco, they were exhibiting international dances to the general public. At the same time, Herman was teaching passersby and getting strangers to dance together on the American Common at the New York Fair. In short, while in both regions the activity was viewed as "folk art," the emphasis was on "art" in the West and on "folk" in the East. It is from these different general tendencies that other differences in attitude grew: toward folk dance material, toward its interpretation and public presentation, and toward folk dancing in general.

Both cohesive and disjunctive forces can be seen in the IFD movement during this period (and to the present day). There were simultaneous ef-

forts to unify the folk dance movement nationally and to create subgroups with different regional, personal, and ideological alliances. For an activity that touted the value of "bringing different people together" there was an extremely high degree of "othering" among its various segments. Whatever the basis of people's perceptions and accusations, the presence of such distinctions and negativity toward any difference in approach is interesting. Throughout the various folk dance periodicals, criticisms of the doings and ideologies of others enabled writers to claim the purity and authenticity of their own approach to folk dance without grappling substantively with their own positions on issues like authenticity and representation, and without clearly identifying their reasons for adhering to a particular ideology.[44] Despite, or perhaps even because of, the rancor such rhetoric and "dialogue" fomented, it apparently served to strengthen feelings of group and regional identity and played a part in strengthening folk dancers' commitment to their movement and its underlying goals.

7

Folk Dance as a National Trend

The place and meaning of international folk dance at the beginning of its existence as a truly mass cultural phenomenon was complex, demanding the more detailed analysis offered here. The use of IFD at the World's Fairs and related events involved often-subtle dynamics of nationalism and internationalism, modernism and romanticism, technophilia and humanism, capitalism and community, aesthetics and politics. A further investigation of the World's Fairs is followed by a discussion of "virtual tourism," the importance of "authenticity," and the rationale behind the belief that true "folkness" might be attainable by the average American while inaccessible to the improperly educated "ethnic." This reasoning led, finally, to the concept of the "true ethnic" as preservationist, and the ongoing frustration with those understood to be "ethnic" yet inauthentic. There is much in the dynamics discussed here that has continuing resonance in the Balkan scene and in American culture in general.

World's Fairs and International Folk Dancing

"The folk dance swept the nation. It is done practically everywhere," writes Beliajus in 1948 (Viltis 1948/6, 6). Indeed, during the 1930s and especially the 1940s the movement grew to such prominence that one would not be surprised to find that there was some sort of folk dance program in just about any city, large town, or college campus in the country. We have seen some of the numerous accounts attributing this growth to the World's Fairs: "It was the 1938 Treasure Island Fair which turned international folk dance into a vital, living art and recreation of the people. It was the colorful ethnic exhibits, the folk music and dance performances, and folk dance events which sparked the widespread interest which led to the formation of many clubs and classes."[1]

Michael Herman echoed this assessment, saying "impetus to the present-day popularity of folk dancing was given by the New York's World's Fair . . . when thousands of Fair visitors were enticed to try simple dances of many lands at the American Common. Entranced by the fun and by the

ease with which they were able to do these dances, these people demanded places in which they could folk dance regularly" (Herman 1947 [1956]: vii). But what was it about the fairs that they had such a great impact? How did they contribute to folk dancing's popularity in all corners of the nation?

There is no doubt that Century of Progress expositions had a tremendous influence on the American public in general. The presence of these fairs in American culture of the period was all-pervasive. As Rydell (1993: 1) points out: "These fairs took the nation by storm, firing the imaginations of countless ordinary Americans, including those who saw world's fair newsreels in local movie houses (the New York World's Fair alone generated 236 newsreels that reached an estimated 220 million people), read stories about world's fairs in local newspapers, participated in world's fair contests, and reveled in live radio broadcasts from the expositions."

With such a presence in the society and influence on the American public, each World's Fair was a trendsetter that put a stamp of approval and value on the programs it included. For example, Glassberg (1990: 247) reports that "a collection of twenty homes along a replicated colonial Philadelphia street" offered "a boost to the fledgling historic preservation movement" and led to "the opening of outdoor museum villages such as Greenfield Village and Colonial Williamsburg in the 1930s." Through participation in the World's Fairs, folk dance leaders Beliajus, Chang, and Herman received very wide exposure indeed. Their programs gained tremendous visibility and were crucial in introducing many, perhaps many millions, of fairgoers to folk dancing for fun and recreation. But beyond giving such exposure, the fairs played what might have been a greater, though subtler, role in the development of IFD.

American society was experiencing a multilayered crisis during the Great Depression and the government was using all available means to end it. President Roosevelt endorsed and supported World's Fairs, seeing in them great potential for helping to overcome the economic crisis and restore faith in American society. Through this and many larger scale social engineering projects, he used largely socialist methods to reassure the American citizens of the strength and power of the capitalist system.

Fairs provided Americans an escape from daily life, diverting their attention from the country's economic, social, and political crisis. "Just when the future seemed so bleak," Rydell (1993: 1) remarks, "nearly one hundred million Americans visited the 1933–34 Chicago Century of Progress Exposition, the 1935–36 San Diego California Pacific Exposition, the 1936 Dallas Texas Centennial Exposition, the 1937 Cleveland Great Lakes and International Exposition, and the 1939–40 San Francisco Golden Gate International Exposition, and the 1939–40 New York World's Fair." Through manufacturing fun and leisure time, the fairs created an image of a prosperous American nation whose people were happy and grateful to their country.

World's Fairs were certainly not organized to further the cause of international folk dancing, but international folk dancing was a perfect fit with

the cause of the fairs and an enactment of the vision of America they were intended to convey. In keeping with the then-current rhetoric on preservationism and exaltation of the "folk" and "peasant" in the midst of a crisis of advanced capitalism, folk dance was an example of the harmonious integration of difference in a multicultural society. An association with IFD was not new to the Depression era fairs as, at least since the beginning of the physical education movement, there had been connections between such fairs and expositions, IFD, and the work of molding America's sense of national identity. However, the timing and scale of the great fairs of the 1930s made their influence much more present in the lives of average Americans. They painted on a huge canvas an idealized image of the past and an optimistic view of the future, a vision of unity and harmony among people of different backgrounds, races, and creeds. Hardly an accurate representation of intergroup American relations, this was a carefully crafted vision that obscured real intercultural dynamics. But depicting reality was not what fairs were for. Realism was a low priority not only for Americans. As Greenhalgh (1988: 106) points out: "most nations showed themselves as residing in pleasant holiday-camps, where everybody had plenty, everyone was content and everyone knew his or her folk-tunes by heart." As heirs to romantic and nationalist ideology, the fairs' emphasis on the "folk" and "peasant" as the heart of national difference and identity was hardly surprising. It provided an opportunity for people to visit colorful and distinctive representations of many nations without leaving the fairgrounds. Greenhalgh (1988: 106) sees these villages as "a dream of the bourgeoisie, a grand version of the suburbs they were busily building for themselves. To retreat to pre-industrial life was an attempt to suspend the knowledge that the industrial age gave them their power, and that the ugliness of the urban environment was their doing." The fairs' emphasis evoked the interconnectedness of "the people" and all the other values ascribed to the folk. The exhibition of the folk in their new American context was realized through designated nationality days. The use of international folk dancing to represent the American nation, however, took representation of "the folk" to a different level; it offered a visual and sonic rhetoric of a multicultural American folk united in the celebration of diversity. It is hard to imagine a practice that could depict this vision more effectively than international folk dancing.

It is perhaps ironic that folk dancing at the New York World's Fair took place at the American Common, a space that became available in 1940 when the Soviet Union withdrew from the fair on the eve of World War II. The American Common was "the brainchild of Robert Kohn," conceptualized with "explicit ideological aims." An exposition news release announced that Kohn "suggested that the space be used to demonstrate an idea diametrically opposed to the propaganda of the totalitarian states . . . [namely], that America's greatness springs from the free and democratic institutions that allow her individual citizens and cultural groups to pursue happiness in their own differing ways'" (Rydell 1993: 185–186). Obviously, in this context America's national image could not be separated from

its international image. In the form of an international fair, America was forging a national image opposed to that of other world powers, emphasizing the uniqueness of its "colorful" citizenship. The "differing ways" of its cultural groups were to be shown as peacefully integrated and joined in an abundant, festive celebration of life in America.

The particulars of representing American pluralism were significant. One aspect of Kohn's realization of this task was to update the tradition of "ethnic" days. Rather than randomly scattering these celebrations throughout the duration of the fair, he made the American Common the focal point of weeklong festivals of different ethnic groups. The groups' displays of their "old ways" were seen as a sharp contrast to nearby exhibits of the latest machinery, military technology, and scientific achievements of the new American nation to which they belonged. The genius of this juxtaposition of past and present was the powerful message that the past was not only freely living within the present, but that the present was ensuring the past a life in the future.

> To be certain that old world traditions did not simply reinforce old world loyalties, each day at the Common concluded "with a brilliant patriotic gathering." "Here," a publicity release intoned, "will be America in its richest mingled traditions. Here will be the most direct and powerful answer to the dictators who would mold all peoples into the same rigid pattern." (Rydell 1993: 186)

Rydell evaluates "Kohn's decision to highlight the plural traditions of the American 'folk' instead of the techno-scientific possibilities of the future" as "brilliant but risky, given the hostilities between blacks and whites that lingered from the 1939 exposition season." The emphasis put on folk, however, had less to do with ironing out difficult interracial relationships than with asserting the value of the American system by attaching to it an attribute the value of which was already widely accepted.

This sets the stage for Michael Herman's participation in the New York World's Fair in 1940. The crowds of up to a thousand fairgoers who joined Michael Herman at the American Common were able to sample different folk dance steps as they would sample ethnic foods. The message of hundreds of people joining hands and dancing peasant dances of European countries was clear. Whatever the background of the participants, they were Americans partaking in the vision of a united nation and a united world. The display proved that America was on the right path, and that industrialization was not destroying the real "folk" but, on the contrary, providing them the leisure time to dance and be merry. Not unlike the Vacationland Palace and the Hall of the Western States at the Golden Gate exposition, presentations of IFD at World's Fairs were designed to highlight "Recreation as the Heritage of the Machine Age" (Rydell 1993: 129, n. 24). A souvenir publication from the San Francisco Golden Gate Exposition clarifies the "precise relationship between the pursuit of pleasure and industrialization of the American West":

This is adventure, and adventure is a product of leisure, just as leisure in America is a product of industry's efficiency. So adventure sets the pace for the fair—leisure, travel, recreation, the yearned-for opportunity to gather into one beautiful setting the color of the Western World, not at work, but living, playing, roaming over its finest country. This makes industry important only as a contributor to Romance. This makes the Fair, instead of a factory manual, a saga of the West—a Pageant of the Pacific. (Quoted in Rydell 1993: 129–130)

The implied vision of capitalist order as, not manipulative or exploitative, but caring and helpful was hardly subtle. Folk dancing fit perfectly into this romantic picture. Here people were engaged in an activity that demonstrated to participant and passerby alike that industrialization did not set people apart but encouraged them to join hands and celebrate their diversity. In a somewhat roundabout way folk dancing was used to celebrate technology and indeed to exalt the capitalist system. Its presence did not suggest a need to restructure the capitalist order, nor did it advocate turning back to the "earth." Its message was, in fact, that no matter how the industrial world evolved, Americans could have their cake and eat it too. "It has frequently been declared that the much-maligned machine age is lethal to culture and destructive of everything simple and human; yet this same age has made a special point of discovering and preserving the fine simplicity and rich humanity of the peasant arts which preceding periods have been prone to pass over as crude and uncouth," wrote John Martin, the dance critic for the *New York Times.*[2] The fairs took this line of reasoning to a new level. As San Francisco Mayor Angelo Rossi proclaimed during the Golden Gate Exposition, the citizen-tourists could realize the "dreamy enjoyment of manjana-land, spiced with American efficiency" (Rydell 1993: 130).

In the apt term "citizen-tourist," "citizen" represents the hard work, honesty, and decency of people devoted to their community and country, while "tourist" speaks of the leisure, enjoyment, celebration, and experience of the world made possible by American modernity. In the search for an embodiment of such a citizen-tourist, one might look no further than the folk dancer. Although I have found no explicit acknowledgement of folk dancing as the pastime of the model American, President Franklin Roosevelt's vivid interest and support of the practice might have suggested as much.

It is important to remember that surrounding the folk dancing on the American Common was a firm belief in the images of unity and harmony being presented there, certainly on the part of the dancers and probably many fair organizers as well. If the purpose of the American Common was to help "make loyalty to our country the only test of Christian or Jew, white or black, native or foreign born" (Rydell 1993: 186), folk dance represented the cause admirably. However, just as the fairs' peace rhetoric was being "ridiculed by the displays of military technology,"[3] the "integration of difference" at the American Common remained, not entirely, but largely

symbolic. Folk dance material from different immigrant cultures was appropriated to support an idea of their innate sameness. Like a museum exhibition of art objects from around the world, this exhibition of international folk dances did not substantively unite the different American cultural groups. But what it did do was help to articulate a vision of a harmoniously integrated American society in which every citizen could dance and be merry. In so doing it encouraged hope for a united nation, a united world, and trust in the American way to make this hope a reality (figure 7).

International Folk Dancing as "Virtual Tourism"

If the true American citizen was to be a tourist, international folk dance facilitated the expression of this identity in part through theatricality. Firstly, dancers entered a different temporal, social, and spatial sphere to partake in this activity. Secondly, they imaginatively took on multiple roles during a single evening (Russian kozak, Serbian shepherd, Hungarian townsman, Dutch shoemaker). With an audience or without it, folk dance was a kind of theater.

Figure 7. National anthem follows folk dancing at the Waldorf Astoria Hotel (photo courtesy of Sally Ray)

The "othering" of identity through marking the folk dance experience as different from one's everyday life and everyday self is clearest in participants' dressing up in folk costumes, not only for festivals and performances, but also for regular folk dance classes. As Vyts Beliajus noticed, "at the drop of a hairpin a costume is worn." Folk costumes figured highly in the international folk dance scene as stage props, but also as valued objects that could be collected, possessed, used, and recreated. Many folk dancers viewed folk costumes with reverence. These objects of beauty were particularly admired for the intense labor invested in their making. There was no clearer way to identify one's self as "of the folk" than to wear a folk costume. As intensive manual labor was recognized as one of the attributes of real folk, people would spend "days and months of sleepless hours to create tenderly and meticulously creations of utmost beauty" (*Viltis* Oct.–Nov. 1949/7). Models and directions for making folk costumes were printed periodically in folk dance books and magazines. Most commonly, however, pictures from *National Geographic* magazine were used as the pattern.

As *National Geographic* provided its readership an opportunity to explore the "other," or as Jules Verne's *Around the World in Eighty Days* led readers on an exotic tour, international folk dancing enabled people to "explore" different countries without actually going there. This "virtual tourism" had a particular appeal during the Depression when it was the only travel most Americans could afford.

What was the most desirable destination for folk dancers? Generally it was the "Folk Land" that they yearned not only to visit, but also to embody. Whether from Bulgaria, Italy, or Denmark, dances from "Folk Land" had quite identifiable characteristics. "Most of them are confined to space limitations without flourish, wild twirls, lifting of dress, throwing of head and shoulders, undue and wildly exaggerated hand clapping, or executing steps as if one is ready to take off on an airplane ride," explains Beliajus, clearly dubious about such showiness. "Most of the European folk dances require simplicity and humbleness in bearing, to be one of the folk," he further asserts. To be "one of the folk," a dance needed to be devoid of seductiveness, competitiveness, exaggeration, spectacle, and complexity. Mary Ann Herman (*Viltis* Dec. 1956/15) wrote: "We'll settle any old time for the wholesome, non-competitive, unselfish type of folk dancing we have here, with folks making up with a friendly helping hand for what they may lack in polished dance techniques."

It should be clear that these ideas were based on an imagined "Folk Land" rather than an actual understanding of ways in which dance functioned in traditional societies. This vision of the folk had very little to do with the values of "peasant societies" and little more to do with the reality of the international folk dance scene, yet leaders and followers alike perpetuated it. Despite statements to the contrary, the emphasis in the IFD scene was, in fact, much more on the quantity of dances than on quality, and the structure of the average folk dance club was hierarchical; members were divided into classes for beginners, intermediate to advanced classes, and exhibition groups. In traditional villages, only a handful of

dances would be danced in a lifetime, and dancers were divided into categories based, not on skill and the organization of a school, but on differences in, age, gender, and social and marital status.

The theatricality of IFD events was sometimes full-blown, as in Michael Herman's description of the virtual culinary travel at his folk dance camp:

> The food is authentic, and plenty of it, prepared by excellent cooks. Volunteers sign up for a committee whose function is to create the proper atmosphere for each meal. They may, and have, turned the dining room into a Turkish harem, an American Indian teepee, a German Rathskeller, a French Art Gallery, if need be. Authentic costumes are usually available from the Herman collection and many of the campers bring their own. If not, they are made from available materials. These are worn by the committee who serve the meal. Authentic music is played in the background. Food customs are observed and there is always someone at camp who knows some interesting things to tell about the country whose food we are eating. (Folk Dance Syllabus, 1953:1)

What Herman describes is a homemade fantasy of being somewhere else and somebody else. Cultural difference is reduced to stitching patterns, colors, and spices used to enrich the perceived colorlessness of American culture. This travel around the world may have been recognized as an entertainment, but what are its implications?

One of the activity's important premises is that elements of symbolic culture can be recreated and appropriated for an enactment of difference. Needless to say, real difference has not been explored. The choice of a harem or a teepee, rathskeller or a gallery to represent a particular cultural environment does not just fail to break stereotypical representations of these cultures it affirms them. Furthermore, the harem is assumed to be the place where the Turk is most Turkish, just as the French express their greatest Frenchness in the art gallery. Regardless of their different connotations, these were places where people were imagined to make merry. The assumption that Turks are the merriest in the harem and the French in the art gallery is inconsistent with the statement that "folk dancing is a recognized instrument for breaking down prejudices and for creating in their place a spirit of good will towards all men" (Herman 1956: viii). It is one thing to say that "all over the country people discovered that one didn't have to be Swedish to enjoy doing the Hambo, or Russian to enjoy the Troika" (ibid.), but it is another thing to assume that because one can dance the Hambo and the Troika one has an understanding of the Swedes and the Russians. The still-common belief that folk dancing involves "'painlessly educating' people in the cultural backgrounds of the countries where the dances originated (ibid.)" and, in so doing, "develop[ing] good fellowship" must be scrutinized. Such painlessness comes from the virtual nature of the intercultural encounter. Doing the steps of a Russian dance might build "good fellowship" among the "Syn-

thetic Slavs," to borrow Beliajus's term. But only symbolically can that activity be viewed as synonymous with cultural exchange, dialogue, or interaction.

A major presumption of IFD is that folk dancing is fun, and that people are most themselves when celebrating and making merry. In her critical analysis of folk festivals, Barbara Kirshenblatt-Gimblett (1994: 419) writes: "in festivals we have . . . the life world of others as our playground, the view that people are most themselves when at play, and festivals as the quintessence of a region and its people." The world of others was, sometimes quite literally, used as a playground when folk dancers would crash a local ethnic party, oblivious of the cultural etiquette in place at these events. How little folk dancing contributed to the understanding of another culture becomes clear from the fact that sometimes "ethnic dancers boycotted their own affairs" because "those 'pesky folk dancers'" were there.[4] The failure to understand that within ethnic communities dancing meant something more than entertainment and recreation led (and still leads) to conflicts between "ethnics" and "folk dancers." Some ethnic communities have used various means, including high cover charges, to keep the folk dancers away. It was not rare that, when actual intercultural encounters happened, folk dancing did not prove to be "of great value as a harbinger of good will toward fellow men."[5] Learning was not painless in these situations, nor was it as much fun as it was within the safe and predictable environment of a folk dance club.

This is not to say that real exchange, communication, and meaningful relationships did not take place between individual folk dancers and ethnic communities. Some folk dancers regularly attended ethnic events with a sincere curiosity and willingness to abide by the standards of the hosts. Such individuals were often welcomed without distinction and respected for their interest in the culture. Problems more often arose when a large group of folk dancers imposed their own values and expectations on an event as if it was their own, but with the advantage of live music.

Treasure Hunt: A Search for Authenticity

The growth of international folk dancing and the subsequent need for new material led to a situation in which many were "out on a folk dance 'treasure hunt,'" as Beliajus wrote in 1950. The metaphor of a treasure hunt is well suited to a situation in which "Everyone explores and everyone gathers materials from anywhere and everywhere. Many gather it from books, others from special institutes for instructors, others from observing other groups, and still others through obtaining it anywhere from 2nd- to perhaps 12th-hand handing over." The problem, as described, did not lie in the method of hunting itself, but in the difficulty of evaluating the value of what was found. In the article "How Is One to Know?" (*Viltis* Summer 1950), Beliajus draws attention to folk dance teachers' lack of ability to recognize pure and authentic folk dance form. While seeing nothing

problematic with the idea of folk dance teachers as treasure hunters, Beliajus concluded that the greatest problem was not teachers who "religiously follow written descriptions," nor those who "willfully adulterate a dance to suit their own needs," but "the ethnic representatives who misrepresent and the material hunters, bona fide people, who are their victims." He asked:

> how is the "treasure hunter" to know? He goes to a concert mainly because an "ethnic" group will be there and they will dance "ethnic" dances and it will prove to him a well from whence he will bring forth a wealth of new "authentic" material. Then they will come back to their groups and teach them the "real" thing as they saw an ethnic group present. . . . Many of the researchers, as mentioned above, are sincere, true and "bona fide" people. But how are they to know what they just saw and were thrilled with is something that is not folk but highly glorified stuff?

For a "treasure hunter" to be deceived by the natives, tricked into being thrilled by something that was not real and folk, appears a terrifying thought. "It is the researchers who are the greatest victims, and they, in turn, unintentionally, plant the wrong seeds and help it grow," Vyts continues. He fails to mention that the treasure hunter didn't think to ask the "natives" about the dance they were doing, and certainly didn't solicit their thoughts about the researcher's impending status as authoritative representative and teacher of it. Beyond the ethical issues it poses, this passage demonstrates the belief that, even with the best intentions, the "treasure hunter" could not recognize real treasure. It is implied that the beauty of the dance and the thrill that it induces can be not only erroneous but also harmful. The value of the dance is not in its appeal, in its form and accompanying music, nor in its origin or popularity among the ethnic group that performs it, but in its "authenticity," its "realness." But if it is indeed so hard to tell what is real and what is "dressed up," then why was it so important? Why was it important that the dances be "folk" rather than "recreational"? What value was there in "folk" status? Like the reliance of art collectors on external information about an art object to determine its value, a folk dance needed to be authenticated as such by a "researcher" who would not assume that material from a "genuinely ethnic source" would automatically be of value. What gave value to a dance was the imagined antiquity and purity of its origin. "The obsession with authenticity of the object and the rationale for its collection in science, not in plunder, would soon encourage and justify the acquiring of objects from all over the world by Western museums" (Greenhalgh 1988: 88). The folk dance movement had largely adopted this "museum attitude," even though a dance or piece of music cannot be possessed and displayed in the same manner that objects in a museum can.

Folk dancers of this period often expressed double standards with regard to the appropriation of dances from different cultures and were con-

cerned with "ethnics" who were not maintaining the purity of their dances. Beliajus found it bothersome and difficult to understand why a New York Swedish group would decide to improve on Tantoli, a simple ballroom type of dance of Finnish origin. "Why bother with Tantoli when the Swedes are noted for so many beautiful 'knock-out' dances," he asks. In the same article Vyts writes that "the true ethnic groups value beauty, the meaning, and the age of their dances. They do not want them distorted, after having survived for centuries, by a group of disinterested people, disinterested at least in the peculiarities that distinguish one dance from the other in national traits." In response, apparently, to his incomprehension of ethnic groups who were not obsessed with preservation and the purity of national style, Beliajus here introduces the category of "true ethnic groups."

In order to be considered one of the "folk" one no longer needed only to be born into a particular ethnic group, but needed to be involved in the preservation of that group's cultural heritage. It is only a small step in logic to conclude that "folk" and "folkness" could be achieved through the right mindset, and that one could learn to determine categorically what was folk and what was not, thus surpassing the authority of the unenlightened "ethnic."[6] Emphasizing the unreliability of ethnic sources, Beliajus argued (*Viltis* December 1954/13) against the proposal of the FDF of Southern California that "European dances should be learned from 'ethnic groups.'" "To this I can only say," he writes, "'they used to woz but they ain't no mo'"(ibid.). This anger with "ethnics" who are not preservationists has troubled folk dancers ever since. It seems to be a problem for the movement that, before its very eyes, folk dances within ethnic communities change. "Whenever I asked a Jugoslav as to what happened to a certain step previously popular and now replaced with something else I got three answers: 1) the other step is old fashioned now, 2) their uncle (or father) danced that way but it is not done that way anymore, 3) the DP's do this new way. . . ." What Vyts describes here is a normal process of change initiated both from within and without. But the very thought of constant change in folk dancing is a nightmare for the folk dancer who hopes to find the essence of a live cultural form in a single rendering, stable, constant, and unchanging. The belief in a "single right way" of doing a particular folk dance was so generally accepted at this time that any variation was perceived as degeneration. This belief helped teachers establish authority, inhibited the spread of variants, and set interpretive boundaries. Many shared a conviction that a folk dance was not a complex set of possibilities but, like a costume, an object that could be acquired, collected, and exhibited. The authentic, and therefore valuable, needed to be tangible and definite. Multiplicity could not be owned or prescribed and was seen as emblematic of personal expression rather than the communal expression of "the folk." For various reasons the question of whether or not the material used in the IFD movement was authentic is somewhat moot, especially since little attention was given to the quality of the execution of dance steps and even less to the quality of the music. It was important that a dance could be "proven" to be an authentic Russian or

Yugoslavian folk dance, but it mattered very little to the folk dancer where the dance came from or how it was to be danced as long as it was "folk."

The qualities of "the folk" were more often implied than defined, with a lot of sentimental values and judgment attached to them. "The folk dance means that it is the dance of the people," writes Beliajus (*Viltis* October 1948/6, 6), "for the most part, the dance of the European peasantry. People who are still close to earth." If "folk dance" was the dance of the people, one might wonder to whom the other dances belonged. The vision of European peasantry as people "still close to earth" is already familiar to us from the beginning of the century, and is echoed to the present day. An implication is that folk dance stands in opposition to the dance of modern industrial societies, which are no longer close to the earth.

This thought is part of what motivated Mary Ann Herman's statement, "We don't believe folk dancing should be promoted or glamorized. A nice, steady, healthy, natural growth with emphasis on quality not quantity, emphasis on people not dance . . . that is our philosophy" (*Viltis* December 1955/14). When folk dancing became what was clearly a fad, especially in California, folk dance leaders became terrified and did not dare rejoice in the development. The reason for their concern was that folk dancing was "supposed to be" a natural, spontaneous, steady activity belonging to "the people" rather than to popular culture. The promotion or popularization of folk dancing was seen as an almost subversive, harmful activity because of the possibility of aligning "folk" with "popular."[7] It is imagined that in peasant societies everyone is a "culture bearer," but that it is up to self-appointed culture bearers in "modern societies" to carry the important cultural traditions and keep them safe from the influence of the majority who are merely living in the culture.

PART IV

The 1950s and Beyond

8

International Folk Dance and the "Balkan Craze"

The explosion in popularity of Balkan circle dances after World War II presaged the exclusively Balkan scene that was to come. Some in the IFD world found this "kolomania" problematic for a variety of reasons. This specialization created a demand for the constant introduction of new dances, a demand that was met by a new breed of "teacher/ethnographers," many of whom traveled to the Balkans to find material. The work of several of these teachers, particularly Dick Crum, is outlined, followed by discussions of the work of some important teachers from the former Yugoslavia. The infrastructure and inner workings of the folk dance world are examined, with particular reference to the emergence and importance of large performing ensembles at home and abroad and the growing importance and availability of Balkan records of various kinds. A discussion of conflict and continuity between IFD and the emerging Balkan scene concludes the chapter and sets the stage to bring our history full circle.

Seeds of "Kolomania"

Music and dance from the Balkans had long been included in international folk dance repertoire, but it was not until the middle of the twentieth century that the movement experienced its "Balkan craze" or "kolomania." While the Serbo-Croatian term "kolo" refers to the nonpartner dances of Serbs and Croats done in a circle or open-line formation, in the folk dance world it came to be used for any similar dance from the Balkans. What we will consider the third phase of the IFD scene emerged with new enthusiasts who were increasingly interested in ethnographic work and traveling abroad to experience and learn dances in their original context. This growing interest in focusing on a single region or tradition rather than running through the dances of many cultures in an evening paved the way for the fragmentation of IFD, beginning with the emergence of a nascent Balkan scene.

The first dances to become popular in the movement were Serbian and, to a somewhat lesser extent, Croatian dances. As we have seen, by the 1930s

prominent folk dance teachers were regularly introducing circle dances, particularly from Yugoslavia, to their classes and performing groups. Vytautas Beliajus was "teaching kolos 'fullblast' in and around Chicago—first having learned them from native Yugoslavs and later teaching them to the 'second-generation', as well as to his early folk dance groups" (Filcich, in *Viltis* Oct.–Nov. 1955/14).[1] Michael Herman was teaching kolos in New York at approximately the same time. Changs International Folk Dancers was probably the first group to have a separate kolo class, with "one evening a week being devoted to kolos alone" (ibid.).

There were many other occasions on which the American public, and folk dancers in particular, were exposed to Yugoslav folk dances. As a part of the Yugoslav program at the San Francisco Golden Gate exposition in 1939, "an ethnic group from Sacramento performed the 'Srpkinja'" (ibid.). Perhaps the public display of this type of folk dancing contributed to its increased popularity in the years to follow. World War II reports on Balkan cultures may also have had an impact on the subsequent rise in popularity of kolos. John Filcich provides at least one account of a direct relationship between "war-effort" programs and the introduction of kolo dancing to the IFD community. During World War II, two U.S. Marines, Milan Palaski and Phil Hodak, organized a performing group in San Francisco that was "frequently exhibiting at ethnic and 'war-effort' programs."[2] After an exhibition at such an occasion, Marvin Hartfield, then the leader of Changs International Folk dancers, "persuaded the exhibiting group led by Phil and Milan to demonstrate and teach kolos at Changs" (ibid.).

The popularity of kolos grew steadily throughout the 1940s, and by the mid 1950s became full-blown kolomania.[3] One can find many accounts that depict the kolo dancing scene as exuberant, vibrant, and growing, particularly in California at this time. As Suzanne Jenkins (*Viltis* May 1957/16:21) remarked, "In the Bay area you have to go as fast as you can just to keep up with kolos. There is a kolo class every night of the week and a kolo party every weekend." An Annual Kolo Festival was added at "the height of kolo activity in the West." The first of these festivals was organized in the fall of 1952 as a benefit for Vytautas Beliajus, who was at that time recovering from a severe illness. Filcich recalls how he and his fellow folk dancers from California "thought of holding a Kolo Festival to do our part. It was a two-day affair held over Thanksgiving week-end and patterned generally after an ethnic activity." As the event was a great success, showing that there were many folk dancers excited about doing only kolos, the scope of the Kolo Festival continued to expand in the following years. "Each year the Kolo Festival has grown with the addition of another day," wrote Filcich (*Viltis* Oct.–Nov. 1955/14).

The Response to the Balkan Craze in IFD Circles

During the 1950s the popularity of kolos spread like wildfire, not only in California but also throughout North America. However, the fact that kolo

dancing had become the latest fashion was not received with universal enthusiasm. Some people, including Beliajus and Michael and Mary Ann Herman, were sincerely disturbed and worried by this fad. Why would one view the popularity of the kolo "as an evil instead of a bless" as Vyts[4] put it? For one thing, in the scene's philosophy of internationalism and egalitarianism there was no room for one region's traditions to be so highly favored over another. More important, echoing the fear generated by folk dance's growth following the San Francisco Exposition, the popularity of kolos was seen as a threat to the very essence of the scene's folk appeal. As in the inevitability of "rock" smashing "scissors" in the children's hand game, so "popular" was the dreaded antithesis of "folk."

There was also a more pragmatic concern. Kolomania threatened to convert a large number of international folk dancers, causing them to abandon groups and teachers still operating on the "forty dances/forty countries" model. According to Vyts, the threat was not evenly spread across the country, but was serious.

> Kolo dancing out East, tho popular, is not the craze. Nor does it share the West Coast enthusiasm within any reach of proportions. . . . On a whole and for the most part the East Coaster and all Central States take kolo on an equal footing as a part of international dancing which is by far healthier and should be highly commended. For kolo seems to be a mania which also inspires tendencies of selfishness. (*Viltis* December 1957/16: 17)

Kolo enthusiasts were perhaps the first of the international folk dancers to be so deeply affected by specific music and dances, as opposed to simply enjoying participating in the scene as a whole. Up to this point the average folk dancer, though he or she certainly had favorites, received the repertoire from all corners with similar enthusiasm. The passionate attraction to the Balkan, specifically Yugoslavian, circle dances appeared somewhat suddenly and was seen as unhealthy and threatening. Vyts went so far as to claim that "the catchy tunes and intricacy of some of the steps, hypnotized a great many victims, rather than beneficiaries, like dope. They have tendencies of aloofness and a craving to be by themselves away from general participations" (ibid.). Clearly, he seems to argue, there was something wrong, irrational, almost abnormal, in this attraction toward one particular kind of folk dancing, particularly this one.

That someone could appreciate a folk dance but not "folk dancing" was incomprehensible to many in the "old school." The desire to dance kolos was insatiable among enthusiasts and resulted in impatience with other kinds of folk dance. Vyts advocated teaching "the kolomaniac restraint and civility when in a 'mixed' dance crowd," but to no avail:

> In spite of the hour set aside for kolo dancing at many festivals, in spite of the additional kolos during the regular evening program which seem always to be above proportion to any other nationality, in spite

> of strictly kolo festivals of two-three day durations, one will still find kolomaniacs who will want to dominate an international folk dance evening. They'll try to put on kolos during intermissions, hog the request period, or do something ethically wrong which will be hurtful to the group and slight the visitors . . . It would not be surprising at all if a Kolo Federation will soon be formed which will be the first major break with the folk dance movement. (ibid.)

Although a "Kolo Federation"[5] was never formed, the emergence of the independent Balkan music and dance scene would later prove Vyts's fear to be well founded.

The "Kolo-nization" of America

Many factors contributed to the "kolo-nization" of America, to borrow Mary Ann Herman's expression.[6] The period after World War II was a time of economic prosperity in the United States. Membership in clubs and involvement in group activities outside the home reached an all-time high. Car ownership, transatlantic flights, and travel abroad were becoming much more within the reach of average Americans. Objects and images from around the world were becoming easily available. More specific to interest in things Balkan, a number of folk troupes from the region toured the United States in the 1950s, and recordings of Balkan music, either made by ethnic bands in America or imported from Europe, became more easily available. Children of immigrants fled their urban roots for the suburbs, and the growing importance of youth culture and the beginnings of rock and roll additionally marked the period as one of transition. In light of all that was going on, the old IFD repertoire must have seemed rather staid. Balkan repertoire, on the other hand, resonated with the times. It seems everything was in place; the fire of a Balkan craze was laid and just waiting for something to ignite it. The match was the excitement Balkan music and dance inspired, particularly among younger folk dancers.

The Aesthetic Appeal of Kolos

But what was all the excitement about, and where did it come from? It is perhaps impossible to trace all the strains of influence, but we can begin by returning to a discussion of aesthetics. In the introduction to his book *Igra Kolo, Dance Kolos*, John Filcich, the prominent folk dance teacher of the period, explains what he saw as the attractive qualities of kolos:

> Kolos are among the liveliest, gayest, and most enjoyable dances in the world. They are very practical dances and should be adopted by all dance groups; most of them do not require partners, but reflect a very high community spirit. There are easy ones and there are hard ones. Then there is that ever present urge to reach higher degrees of

> executing the steps and learning new improvisations that makes one enjoy them so much and never seem to get enough of them! (2)

Filchich mentions first the dances' "liveliness" and "gayety," the appeal of which in an activity designed for "fun" is obvious. The various levels of difficulty of kolos meant they could challenge beginners and experienced dancers alike. When folk dance leaders such as Dick Crum appeared on the scene, the introduction of the idea that there were many "right" ways to do the same dance proved it possible for dancers of different levels of experience to dance kolos together and still all feel equally challenged. This opening up of opportunity for individual expression was appealing to folk dancers who were often bored with a dance once they figured out its basic steps. The possibility of people of all experience levels dancing together had both a practical and aesthetic appeal.

Perhaps the most important part of kolo's aesthetic appeal is that it did not require partners. Nonpartner dancing in general was on the rise in 1950s America, reflecting changes in perceptions and behavioral standards with regard to gender and sexuality, and an increasing informality. The very form of the kolo was perceived as congruent with contemporary social and aesthetic demands. This resonance with the times would be even more amplified in the sixties and seventies. In the biography of Mark Morris, the professional modern dancer and choreographer who started his career in the Balkan folk ensemble Koleda,[7] the author explains how "Koleda was like a sixties commune, and the project on which they were embarked was itself a symbol of community. Holding hands in a circle, dancing and singing in harmony, they made art out of friendship and love, and friendship and love out of art" (Acocella 1993: 29). The IFD repertoire had the appeal of being *folk*. The appeal of Balkan dances, on top of being folk, was in their very form—the circle—an embodiment of community, harmony, and humanity united by joining hands.

The novelty of the material, and the novelty of its teaching and presentation were certainly important to their charm. It makes sense that, in a scene that was partly about enjoying things exotic and peasant, eventually some people would turn to the things that seemed the most exotic and most peasant. For most folk dancers, the music and the dance involved in kolos was, of everything in the IFD repertoire, the furthest removed from the mundane. The relative strangeness of Balkan music and dance most likely contributed, and still contributes, to the perception that it must be older or more rural than, say, a polka. Bill Vanaver (in McLaughlin 2004 [1977]) referred to Balkan repertoire as "the bluegrass of folkdancing." Explaining his interest in Balkan music, he drew parallels between the division of IFD and folk music movement in general: "In the same way that folk music split off into a popular, a political, and a traditional music group, folk dancing too split up—almost exactly the same lines. There was a social-recreational type, there was kind of a left-wing type that emphasized peoples getting together, and there was the traditional. And I was into the traditional, and that tended to be Balkan."

Also new in kolomania was the idea of focusing on a relatively narrow geographic/cultural region, as bemoaned by Vyts Beliajus. Elizabeth Bernstein reported in 1957 that "The kolo festival and jamboree at Herman's this year was a gala affair and the peak was the workshop. For a few days I was in another world—the world of the Balkan peoples. I was in the regions of Macedonia, Montenegro, Serbia, Bulgaria, Yugoslavia, Romania, Bosnia, Voyvodina, Croatia, Slovenia, Dalmatia."[8] The focus enabled participants to get into a kind of cultural groove, firing their imaginations to feel a particular sense of place. This provided, at once, a more focused and intense experience of "virtual tourism" and an opportunity to specialize, directing rather than scattering participants' energy, desire, and appetite.

In kolomania the music began to play an important role in drawing people to the material, probably a first in the IFD movement, and this was to be one of the most significant jumping-off points for the Balkan scene. The love of the music not only stimulated people to choose Balkan dance as their "area of specialty," but also to make first steps toward learning related musical traditions. As John Filcich (*Viltis* Oct.–Nov. 1955/14) recalls, "it is in the field of kolos that we turned from records to live tamburitza music at larger parties and Festivals." The formation of "non-ethnic" music groups for the purposes of providing live music for the folk dance classes came spontaneously within the folk dance movement. Only a few years after the beginning of the kolomania the Ruža Tamburitza Orchestra of San Francisco was formed, modeling themselves after numerous first- and second-generation Yugoslav-American tamburitza orchestras on the West Coast. "This group," Filcich writes in 1955, "is to the best of our knowledge, the only non-Yugoslav tamburitza orchestra anywhere. It is composed of young men from our 'Balkan Dancers' who were inspired by the kolo movement to channel their talents in this constructive and highly beneficial manner. They now provide live music for many parties, dances, and the Annual kolo Festival, as well as playing for 'the Balkan Dancers' during their exhibitions."

In tandem with the growing interest in music, folk dance underwent a transformation from recreational hobby to something involving considerably more time and emotional investment for those who began to wrestle with the intricacies of Balkan forms. The constant influx of new dance material kept enthusiasm for kolos high. As Filchich observed:

> Just as the Stockton Folk Dance Camp gave kolos the first good shot-in-the-arm, so again is it responsible for the latest booster shot. Dick brought us a new concept of kolos. . . . Perhaps even of greater significance and importance than the dozen or so new dances that he introduced, was the introduction of singing.[9] In Yugoslavia much of the dancing is accompanied by singing. . . . Having been initiated to this new concept, we are now in the midst of a new wave of enthusiasm —copying and compiling verses in native Serbo-Croatian and learning to sing these kolo-songs while dancing. (ibid.)

This passage illustrates not only the significance of an influx of new dances and the growing importance of musicmaking, but the effects of a new breed of folk dancer, the teacher/ethnographer. Improvements in overseas travel opportunities and the American economic picture, particularly the extreme imbalance between the American and Eastern European economies, made it feasible for Americans to gather dance and music repertoire firsthand in the Balkans. The appeal of such new repertoire included its novelty and the described attraction to the material itself, but also included the appeal of much closer contact with peasantry. Luther Gulick had detailed his frustrating difficulties in finding real peasant culture in Europe as early as 1911. With travel to the Balkans came unprecedented access to "the real thing."

The new generation of folk dance teachers began to travel as often as possible to the Balkan countries of their choice. There is no doubt about the appeal for folk dancers of learning, not third- and fourth-hand from textbooks and people who had learned from them, but from teachers who had learned from genuine peasants living in genuine villages. Thus, the Balkans became an actual destination, although many folk dancers' imaginative "virtual tourism" was rather supplemented than supplanted by the budding contact between folk dancer and "folk."

Nowhere in Europe could one get to the "real folk" more easily than in the Balkan countries, especially the former Yugoslavia due to its open tourist policies. For aesthetic and practical reasons, the region became a Mecca for the teacher/researcher—the real counterpart to Beliajus's imaginary "Folk Land." In this light, kolomania was a logical extension of ideology and practices well established and accepted in the IFD movement. This access to the "source" helped create and feed an insatiable appetite for a new sense of authenticity among folk dance enthusiasts, and the model of folk dance teacher as "ethnographer" brought a fresh perspective to the movement and its existing teaching models.

A New Breed of Folk Dancer: "Teacher/Ethnographer"

The beginnings of what I refer to as the "ethnographic" phase resulted in a rapid and massive increase in available folk dance material. With new advancements in recording technology, teachers would not only be able to find descriptions of dances but could get adequate recordings of music appropriate to a given dance. A growing number of folk dance teachers were soon able to introduce the folk dance public to hundreds of new dances, rather than being limited to a few Balkan dances learned out of books or from immigrant groups in the United States. Balkan villages proved to be an inexhaustible source of material for these researchers. And with the growing fad for Balkan dance, more teachers began to specialize in it. By 1979, Dunin (1979: 71) would find that "at least ninety-two teachers are responsible for teaching the dances [South Slavic] throughout California." Although she writes of a later period, most of the teachers she

mentions started in the 1950s and '60s, and the statistical information Dunin acquired in her research is revealing of the scope of the repertoire introduced to the folk dance communities. "Two thirds (67%) of the 1,810 dances are taught by only nine teachers and the collective Aman[10] staff: Filcich (247), Crum (204), Moreau (117), Boxell (116), Kolarovski (107), Dunin (100), Aman staff (88), Engler (79), Joukowsky (78), Gajicki (68)."[11]

In their research trips the new folk dance teachers were doing more than just accumulating dance steps and transcribing melodies. While Mary Wood Hinman, Elizabeth Burchenal, and others had earlier advocated going to the "source," they were primarily looking for more dances to suit an existing understanding and agenda. Many in the new generation were exposing themselves to experiences that challenged their very understanding of what dance was, how it was used, and what it meant.

Dick Crum

Dick Crum (figure 8.1) was hardly the first to introduce Balkan dances to the folk dance community, but he became the most influential teacher of the kolo repertoire and one of the first researchers to gather his material "from the source." His position in the history of international folk dance somewhat parallels that of Mary Wood Hinman, who in the 1930s acted as a bridge between the settlement house movement and the introduction of recreational international folk dancing to the American public. Crum, likewise, was an important bridge between the IFD scene, as we know it from the early days of Beliajus and the Hermans, and the contemporary Balkan dance and music scene. His perspective is, thus, extremely valuable to an understanding of this historical period.

I am very fortunate to have been able to record many hours of conversation with Dick Crum, who remained an active teacher and an advocate for Balkan music and dance until he passed away in December 2005. His vivid and detailed memory, years of devoted research and scholarship, and remarkable storytelling ability have contributed substantially to my understanding of the IFD world and the dramatic changes it underwent when some of its representatives began researching dances in the countries of their origin. The scope of this work does not allow me to do justice to Crum's life work, as is true for many other prominent individuals of this time period whom I have not had the privilege of knowing. The information here presented should be understood as selective and pertinent to an understanding of larger issues.

Except for the fact that he was of Irish-Scottish background, the description of Richard Crum's upbringing does not sound much different from the stories of Michael Herman and Vytatuas Beliajus. Born in St. Paul, Minnesota in 1928, Crum grew up in a Romanian neighborhood. Although Romanian dances were his first contact with folk dancing, he does not consider them to have been influential on his future career. As a teenager he became involved in ballroom dancing and developed a special interest in Latin American folk dances. His first dance research trip was to Mexico

Figure 8. Dick Crum, Mendocino, 1997

in 1948 where he spent nine months learning Mexican folk dances. Upon returning to the University of Minnesota, Crum became active in the recreational folk dance movement, particularly within the International Institute in St. Paul. Through the International Institute's yearly Festival of Nations, Crum became acquainted with the folklore of various local immigrant groups. When the need arose, he volunteered to fill in with the Croatian dance group for the Festival exhibition. Crum learned his first Serbian kolo, "Seljančica" in 1949 from "a fellow who had traveled to a place where Michael Herman was teaching. He learned some Serbian kolos from Herman and brought them back to St. Paul" (Crum, phone interview).

Up to this point in Crum's folk dance career he was following in the pathway of leaders including Beliajus and Herman. "Vyts was my folk dance God when he came to Minnesota in the late forties," said Crum, recalling the time when he first met Beliajus. However, Crum's pathway through the folk dance world would take a dramatic turn when, intrigued by the possibility of receiving a scholarship from a folk dance group at the Duquesne University in Pittsburgh, he decided to audition for the Tamburitzans. It so happened that the Duquesne University Tamburitzans gave a concert in Minnesota in 1950, and Crum performed for them the few Yugoslav dances he knew from the IFD repertoire. He was accepted into the group, and the decision to join the Tamburitzans changed his life profoundly. In February 1951 he moved to Pittsburgh.

The Duquesne University Tamburitzans were, at the time Dick Crum joined them, largely an ethnic ensemble in which most of the members were not only of Yugoslavian background but also spoke Serbo-Croatian. In such an environment Crum was learning music and dance as well as the language and other aspects of the culture. In 1952, he went with the ensemble on his first tour to Yugoslavia. This tour was a turning point for Crum, and his experiences to a certain extent embody the sharp differences between the two periods in the history of IFD that he bridged.

Crum did not think of this as a research tour, but, as he says, "I was eager to learn, and they were all forthcoming. Every waking moment I was learning." At that time Crum was unable to distinguish between a staged and non-staged dance, and he did not necessarily understand where the material was coming from and how it was represented. When the Tamburitzans performed along with the prestigious Croatian folk dance ensemble Lado, Crum felt that what the Tamburitzans took to Yugoslavia was "not a show but a cheap Vaudeville. I was very ashamed of the program." Watching the other ensemble was revelatory. "When Lado performed the second half of the concert I saw for the first time Croatian dances, and I was numb. I was completely numb . . . I almost fainted when I saw Lijevakovićev's *Slavonsko kolo*." This intense aesthetic experience is something Crum never experienced at IFD events. One of the major points of departure from the IFD scene as we know it up to this point was a motivation in which the aesthetic might outpace the ideological. What moved Crum, and soon many others of his generation, was this intense aesthetic experience, accompanied by his recognition of the dance and its accompanying music as a living art rather than a representation of an idea. Due to this realization Crum was perhaps the first folk dance teacher to try to capture the "spirit" of the dance, going beyond the mere execution of steps and beyond the well-intentioned but stereotyped sense of "spirit" employed by Hinman and her peers. On his first tour to Yugoslavia, he witnessed a non-staged dance in a market place in Sarajevo. When in later years American folk dancers would ask him, "What approach do you use when you see a non-staged dance and you want to join it?" he would recall this experience and reply, "It will not even occur to you to get into

that circle. And, believe me, when you are faced with a *real* dance . . . you will not even think of joining it. . . . When I saw *Trusa* on Baščaršija, I realized I did not belong there. Then I realized—I am seeing something here that is very different from all the other folk dancing I have seen." This observation is extremely important and could not have been made before folk dance teachers began to do ethnographic research. Crum distinguishes here between the different levels on which a dance exists. Just as Hinman came to feel that immigrant teachers were needed to give a sense of the qualities of dance steps beyond their simple execution, Crum realized that there was yet another level. Although he did not articulate this at the time, he acknowledged the depth of interaction between the dancers he happened upon in Sarajevo. He saw that simply executing the proper dance steps could not make one a part of such a dance any more than walking into a stranger's funeral could make one a mourner. What Crum calls here a "real dance" is obviously different from IFD repertoire, and even from the choreographed staged presentations he saw while in Yugoslavia. Similar experiences have compelled some enthusiasts to completely drop out of the scene after their first visit to the Balkans.

Although Crum's experiences, as he recalls them, were colored by his folk dance training in the line of Beliajus and Herman, he could not avoid noticing the differences even within familiar dances he saw in his travel. "When I saw people doing *U šest* I was very confused. They were all doing the dance differently and that was not at all true in the folk dance world. I remember thinking, 'Oh, I wish Michael was here to tell me which one of those people are right.' This was the state of my mind." Being so accustomed to the packaged presentation of folk dances in which "dances were normative, and you can go and find the correct way of doing them in one of those books," Crum struggled, "trying to make the real world match what I assumed to be the laws." The experience of trying to make the real world match one's perception—something we all do in trying to make sense of our surroundings—would be shared by many enthusiasts of folk dancing when they set out to explore the Balkans. Such experiences will be explored in more depth in chapter 9, but at the moment it is interesting to consider Dick Crum's experience in light of its occurrence between two historical phases of IFD. Faced with the obvious discrepancy between the empirical data and the IFD mode of presentation, Crum did not know how to reconcile the two. He "followed the formula of Burchenal, Hinman, and Herman" and decided to create one "packaged" dance out of the many different ways the people were executing the steps. He translated the different personal styles of dancing into different "figures."

> I said, OK, since I don't know who is right here I would take various figures and put them together and then I would say do figure one two times, go to figure two, etc. Now I look back and say, "God, Crum, how could you be so docile, so spineless." . . . I am an intelligent person, why did not I see that? Somehow, all those 600 people in Yugoslavia were wrong, and Michael was right.

Beside the fact that Michael Herman's authority may never have been called into question in the folk dance world, there were ideological obstacles to accepting the possibility of there being many right ways to do a particular dance. An acknowledgment of such individuated expression within the same circle conflicted with the near sacred concept of "folk" as communal creation and expression. "Folk dancing is the creation of the people, of the masses, and not of the individual," wrote Beliajus.[12] This widely shared belief is so deeply engrained in the folk dance world and American society at large that, even today, it can be seen as provocative to question it. Crum credits Bob Leibman[13] and other teachers "who had no burden of Herman's tradition," with beginning to take the scene beyond presenting the dances in the old manner. Still, the emerging Balkan music scene continued to wrestle with related issues, as in instances when musicians were expected to replicate a familiar recording of a particular dance with its exact tempo, number of repetitions, and duration (see chapter 9).

Upon returning to the United States after the tour, Crum was in great demand, with requests from numerous clubs and camps that wanted him to teach the new material. With further research trips and fluency in several Slavic languages, Dick Crum became the first expert in Balkan dance within the folk dance community, setting an example for many to follow and inspiring enthusiasm for Balkan dance around the country.

Other Teachers

A defining characteristic of the kolomania period was the remarkable diversity of the teachers. Their sources, methodologies, and pathways differed considerably. On one hand there were old schoolteachers like Herman, Beliajus, and many others who began trying to accommodate audience and student demand for popular Balkan dances. However, they stuck with their old methods, either reconstructing steps from available folk dance books, hiring a teacher to come to their club and present the dances to the membership, or learning them directly from one of the new folk dance teacher/ethnographers at a camp or special class. Once the material became part of their repertoire, it would be passed through the established lines within the folk dance world. On the other hand there were the folk dance teacher/ethnographers themselves, including Dick Crum, Dennis Boxell, Michael Cartier, and, later, Yves Moreau, Martin Koenig, Bob Leibman, Steve Glaser, Ron Wixman, Michael Ginsburg, Steve Kotansky, and Joe Graciosi.[14] Acting as the extended arms of the IFD scene, they gathered Balkan music and dance from "the source," which for most meant seeking repertoire in villages, while for others it meant studying primarily with state folklore ensembles. In either case, this work made these teachers important sources of new material, helped them become authorities on related issues, and eventually led them to become some of the main leaders in the emerging Balkan scene.

There were also various types of "ethnic" teachers. John Filcich, for example, is of Yugoslav origin, but he got involved in Balkan dancing

through the IFD scene after attending the "Oakland Festival" on December 12, 1947. After six months or so of general folk dancing, his "complete attention began to center on kolos, having remembered them somewhat as a boy in Gary, Indiana." Since Filcich was of the "appropriate" ethnic background, his sources were not questioned. As was the case with Beliajus and Herman, it was generally assumed that, as an "ethnic," he simply knew all these folk dances. Filcich himself explains, however, that "Contrary to popular belief, I did not learn them [kolos] in Yugoslavia, or even 'back East', but right here in the Bay Area—partly from the few teachers who knew them somewhat, partly from Easterners living here, but to a large extent by continual research and hours of practice" (*Viltis* Oct.–Nov. 1955/14). Along with teaching and introducing new repertoire, John Filcich's contributions include the San Francisco Kolo Festival, which he and his family have run from its inception in 1952 to the present day. Another important contribution was the maintenance of a record shop featuring Balkan and related music.

An "ethnic" teacher of a different sort was Anatol Joukowsky. "Kolo dancing of a highly polished exhibitional and theatrical nature was added in 1951 with the arrival of Joukowsky from Europe" (*Viltis* Oct.–Nov. 1955/14) Joukowsky spent several years with the National Folk Ballet in Belgrade and then lived and performed in France. His experience was broadly comparable to that of Louis Chalif and Vasille Avramenko at the beginning of the century, or perhaps Tashamira in the thirties. Many of the dances he taught were balletic and highly choreographed. Dick Crum provided an anecdote about the folk dance tune "Žabarka," named for its village of origin, Žabari. The tune was included on a record made in Belgrade (Radio Televizija Beograd) that was imported to the United States for the folk dance market. When Joukowsky bought the record in San Francisco he interpreted the title "Žabarka" as if it were derived from the word *žaba* ("frog") and "made up a dance that incorporated frog-like movements. . . . So, along comes the story that Serbs in Šumadija were interested in frogs, and frogs were important in their lives and it was natural that there would be a mimic of a frog."

This anecdote is not included as a critique of Joukowsky's teaching, but as a glimpse into one of the strains of influence and tradition coming to the scene through the various backgrounds of dance teachers. It is also an interesting illustration of the folk dance world's own folklore. Dances were often similarly "contextualized" by teachers and others. The stories, often wholly fictitious, were introduced to situate and add value to a dance, and in doing so they often perpetuated existing stereotypes and created new ones. Folk art, it is often thought, always comes with an explanation, a "reason" for its existence. Dick Crum observed that "regardless of what the teacher's intentions were, people in the class will make out of the material what they need to. . . . One of the things that dogs a dance teacher that is trying to be ethnographically accurate are these stories. They are always around, and they are made up by anybody." The practice persists for various reasons, including the "museum" view of folk dance as an

object, the value and meaning of which is increased or discerned through explanation.

Filcich and Joukowsky have a lasting legacy, particularly within the Folk Dance Federation. But three "ethnic" teachers of a somewhat later date had a tremendous and more direct impact on the development of the Balkan music and dance scene per se: Mile Kolarov, Atanas Kolarovski, and Pece Atanasovski, all native Macedonians. An account of their teaching and performing activities in the United States and their work with Americans traveling to Macedonia, might be a book in its own right. Although they arrived after the blossoming of kolomania, these three "ethnic" teachers, along with Americans such as those above, played a significant role in shaping the budding Balkan scene, particularly in the sixties and seventies. An important source of the Macedonian teachers' influence stemmed from the fact that they were not only traditional dancers and musicians, but choreographers, arrangers, and leaders of distinguished folk ensembles in the former Yugoslavia.

Folk Dance Ensembles

The development of large folk ensembles and dance troupes in the late nineteenth century was a logical outgrowth of the romantic nationalist ideology of the time. The trend ranged in its manifestations from giant outdoor pageants in the United States to the beginnings of folk ballet and the balalaika orchestra in Russia. The former Yugoslavia saw the creation of Tamburitza orchestras, a form that traveled with Yugoslav immigrants, giving rise to groups like the Duquesne Tamburitzans in the 1930s.[15] With socialism came an explosion of state folklore troupes, beginning in 1937 with the Moiseyev Ensemble (State Academic Ensemble of Folk Dances of the Peoples of the USSR), a model for the large ensembles of highly trained, colorfully costumed musicians and dancers that would follow. Tremendous interest in folk dance was sparked by the American tours of these groups beginning in the 1950s. Although they were not the first to tour the United States, Moiseyev's first visit in 1958 was probably the most influential. "The impact of the one hundred Moiseyev dancers, performing never-before-seen synchronized choreographic feats with the power and ease of circus acrobats, created an electrifying impact on audiences worldwide that is difficult to imagine for those not present or unaware of this phenomenon," writes Anthony Shay in his *Choreographic Politics* (2002: 4). Less than a year after the Soviet group's visit, San Diego could boast of its own "Moiseyev troupe" called "Dolina Cigany," organized by John Hancock.[16]

Rather than adopting the model of Changs International Folk Dancers and other earlier groups, the new breed of folk dance exhibition troupes modeled themselves after Moiseyev and other European ensembles formed shortly after the end of World War II. The groups Lado (Croatia, formed in 1949), Tanec (Macedonia, 1949), Kolo (Serbia, 1949), Kutev (Bulgaria,

1951), and Dora Stratou Greek Dances Theatre (1953), all provided their American counterparts not only models for the presentation of folk dance material, but much of their repertoire. It is interesting and somewhat ironic that such highly polished and idealized nationalist presentations of the "folk" constructed by the socialist states would be adopted and perpetuated among Americans as true representations of peasant cultures.

In any case, the excitement surrounding the American tours of these ensembles "not only changed the lives of many individuals in the United States, but also irreversibly altered the nature of international folk dancing and the personal lives of many of its participants," recalls Robin Evanchuk. When Tanec and Kolo came to the United States, "Some followed the groups to other cities and by the time the performers left the area these devoted individuals had acquired a strong familiarity with the dances, music and style of the companies and had begun to pattern their own dance styles after what they had seen on the stage. Contacts were then made with local members of the Balkan community. . . . In time, these devotees became strong supporters of this ethnic culture and wished to become a part of such a culture locally" (Evanchuk, 1987–88: 117–118). With the tours came opportunities for contact with Americans who were eager to learn what the ensembles had to offer. Moiseyev himself visited Michael Herman's Folk Dance House with his troupe, and even learned an American square dance from Herman that became a popular encore for the ensemble. A number of dancers, including Atanas Kolarovski, Bora Gajicki, Athan Karras, Pece Atanasovski, and George Tomov, all members of premier national ensembles in their respective countries, either immigrated to the United States or came on solo teaching tours. Some organized folk dance workshops in their native countries that were attended by many American enthusiasts. In this manner an intertwined network of people, clubs, ensembles, repertoire, and ideas stretched across the ocean. Almost everyone in the Balkan dance scene at this time was, at most, one step removed from this network.

For many years large ensembles were the most publicly visible face of the American folk dance world. Whether formed in the 1930s or 1960s and 70s, many of the most influential American folk dance giants are still active either professionally or on an amateur basis. Often starting small, under the initiative of one or two people, the groups sometimes evolved into sizable establishments with up to a hundred performers, whole administrative and managerial divisions, and costume and property departments.

The size and aim of these ensembles were incompatible with an existence within the limitations of the IFD scene. Instead, they reached out to the general public, offering performances and lecture-demonstrations in schools, colleges, clubs, hotels, and festivals throughout the country and abroad. Through these tours and performances untold thousands were introduced to music and dance repertoire that was either "international" or specifically Eastern European or Balkan. While this resulted in many new folk dancers, the ensembles were sometimes seen as having a negative impact on local international folk dance clubs as well. It was not

unusual to encounter accusations that a big ensemble was ruining the livelihood of a local recreational folk dance scene by recruiting away the most talented and enthusiastic of young dancers.

The performing groups can be considered folk dance schools through which numerous dancers and musicians passed over the years. Many of the groups' members later branched out, either founding their own troupes or pursuing some kind of folk-dance-related career. The most popular folk dance leaders of this period often had a large performing ensemble at their side, as we have seen in the case of Dick Crum, who came out of the Tamburitzans and was later their artistic director. Among others closely tied to the folk dance scene, Vince and Robin Evanchuk formed Westwind in Los Angeles (1960)—Neal Sandler later took their repertoire north and formed Westwind in San Francisco—and Dennis Boxell founded and directed Koleda in Seattle (1967). Other ensemble directors, including Anthony Shay and Leona Wood of Aman, formed in Los Angeles in 1963, and George Tomov of Tomov, formed somewhat later, in 1974 in New York, did not have much to do with the folk dance world outside of their own ensembles.

The relationship between the recreational folk dance world and the big performing ensembles is complex, with both cohesive and disjunctive forces in operation. They fed off of each other while still attempting to remain in their separate spaces. The obvious distinction between the two is an emphasis on performance and representation versus an emphasis on participation and personal enjoyment. The difference in orientation resulted in clear differences in approach to folk dance material and in its interpretation. While in folk dance clubs it mattered little how one danced as long as one danced, the way the dance looked was obviously crucial to the success of a performing group. The ensembles' polished presentation of folk dance inspired both the resentment and admiration of average folk dancers.

The high production standards set by the socialist groups and demanded by the public contributed to making authentic costumes an expected and integral part of folk dance presentation, and every large troupe had to have a large costume collection. In the attempt to perform dances in appropriate costume, choreography was often structured around costume changes. Several sets of costumes were needed for a single show. Koleda director Dennis Boxell is reputed to have had, at one time, a collection of some three hundred costumes. Ensembles often purchased costumes from abroad or from the specialty shops that sprang up at home to serve the folk dance market. Sometimes group members made their own costumes, copied from an original or a pattern. Specialized folk dance and music libraries and museums became an integral part of the largest performing ensembles. Along with costume collections, musical instruments were acquired in order to add live and "authentic" music accompaniment to the dance repertoire. Even if used only as stage props, effectively extensions of the costumes, exotic instruments added to the atmosphere. In many cases, though, they were much more than props. A significant number of

ensemble musicians approached their instruments quite seriously and went to great lengths to try to master them. The curiosity and determination of these musicians, working under the wings of large ensembles, was of critical importance to the development of a Balkan music and dance scene (see chapter 9).

The Workings of the Folk Dance World

In the making of any popular culture phenomenon there occurs what is almost a chemical reaction, a back and forth between desire and the things that alternately fulfill and create it. The variables of the actions and interests of individuals and organizations and the imminent qualities of things and ideas are joined together to fit in the mobile of a culture's world of ideas and systems (political, economic, etc.) Untangling the intricacies of aesthetic/cultural supply and demand can get bogged down in "chicken or the egg" questions. Although it is not always clear what led to what, kolomania, and later the Balkan scene, emerged from interpenetrating systems of activities, commodities, and ideas—a crucible of newly discovered and inherited practices and possibilities. The bigger the folk dance phenomenon grew, the more complex, multifaceted, and systematized became the inner workings of the scene.

Increased access to sources of material brought many changes to the ways in which the folk dance world operated, not the least of which was an expansion in infrastructure. The establishment of supply routes from the Balkans aided the expansion of the folk dance market and the creation of many small businesses to distribute and meet demand for the newly available supplies. Fueled in part by the nation's growing economic power, record and costume shops opened; several record labels were established to serve the needs of the folk dancers; festivals, folk dance camps, holiday and weekend workshops were organized throughout the country; and there was an upsurge in the collecting of everything from folk costumes and records to musical instruments and various other art and utilitarian objects.

Once it took hold, kolomania was characterized by an insatiable appetite for new kolos. What's more, the new folk dance groups and classes that were focused exclusively on Balkan material needed a constant supply of fresh material just to maintain the standard class format, which involved teaching new dances every evening. Over the years, thousands of Balkan dances would be transmitted to the American enthusiasts. New teachers "conquering" new territory fueled new trends and a market for new commodities. Reports on these conquests were published in folk dance papers and magazines, generating widespread interest in aspects of Balkan music and dance culture that were previously unknown in the scene.

An interesting development of this period was the spread of folk dance coffeehouses, which became social hubs for college students in the 1960s. In places such as Askenaz, Mandala, and the Intersection[17] rather than folk dance taking the formalized structure of a dance class, dancing became

an integral part of an evening along with the other activities of a social club. These hangouts had much more in common with immigrant community social clubs than did other folk dance institutions, although the repertoire was more "international." While they remained popular on the West Coast, particularly in the Bay Area, folk dance coffeehouses never really took off in the East, and those that started were apparently unable to sustain community interest. "Community, universal harmony, the quest for 'roots,' the longing for innocence, the search for a popular art rather than a high art: these aspirations . . . produced a folk dance renaissance, and the West Coast, where utopianism always runs high, and ran highest in those years, contributed heavily to this trend" (Acocella 1993: 26). The popularity of folk dance coffeehouses and related venues was such that, according to Dick Oakes, even Hollywood took notice. The Intersection, founded by Rudy Dannes and Athan Karas in 1964, was in its heyday frequented by Hollywood celebrities such as Marlon Brando, Bo Derek, Ginger Rogers, Telly Savalas, and Omar Sharif.[18]

Along with infrastructural developments, we have seen some of the ways in which methods of acquiring repertoire and the profile of folk dance leaders changed with the accessibility of Balkan resources. Before long, Balkan folk dance became a career option with its own professional paths and rules. Upon return from the Balkans, folk dance teachers and their new material were in great demand. Folk dance camps, such as Stockton and the Maine Folk Dance Camp, functioned as trendsetters and centers of dissemination. Upon presenting the new material there, well-known teachers would typically embark on a teaching tour throughout the country and even abroad, transmitting the new batch of dances to the local clubs and teachers, who would then teach the material on *their* teaching tours, usually on a more local level. When a new dance was presented at one of the major camps (still largely "international" in repertoire) the instructions would also be written down in a camp syllabus. These syllabi functioned as inexpensive, miniature versions of folk dance books and, while in most cases they were intended as a reminder to class participants, they would also be used as guides to learning new dances by those who did not attend the camp. Thus, starting with an individual researcher who learned a dance in a particular part of the Balkans, the dance was transmitted through the grapevine of the folk dance world, reaching a wide number of folk dancers in a short period of time.

The work of the new teachers affected not only the mechanics of the folk dance world but also the status of the older generation of "giants" in the field. The decline of the older teachers' influence was all but inevitable in light of the number of teachers returning from the field with empirical evidence not in keeping with established beliefs and practices. Although Herman, Beliajus, and others of their generation remained active in folk dance for many years, and remained prominent in the old-school IFD scene, their virtual monopoly on aspects of the overall scene crumbled under the weight of new ideas, new teachers, and new scene mechanics.

Balkan Records

Like improvements in international distribution, the frequent Balkan trips by interested folk dancers, teachers, and otherwise, was an extremely important point of access to new music resources. The quality and quantity of recorded music improved dramatically in this period, as recordings increasingly became a commodity as well as a necessity. Teachers at the top of the folk dance distribution and teaching pyramid needed to have dance/music packages that could be made available to other teachers down the line. As with dances, recordings direct "from the source" were prized and recognized as much more exciting and interesting than the folk dance material that had previously been available.

Several kinds of folk dance recordings were available during the kolomania period. These included imported records (brought back from Balkan travels or acquired through shops serving ethnic communities), commercial recordings made by Americans of native musicians in the Balkans, and pirated recordings (mostly reprints of releases originally put out by record labels in the Balkans[19]). There were also recordings made in the United States. These included recordings of Michael Herman's type, as well as recordings of groups comprised solely or primarily of "ethnic" musicians. The latter, released privately or through a record label, produced within immigrant communities or by other Americans, were intended more for an immigrant than a folk dance market.[20]

Demand for these recordings was accompanied by the emergence of various folk-dance-friendly labels such as Worldtone Records, Festival Records, Balkan Records, Folkways, and Folkraft, which often included recordings from several of the above listed categories in a given year's catalog. Recordings were available at folk dance events and record stores including specialty outlets like Joan Amsterdam's "International Folk Rhythms" in Chicago, a store specializing in imports run by John Krilčić in Beaver Falls, Pennsylvania,[21] and the Festival Records shop run by John Filcich and Ed Kramers in San Francisco.[22] Both Krilčić and Filcich produced and released records as well.

As folk dance teachers could not work without musical accompaniment, recordings became a logical byproduct of ethnographic work. Most teachers purchased records, but Dick Crum, Dennis Boxell, Martin Koenig, Yves Moreau, and others also found ways to make them. Crum recorded a lot of material for Michael Herman's Folk Dancer label, while at the same time Dennis Boxell produced records with Folkraft.[23] Boxell also put out some records on his own record label. Yves Moreau worked with Kenny Spear in New York with Worldtone Records and also put out a record on Balkantone, the Bulgarian label. These recordings served their purpose as teaching aids in folk dance classes, but were also an additional source of income for the producers/teachers. Not only would teachers sell the records during their workshops, but sometimes the record company would cover part of the travel expenses to the Balkans or provide recording equipment as well. However, rather than sharing profits with the record company,

teachers preferred to produce the records themselves, or to make cassette tapes of teaching material available. Michael Ginsburg suggested that this practice "put all these record companies out of business. The teachers go to a studio and hire some musicians to play, they pay them, bring the master some place and make it into a recording. They make more money that way than having to share the profits with some other company" (Interview, 1994).

It is hard to quantify the impact of the presence of all these types of recordings. But to say the least, the folk dancers' musical horizons were expanding. No longer limited to hearing Michael Herman's orchestra or tamburitca orchestras' renditions of various Balkan dance tunes, people could listen to an ever-wider array of regional musical styles and instrumentation. For many, the excitement this exposure generated developed into an avid interest in Balkan music. A number of imported commercial recordings, such as that of Fillip Kutev's arrangements for the Bulgarian Women's Choir and A. L. Lloyd's recordings, for example, had a tremendous impact on some who would become influential in the coming Balkan scene, and also created greater public awareness of Balkan music in its own right, not just as an accompaniment to dance.[24] Along with the importance of all these recordings to the dance scene, it is largely due to their circulation that a Balkan music scene emerged in the United States.

The Balkan Scene and IFD: Conflict and Continuity

Although greatly reduced in membership and visibility in American society, international folk dancing is still practiced throughout the country and abroad, despite the exodus of participants to the Balkan scene and other emerging specialty music and dance worlds. Continuity between IFD and these scenes is found in membership crossover and ongoing ideological and practical connections. *Viltis* and several smaller magazines are still published, and the Society of Folk Dance Historians maintains a yearly publication, "International Folk Dance Problem Solver," and a directory of folk dance clubs throughout the country. Some public schools still have IFD classes, too, many of which are remarkably similar in form and content to those Burchenal and Hinman taught in the early twentieth century.

Recreational folk dance clubs throughout the country still dance to scratchy 78's of Michael Herman's band played on the old variable-speed record players. This touches on some unaddressed reasons for the conflict that developed around kolomania. A large number of international folk dance clubs still do not like the idea of dancing to live music or unfamiliar recordings, both of which became very popular in the Balkan scene. For some, the familiarity and safety of dancing to the same three-minute records one has been using for decades is preferable to the uncontrollable noise, unknown tunes, unpredictable tempos and endings one can be subjected to by live musicians. "Some of the people," Colin explained (EEFC list, July 17, 1995), "have been dancing to recorded music for 25 years or

more, and refining their dancing to fit the record exactly. A difference in tempo or an extra measure or two throws this off completely." There are also sentimental attachments to the old recordings, as shown in the following excerpt from an e-mail message written by an old time folk-dancer (Jim, EEFC list, March 21, 1997):

> We are celebrating old things, traditional things. Some of the oldest recordings preserve an art form that fewer and fewer really know. That sound is something I connect with my earliest memories of folk dancing and those are golden memories. . . . It's the same thing as listening to original Louis Armstrong recordings from the '20s or looking at old black and whites of my great grandparents. It symbolizes continuity.

These records do more than symbolize continuity—they provide it. While Balkan music and dance is often seen as an abstract ancestral tie to peasant village life, the old 78's are, by now, a far more literal tie to personal and community history for many dancers.

The emerging Balkan scene's focus on a single region and love of dance events where one can get into a groove doing the same dance for half an hour or so continues to be a turn-off for some. Many in the IFD scene were initially attracted, in part, by the appeal of its image of a world united through dance, and enjoyed concentrating on three- or four-part choreographies and the variety of tempos and movements the IFD repertoire offered:

> Back in the old days in my culture, we danced to records that were 3 minutes long. And anyone who was running the records had to do a variety of dances, mixing nationalities, line/couple/set dances, fast/slow dances, easy/hard dances, etc., or it wasn't a good night. Now you young whipper-snappers come along with your new-fangled notions of doing one dance at one speed for 15 or 20 minutes! (Warren, EEFC list, July 17, 1995)

A successful IFD teacher had to develop a sense of pacing, treating, in a sense, the whole evening as a long piece of choreography, adjusting and responding to the energy level of a group, and building up the excitement level over the course of a class. In this respect, it mattered less where exactly a dance was from than how it related to the previous one. The highly choreographed two- to four-minute dances "are of most interest to the widest (but certainly not all) number of folk dancers, and 4 minutes is short enough to allow an evening of international dance to include a lot of variety. In addition, many dancers really do like the complex choreographed dances and actually do get bored with doing 3 hours of basic pravo and lesnoto" (Rick, EEFC list, July 17, 1995). Focusing on the folk dances and music of a particular cultural group or region was, for many, an unreasonable act, but the popularity of kolos would not diminish but flourish in the coming decades.

Since the late 1970s and early 1980s IFD has been unable to regain its former cohesiveness and attract new adherents as it once could. It both contributed to the growth of, and lost membership to, many emerging specialty scenes. There are, however, people who specialize in Balkan dance, for example, but continue to attend IFD events or to cross over into several different specialty scenes. Some people will attend both Hungarian and Scandinavian classes and camps, while others are involved in both contra and Balkan dancing. Balkan dances remain in the IFD repertoire to this day, but from this point forward changes and developments within the IFD movement will be mentioned only in passing as we turn our attention to the Balkan scene, which by the late 1960s was unmistakably becoming a scene in its own right.

9

The Rise of the Balkan Scene

Most participants in the contemporary Balkan music and dance scene date its origins to the hippie days of the 1960s and 70s, the jumping-off point for this chapter. A number of factors, in addition to its regional focus, distinguish the scene from its IFD roots. One of the most important developments was an interest in music for its own sake, and in learning to play and sing. Early Balkanites learned from records, figured things out collaboratively, put together ad hoc bands using available instruments, and went in search of teachers from the Balkans. While much of this activity was focused on providing live music for dancing, vocal music, previously of peripheral interest, found its own adherents, especially in the American women's movement. Americans came to Balkan folk music and dance through a variety of channels and with a variety of interests. Newly created organizations including the Balkan Arts Center and Eastern European Folklife Center became focal points for this diversity and provided the scene with logistical support and a degree of stability. Finally, we will trace the evolution of the Balkan camps and the steady expansion of genres and cultures embraced by them and otherwise represented in the scene.

The Balkan Music Scene Is Born

With the rise of the large ensembles and increased availability of excellent recordings, it wasn't long before a whole new category of performing group emerged: bands comprised of mainstream American musicians, mostly from the folk dance scene, performing various regional and national genres of music from the Balkans, largely on traditional instruments. As Larry Weiner said of the early American dance troupes, "If you have a performing group you do not want to have people in costumes dancing to records." Orchestras, which originally consisted entirely of classical music instruments, began to include traditional instruments from the Balkans. Stewart Mennin, an early member of the Aman orchestra, explained how the musicians would pick an instrument and then get tapes and records from which to learn the repertoire. "Around 1968–69 we were all fooling around on *gaidas*, *kavals* . . . I taught myself how to play *zurna*." By this

time many students had begun to search for teachers of these instruments, either going abroad or scouring immigrant communities. This was a far cry from the approach of the Victor Military Band, Michael Herman's Orchestra, or even the Banat Tamburitza Orchestra (**CD 4**). It is to this time in the mid to late 1960s that many of the people I met at the Golden Festival in New York more than two decades later traced the origins of a bona fide Balkan music and dance scene, the "village" that would become a home to so many. One of the most important features distinguishing the Balkan scene from its IFD roots was its growing and vital musical component.

Learning Balkan Music

"When Dennis Boxell came with recordings of gaida and zurna, it was a completely new sound!" remembers Yves Moreau. Such new recordings generated the initial fascination that led many folk dancers to try to master the styles themselves. Moreau (1990: 114) noted "the ever-growing accessibility to resource persons and material—as well as the increasing disenchantment of dancing to recorded music" as determining factors in the evolution of the Balkan music scene. Folk dancers had discovered the advantage of dancing to live music through attending ethnic community events or festivals featuring musicians from these communities. These ethnic ensembles would sometimes include members from other backgrounds when the need arose, but such collaboration had nothing like the motivational impact on the Balkan music scene that recordings and travel did. Travels to the Balkans gave many folk dancers a better understanding of the connection between music and dance and enabled them to feel the give and take between musicians and dancers. "I was on another level now," Moreau said. "I was on a high, and went through a withdrawal when I came back home. I did not wanna go to a church basement to dance with records."

Unlike the development of the folk dance scene, marked by prescriptive and normative teaching in groups surrounding a central authority figure, the early development of the Balkan music scene was characterized by a type of peer "instruction" described to me as "the deaf leading the deaf." Experimentation with Balkan tunes on familiar Western classical instruments was among the first steps, followed by the transfer to traditional Balkan instruments when circumstances permitted. Mark Levy's recollection of joining the group Balkanske Igre at the University of Chicago illustrates the exploratory nature of this process: "someone had a gaida that did not work. And I remember just sitting around in this room and we were all trying to figure out where to blow it . . . Somebody started learning tapan. Somebody made their own tapan just from seeing pictures. Somebody played clarinet. I got a *frula* from somewhere. . . . So, gradually we got live music going." The bands were often formed ad hoc with any available instrumentation. The musicians were, as a rule, self-taught, needing to figure out for themselves even how to get a sound out of some of the instruments they had acquired. "We were really awful, we were so

awful," recalls Levy. "I mean, these people [in contemporary camps] are so spoiled here having teachers. God! We were just trying to teach ourselves . . . We had no models, just recordings. We imitated the records."

Learning from records is the method of choice for many in the rock and roll generation, as well as a convenient, inexpensive alternative to lessons. And in the absence of a teacher, it was often the only choice. The aural, exploratory nature of this process is part of its challenge and appeal. An important difference between the early American Balkan musicians and their successors is that the later group had opportunities to see the instruments being played live and to get crucial tips from players, even if they did not engage in formal training.

One of the most influential bands in the early development of the Balkan music scene was Pitu Guli, co-founded and directed by Mark Levy **(CD 6)**. Levy had moved from Chicago to Los Angeles in order to be in this Balkan folk dance hot spot, and there he joined the Aman ensemble, from which Pitu Guli emerged.

> In Aman they had tamburica orchestras and they had orchestras of Western instruments, but we were getting so involved with traditional instruments . . . I fell in love with the bitov ensemble—really, with these recordings of the Strandzanskata Grupa from Radio Sofia. I loved how everybody was playing pretty much the same melody. I loved the bitov sound, and since there was no opportunity to get Aman to play this music we just formed our own group. (Levy, Interview, 1997)

According to Mark Levy, Pitu Guli "just evolved": "Lauren Brody, who was then playing gudulka, said, 'Why don't we try to play together?' So we tried it and it was so much fun." From this spontaneous beginning Pitu Guli[1] "became quite a phenomenon in the folk dance scene in California," attracting a large following of folk dancers excited about dancing to live music. "When we started it was 100 percent recordings. We hated the two minute twenty-six seconds folk dances. It was snobbish in a way, but we really looked down on the way international folk dancing and Balkan folk dancing was . . . with recordings and everything" (Levy, Interview).

Pitu Guli's approach and energy made the band a welcome musical counterpart to the young college Balkan dancers. The band made it possible for them to dance Balkan dances for an entire evening and stay in the groove of a single dance for as long as the mood lasted. As a band of Americans playing traditional instruments for folk dancers, rather than backing a big dance ensemble, it filled a void and served as a model for many of the bands that would mushroom throughout the country in the 1980s.

Pitu Guli's East Coast counterpart was Novo Selo, a band from Philadelphia that played primarily Macedonian "izvorno" music for folk dancing (figure 9.1). Eran Fraenkel formed Novo Selo in 1970 with Jim Finn, Dan Kollar, and Alan Zemel. Novo Selo band members had also started by learning from records. "I'd been listening to his [Mile Kolarov's] record-

Figure 9.1. Novo Selo (from *Traditions* 1975)

ings of Berovka and Ratevka on the Folkraft records for years. In fact, I played those two cuts so often that my parents wanted to chuck me and the record player . . . out of the house," recalls Fraenkel (in Shochat 2001: 3). Soon Fraenkel traveled to Macedonia where he studied with well-known kaval and gaida player, Mile Kolarov. In 1974 the band undertook a novel project, bringing Kolarov to the United States for a year to study with him as, effectively, a musical guru. Novo Selo, with its expertise in Macedonian folk instruments, was a complement to Pitu Guli, with its expertise in Bulgarian folk instruments. This was part of Mark Levy's motivation in creating the first bi-coastal Balkan Camp in 1977.

The simultaneous, largely independent "figuring out" and experimentation with Balkan musical forms, vocal and instrumental, was taking place primarily within folk dance circles, although there were important exceptions. There were many points of contact between Balkan music and American society, providing opportunities for people to find their own paths to the music. International choirs and singing societies, the folk song movement, workers' union songbooks, Jewish leftist choirs, and others included some sort of Eastern European and Balkan material in their repertoire. The many intersections and overlaps between dance ensembles, ethnic groups, folk dance enthusiasts, and musicians who had somehow run into Balkan music, included considerable circulation of both repertoire and people between groups. Although the position of international folk dance had long been essentially apolitical, other points of intersection between Balkan music and American culture happened largely within the political left. In the folk music movement of the 1950s and 60s, for example, groups like "The Weavers" and the "Pennywhistlers" included

Yugoslavian and Bulgarian songs in their repertoire. Balkan dance tunes had enjoyed considerable popularity for some time, but this was an early exposure for many in the folk world to vocal music from the region.

The Challenge of Balkan Vocal Styles

The development of Balkan vocal music in the United States is probably most closely tied to the pioneering work of Ethel Raim and, beginning somewhat later, the group Ženska Pesna. Unlike the majority of leaders within the Balkan music scene, Ethel Raim (b. 1936) did not come to it through folk dancing.[2] Being of Eastern European Jewish background and growing up as a "red diaper baby," a child of communist-leaning parents, Ethel was "brought up on Piatnitsky Chorus." To these Soviet records, acquired at the back of New York's Stanley Theater where Soviet films were screened, Ethel attributes the feeling of "connection to women's voices and three- or four-part harmonies." As a child she also attended left-wing Jewish summer camps, where "there was a lot of emphasis on folk music, American, Russian and Yiddish songs." Perhaps not surprising due to the large Jewish presence in the Balkan scene, Ethel was only one of a number of people I interviewed who mentioned a connection between growing up with Jewish internationalism and a later gravitation to Balkan music.

Before hearing Balkan music, Ethel was already a performer, singing a predominantly Russian, English, and Yiddish repertoire with three other musicians as The Harvesters. Given her surroundings it was almost inevitable that she would hear a Balkan recording at some point, and her first encounter was "a powerful experience": "In 1959 I met Michael Janusz in California. He played for me the Angel recording that he picked up in England. It was the recording of Kutev ensemble . . . The song I latched onto was 'Teodora Is Dozing' (*Polegnala e Todora*). I melted. It was so beautiful." The intensity of this experience compelled Ethel to transcribe the words phonetically and teach the song when she got back to New York. "All I needed is four females, I would teach them the parts and we would sing it."

Numerous people had quite similar experiences, being so moved by their first hearing of a Balkan song that, to the best of their ability, they transcribed the lyrics and music and found people with whom to sing them. The many accounts we heard of seemingly unconnected people around the country responding similarly to these musical encounters raises interesting questions about the physical, cultural, and psychological conditions that lay the groundwork for such occurrences. In this case, the event itself was obviously made possible by the existence of a particular recording and traveling in circles where it might be encountered. But also the space for this type of response to music had to be created in one's consciousness. A complex network of cultural practices and ideas about music must have, to a degree, conditioned people to respond actively to a musical experience, attempting to recreate it rather than simply receive it. Both

popular culture epiphany and personal serendipity often result from a cultural object (a song, for example) appearing to be the missing piece of a puzzle—the thing that connects seemingly unconnected thoughts and experiences.[3] The existing jagged, cultural puzzle pieces are often in the periphery of our thinking until foregrounded by something that has just the right shape to suggest (or compel, as it is sometimes felt) the proper alignment to form a clear picture. Thus, whether the missing link is Nirvana's "Smells Like Teen Spirit" or "Mystère des Voix Bulgares," the result is a personal sense of discovery for those people with enough of the right existing pieces; and a ripple effect is felt through the culture, proportionate to the size of the initial "splash" and the prominence of the segment of society in which the splash initially took place.

In retrospect, Ethel would find the Pennywhistlers'[4] performances of Bulgarian songs stylistically "pretty thin," a result of her having "had no firsthand experience with Balkan music." She was guessing, like Stewart Mennin, Mark Levy, Eran Fraenkel, and many others around the country who were trying to solve the "mysteries" of Balkan music.

The realization that it was within the reach of Americans to "solve" these mysteries came as a revelation. Ethel describes the significance of hearing an American woman sing the opening line of the "Ladarke" arrangement in 1964 at the Ashgrove:

> Being face to face in the same room made the difference between hearing something on the recording and feeling it internally. Realizing that it is well within my *physiological grasp* . . . I got on the parking lot and I started letting loose and to my amazement there was this whole resource of sound that I never knew was there. . . . It was important that that woman, Katie, was an American, that it is within our reach.

The concern with physiological differences between Americans and peoples of the Balkans is more frequently expressed in discussions of vocal music even to the present day, but instrumentalists did not spare themselves from this concern. Tim Rice (1994), for example, wittily writes of the "Mystery of Bulgarian Fingers." The "nature/culture" dichotomy is often brought to the forefront in situations of cross-cultural borrowing. The thought that "it is within our reach" articulates a realization that vocal production, like body language, is culturally based, and learned rather then inherited. Ethel considers this moment of realization a turning point in her career, and she began to focus on emulating the sound of the music rather than just the tunes.

An opportunity to see the Kutev Ensemble perform in New York in 1964 and to meet and interview its director further expanded Ethel's horizons. Not long after this meeting she embarked on her first trip to the Balkans to attend the 1965 Koprivštica National Folk Festival in Bulgaria, where she was exposed to a variety of singing styles. These formative experiences opened the door for Ethel's career in teaching Balkan singing: "In 1967 Bill Vanaver had come to me and said, 'Would you teach a group of us

how to sing like that?' That's the first time I did a Balkan singing class, even though I was trying with the Pennywhistlers to get people to shift their vocal production. But those were rehearsals, not teaching. So I started in Philadelphia in 1967 with Bill Vanaver."

Although Ethel was not a folk dancer herself, she met a need for singing instruction within folk dance circles. Soon after the workshops in Philadelphia, she began teaching throughout the country, especially on the East Coast. Workshops were organized and advertised completely by word of mouth. "In 1969 Martin [Koenig] asked me to do the vocal workshop in New York (that was the first one in New York). I had about a hundred people in the workshop. . . . All those songs that I taught in those early days . . . spread like wildfire throughout the country."

Ethel was teaching "two to three classes a week up to 1977 or so," and it appears that, to that point, no one had taught Balkan singing in the United States as extensively. Part of the depth of her work's imprint on Balkan vocal music in the United States came from her thoughts on teaching. She encouraged students to look internally for the very qualities they recognized in the music, and to use their study of Balkan vocal styles as an opportunity to learn about themselves, their own voices and cultural bias as well. In this respect her teaching and legacy have involved not only imparting new repertoire but offering new perspectives on being and sounding, which many of her students speak of as musically enlightening and even therapeutic.

Balkan Song and the American Women's Movement

A distinguishing characteristic of Balkan music is that it is primarily gender specific, most repertoire being clearly marked as male or female. While the dancing and singing of Balkan men, for example, appeared to Americans to emphasize or augment culturally accepted "masculine" qualities, Balkan female vocal polyphony seemed to suggest a set of values clearly contrary to American ideals of femininity. When this singing reached American soil through the *Mystery of Bulgarian Voices,*[5] touring ensembles like Kutev or Lado and other sources, it made a powerful impression, particularly on many female listeners. The "interest in Balkan women's songs," as Yves Moreau (1990: 114) notes, "became especially popular in the wave of the women's liberation movement of the seventies." Many women I interviewed spoke of the intensity of experiencing a Balkan song for the first time. "It makes the hair stand up on my arm still," said Katherine in our interview.

Recognizing the vocal power, musical tightness, and female bonding evidenced in these songs, many women welcomed the contrast to the aesthetic values dominant in the American mainstream. It was a revelation to some listeners.

> It was very exciting to hear women's singing, strong voices like that, and at that time it was a big deal to hear women using grown-up

women's voices, not that little girl suffocated, subservient women's voice. It was out there, real strong, beautiful dissonance, beautiful rhythm, it was so exciting, and lively, and fresh. (Cathy, Interview, 1997)

The women's movement led American women to seek out specifically female artistic expressions, especially those that seemed consonant with the ideals and images of women's identity that was emerging at the time.

This was in the days of early feminism. Women were discovering their voice at that time. This was a vehicle that did not say feminism on it, but it was a way to discover your voice, some power through the use of voice and again it was about taking up space. This music is very loud and it is not done with amplification. So, discovering that you can make that much sound with your voice does empower women! And, especially if there are feelings of fear, once you learn how to make that level of sound you can feel less afraid. (Louise, Interview, 1996)

There could hardly be a more striking contrast between two cultural understandings of the same phenomenon. In rural areas of the Balkans, the aesthetic value of the strength exhibited in loud singing is tied not to women being powerful or speaking their mind, but is part of demonstrating strength, endurance and a capacity for the hard labor demanded by patriarchal village life. Yet, through the agencies of global travel and "code switching" (Slobin: 1979),[6] music that expresses patriarchal societal values in one culture became, in another, a means of resisting patriarchy and expressing women's liberation.

In any case, in the United States a loud, strong woman was neither the norm nor the aesthetic ideal. Loud "dissonant" singing by women was widely received as a form of resistance. As an alternative singing style, Balkan singing enabled many women to make a statement of empowerment. Cathy, who has always been a singer, found this style "so strong for a woman. First of all, as a grownup, I feel there is a place for my voice . . . and I do feel women need to be heard, and I just don't think they are heard often enough, loud enough, clear enough, or respectfully enough . . . And this music helps bring that out" (Cathy, Interview, 1995).

American women have found Balkan vocal styles attractive on more than one level. Ethel Raim explained that, for her, the attraction was in its "affinity for women's voices." Some women felt that "a great sense of injustice . . . addressed in these songs" spoke to them personally and provided a vehicle that otherwise would be lacking for expressing feelings of grief or pain (Group Interview, Becky, 1994). For Lauren, singing women's songs "was not a political statement. . . . For me it was *not* about the fact that this is women's music. It was the music as a whole that I related to." Angela Rodel, leader of the UCLA choir "SuperDevoiche" and a recent Balkan music convert, recognized in this music the same strength and directness

she heard in punk-rock (Interview, 2004), an association with popular music unthinkable to some older Balkanites. Perhaps recognizing some of the same qualities, Ethel Raim brought to my attention what she felt was another important aspect of Balkan singing styles that has contributed to their popularity among American women:

> When I was growing up we were taught to connect to an overlay of sound. It is cosmetic, it's not about "put out who you are," but "censor it immediately and make it sound pretty," which is so destructive. . . . What I hear in this music [is] presence, honesty. . . . There is nothing covered up, no makeup. . . . It can be falsetto, it can be full-voice singing, it does not matter. It has to do with connection, presence, groundedness.

Although Americans' first connections with the music were primarily through stage presentations or records, in traditional contexts Balkan music is not oriented toward performance. Despite its volume, Balkan women's singing is generally introverted, the singers' attention directed not toward listeners, but toward the other women partaking in the song. The realization of Balkan songs in two- or three-part harmony, especially in unmetered songs, demands great interpersonal concentration and silent communication between singers. Many American women who have been active in Balkan song have stated that the consequent female bonding is one of the best outcomes of their involvement with Balkan music.

Whatever attracted them to Balkan songs, there are numerous female singing groups throughout the country, ranging from trios to large choirs, that devote much of their time and energy to the music. There is a distinction between groups reproducing the repertoire of the big state folkloric ensembles and those devoted to village repertoires, learned either from commercial recordings, in the "field," or from field recordings made by group members. Pioneering groups in the American tradition, such as Danica in the San Francisco Bay area and Ženska Pesna in New York, were followed by many others who were directly or indirectly influenced by them. Aman chorus in Los Angeles spawned many later Californian groups, Danica being one of them. Several members of Ženska Pesna were directly influenced by Ethel Raim through her singing workshop in New York. Formed in New York in 1970,[7] Ženska Pesna was one of the first vocal groups devoted to village repertoire rather than choral arrangements; their early work teaching at Balkan camps and workshops contributed to their becoming one of the most influential groups in the country at the time **(CD 6)**. Women's choirs such as the Yale Slavic Chorus (formed in 1969), Kitka (1979), and Libana (1979) are devoted primarily to public performance of arrangements of Balkan music either self-made or borrowed from state folk ensembles **(CD 7)**. These groups and many others like them developed, and continue to exist, largely outside the Balkan music and

dance scene, although there is crossover in membership, repertoire, and approach.

Balkan Arts Center

The first American institution devoted to Balkan music and dance was the Balkan Arts Center (BAC), founded in 1966 by Martin Koenig in New York. An avid folk dancer, Martin began his teaching career in the early sixties in New York.[8] Also a dedicated researcher, he traveled extensively through the Balkans with a tape recorder and movie camera, returning with numerous reels of audiotape and film that he often uses in lectures. He has also recorded numerous 45 rpm and LP records of folk dances from places including Bulgaria, Romania, and East Serbia. His dance classes and parties in New York's Casa Galicia and elsewhere formed a Balkan dance hub on the East Coast in the early seventies, and provided an alternative or complement to Michael Herman's gatherings. The BAC was also the site of the first separation of Balkan material from the general IFD repertoire on the East Coast.

Martin Koenig's vision for BAC was quite different in many regards from Herman's Folk Dance House. Expressing a desire to build bridges between Balkan immigrant communities around New York and the American folk dance enthusiasts who were enchanted by Balkan dance, BAC offered a series of programs designed to reach out beyond the folk dance community. Similar ideas had been oft expressed in other situations, but they were rarely thought through seriously or brought to fruition.

In 1973, Ethel Raim joined Koenig as the co-director of BAC. Together, Raim and Koenig were among the first to make a concerted effort to understand the cultural context of Balkan music and dance. In addition to fieldwork in the Balkans, they turned to immigrant communities in America for a deeper understanding of their expressive forms. Koenig was perhaps the first dance teacher on the East Coast to teach with live music, inviting musicians from immigrant communities to play for dance events. Fliers for these occasions were printed in several languages in addition to English, targeting immigrant audiences. Several versions of the advertisements were printed, written in Macedonian, Serbo-Croatian, Greek, Albanian, or Bulgarian, and advertising musicians from the respective communities.

The professional partnership between Ethel Raim and Martin Koenig resulted in countless projects, including frequent research trips, recordings, articles, films, lectures, and festivals organized in various parts of New York City.[9] For several years in the 1970s the BAC published the magazine *Traditions* that, with its well-researched, well-written articles, exceeded in quality other publications in the folk dance world of the time. The Balkan Arts Center was renamed the Ethnic Folk Arts Center in 1981, and has been operating as the Center for Traditional Music and Dance since 1998,[10] the name changes reflecting a move beyond a specifically Balkan focus.

The Road to Balkan Camps

While bands were being organized to play Balkan traditional music in many American cities prior to this, the musical side of the Balkan scene did not take the shape of a national movement until the formation of the Balkan music and dance camp in 1977. Largely the creation of Mark Levy, the camp did not evolve overnight. Previously, Levy and his band Pitu Guli had been responsible for organizing the first Balkan music classes tied to the scene. As a graduate student in ethnomusicology at UCLA, Mark Levy was asked to direct the university's Balkan ensemble. This turned into a group project also involving other Pitu Guli members, and these first classes in Balkan music formed the groundwork for the subsequent organization of the camps.

> Of course, what I wanted to do is teach people gaida, kaval, gudulka . . . I was very narrow actually, I was just obsessed with these Bulgarian instruments; I wasn't even into Bulgarian singing. . . . I had a lot of help from my friends. They just came to do it for free because they loved doing it, and we took over the whole music school—in one room one friend of mine was teaching kaval, in another somebody was teaching gaida, in another tambura, in another tapan. . . . And we kept expanding; in one room there would be beginning kaval, in another room intermediate kaval, in a third advanced . . . It was like a miniature camp.

In the early 1970s Pitu Guli began giving workshops and weekend Balkan music and dance retreats at Sweet's Mill (near Fresno, California), with live music provided by the band. Several people I interviewed remember these retreats vividly as some of the most exciting experiences of their youth. The combination of a remote setting and traditional Balkan music and folk dancing was so conducive to imagining the experience of rural life that the line between everyday life and the imagined village was sometimes blurred:[11]

> At Sweet's Mill one year a tapan player got married. And we all got up in Macedonian costumes and we set up the camp so that this was the bride's house and this was the groom's house. And there were some knowledgeable people there. Bob Leibman was a folklorist with an academic degree. So, we recreated one weekend a Macedonian wedding, and it was pretty much from people's fieldwork. Bob Leibman spent a lot of time at this one village and we sang the songs from that village. It is fascinating isn't it? We created a Balkan village. (Levy, Interview, 1997)

Although dance instruction was offered, these weekend retreats were, at first, set up as dance parties with live music. The first weeklong workshop was organized in 1974.

> One year the owner [of the Sweet's Mill camp] was telling me about these weeklong workshops sponsored by the University of Santa Cruz. He asked me: 'How would you like to have a week-long Balkan music

and dance workshop?' . . . So, that's how the camps started. It was 1974 at Sweet's Mill, and all we taught was gaida, gudulka, kaval, tapan, and singing. Somehow I got all these instruments to bring and lend out. . . . It was fairly small, seven or eight staff and maybe fifty people. It was for credit, so we had more lectures. I gave basic talks on Balkan music and culture. Bob Leibman taught dance, Ethel Raim taught singing. (Levy, Interview, 1997)

There was another weeklong workshop in Sweet's Mill in 1975. A group of Balkan folk dancers from Humbolt State University in Arcata, California, was inspired by the first Sweet's Mill camp and decided to organize a weekend camp of their own in the summer of 1975 called "Balkan Village Camp." "We wanted a more intimate 'village' atmosphere than that at Sweet's Mill; something to match our own laid-back rural style and nothing like the 'scheduled' approach of Stockton or Kolo," recalls Kim Wollter (2001: 6). Along with the dance instruction provided by Dick Crum and Bob Leibman, Alex Eppler provided live music on gaida and kaval. In 1976 another Balkan Village weekend was held in Mendocino, but this time with Pitu Guli as the house band. These two groups joined their efforts in 1977 in organizing the first Balkan Music and Dance Camp at the Mendocino Woodlands, California. "Mark and friends were in charge of organizing all the teachers, musicians, etc. HFF [Humbolt Folkdance Factory] was in charge of running the camp" (Wollter, 2001: 7). Mark Levy's original vision for the camps was that they would embrace an educational element, but would also serve as gathering places for Balkan music enthusiasts far and wide. It was during the first weeklong Mendocino camp in 1977 that this vision was realized. It is now par for the course for people and groups to come from all over the United States and even from abroad, but at the time this undertaking was quite novel: "Novo Selo was invited to teach at the Mendocino camp in 1977, and everyone wondered, 'Would it work?' I mean, East and West Coast musicians were about as different as East and West Coast anything. I remember Alan Zemel wondering if he'd arrived on a new planet when we got to Berkeley" (Fraenkel, in Shochat 2001: 13).

As Pitu Guli became known in the scene, they began to connect with other groups, including Ženska Pesna and Novo Selo. All shared a strong preference for village repertoire, great respect for the traditions the music was stemming from, and a studious approach to both learning and teaching the material. These three groups comprised the teaching staff at the first Balkan camp in 1977, an event which has taken place annually in the Mendocino Woodlands ever since.

The Eastern European Folklife Center and the Growth of Balkan Camps

With the increasing prominence of the Balkan scene and the popularity of camps, the task of organization grew as well. The East European Folklife

Center was incorporated as a nonprofit organization in 1981, its primary mission being to promote Balkan music and dance in the United States and to facilitate running of the annual camp. The organization, currently based in Berkeley, California, is run by a board of directors and a full-time general manager, at the time of this writing Rachel MacFarlane. The board of directors currently numbers seven people, and along with a secretary, treasurer, and board liaison, it has administrative, long-range planning, publicity, development, scholarship, and program committees. The EEFC is funded primarily through workshop tuition, membership fees, and tax-deductible donations at the annual camp auction, as well as occasional grant support.[12] The fact that organization members are joined by a common interest rather than ethnicity poses an interesting difficulty in acquiring grants. Most grant agencies operate on an ethnic preservationist model and do not usually fund projects in which people participate in something beyond the boundaries of their own ethnicity and cultural heritage. The longevity of this model is perhaps questioned by the nation's changing needs and realities, but currently it constitutes a considerable funding obstacle for the EEFC and groups like it.

The EEFC exists largely due to the efforts of Mark Levy and Carol Silverman (figure 9.2). Levy's original conception of the EEFC was an institution with its own building, with year-round classes, concerts, and other events. This dream first took physical shape at the 1977 Mendocino Balkan camp. An East Coast camp was also started on Levy's initiative with help from David Bilides and Henry Goldberg, long-time Balkan music and dance aficionados, who were at the time in the Boston-based band Evo Nas. The first East Coast camp was held in 1983 in Ashokan (New York). It moved to Buffalo Gap (West Virginia) in 1986, Ramblewood (Maryland) in 1994, Mount Washington (Massachusetts) in 2003, and Iroquois Springs (New York) in 2005. A third camp, the weekend-long Balkanalia, was added in 1997 in Oregon.

From the 1977 Mendocino camp's original seven or eight instructors teaching primarily dance and bitov ensemble, by 1997 the camps had grown to include over twenty teachers offering over forty different classes at each weeklong camp. Along with formal instruction each camp now offers several hour-long folklore talks by staff members, organized group sings, and nightly concerts and dance parties featuring multiple performers, held both in the dance hall and in the kafana until the early morning hours.

As the camps have grown, their structure and organization have also changed over the past twenty-five years. Mark Levy noted campers' growing interest in gaining an understanding of the cultural context as well as in learning the music and dance material thoroughly. An increasing percentage of camp attendees are performers who are trying to optimize their time at camp to expand their repertoire and learn new skills. Many campers expect not simply an opportunity to learn some Bulgarian, Bosnian, or Greek music but to be able to delve into very specific regional styles such as Thracian singing, Rhodope gaida playing, women's songs of the Bosnian highlands, or Pontic Lyra.

Figure 9.2. Mark Levy and Carol Silverman, Mendocino 1997

The increase in camp attendance is sometimes viewed as a mixed blessing. On one hand it has contributed to there being well-attended classes in even the most "obscure" repertoire, large parties, and a tremendous choice of classes and activities. On the other hand, the camps' growth has left some with a feeling of a loss of social cohesion. "You cannot know everybody when there are three hundred people walking around," Melissa pointed out. "The communal feel is very different now in camps. The camp is much more organized now . . . but there used to be much more physical intimacy. . . . Now they have part-timers, strange faces popping out in the middle of the week. It is a stranger in the village! Who is this person?" (Interview, 1995).

There is a great deal of nostalgia for the early camps and the tight bonds that would develop over the course of the week. As there were many fewer classes, most of the campers would be involved together in the same activities throughout the week. "We were all in the same place all the time" (Levy, in Lancaster 2000/2001: 6). In more recent camps it is possible for campers to have completely different experiences and perhaps not even see each other at all during class times. "The first few camps were such a high, so ecstatic, so exciting, such heart opening, such closeness between the campers. Some of the old-timers have this feeling of family which is what it was, very close-knit family . . . you have at least sat or danced next to, or shared something, or sang with each person" (Nada, Interview, 1997). It is perhaps this nostalgia for the early camps that led to the addition of the third annual EEFC camp, balkanalia!, billed as an "ultimate marriage between the manic energy of the week-long summer camps and blissfully drowsy free time" (Weaver 1997: 6).

In the 1970s most of the campers were of approximately the same age, with similar expectations and desires, which contributed to the bonding experience and feeling of rapport and unity (figure 9.3). Currently, there is a wider range of age groups from children and teenagers to seniors.

There has been a marked, though gradual, increase in the number of "ethnics" in the camp, both as teaching staff and campers or guests,

Figure 9.3. Attendees of the Ashokan camp, 1985 (courtesy of Mark Levy)

contributing to further diversification. At recent Balkan Music and Dance Workshops, approximately half of the teaching staff has been from various Balkan countries, which is a big change from the camp instruction of the 1970s and 1980s, provided primarily by American staff members.

In its beginnings, Balkan camp was a meeting place of two groups of people with somewhat different interests and aspirations; musicians and dancers. Carol Silverman (personal correspondence, 2005) explained that "in the 1970s there was a fairly strong division between recreational folk dancers and musicians. . . . Instrument and singing teachers tended to be more involved in travel to the Balkans and language learning than recreational folk dancers. Through the years, however, more dancers at the camps began participating in instrument and singing classes, and since the 1990s the boundaries between the two groups have become blurred."

The duties of camp organization were gradually transferred from Mark Levy to the EEFC Board. Individual responses to this change range from the positive, in which the development is viewed as a process of democratization, to the negative, in which it is believed that one man's clear vision of the camp has been replaced by too many negotiations and compromises. It is clear that over the years campers' interests became more diverse, creating many tensions that are in turn forcing the board to adjust and to act as a negotiator in disagreements on issues that concern all the EEFC members. The camp's policies and directions are constantly changing and adapting to new circumstances.

A major change in camp organization is perceived in the domain of gender-designated roles. Many people I interviewed, particularly women, expressed dissatisfaction with the uneven treatment of the sexes in the past. It was typical at the early camps for the teaching staff to be "all men . . . except for the women singers. That was considered appropriate, and all the bands were male" (Anonymous, Interview, 1995).

> When they started having evening parties at the camp there was no singing, only instrumentalists and they were only men. Women instrumentalists have been feeling that they have not been treated equally. Even now, the men who are good instrumentalists still do not treat female singers or instrumentalists really well. They made room for them because they kind of had to. There are now all female bands that do not need men to play for them. (Anonymous, Interview, 1995)

"My first three years as a teacher there were miserable," remembers percussionist Polly Tapia Ferber (Lancaster 2003: 5). "I cried a lot. I was the first female instrumental teacher on the stage and I felt I was not accepted or appreciated by the other instrumentalists on the staff. It felt really groundbreaking and heartbreaking." This gender division between instrumentalists and singers reflected divisions in American culture at the time, as has the subsequent emergence and increasing prominence of female instrumentalists and all-female ensembles. Gender issues have hardly been confined to the Balkan scene, as American women playing traditionally

male instruments are even more likely to encounter obstacles in the Balkans. Clarinetist Sonia Seaman, for example, recalls dealing with bias against female clarinetists both at home and in Macedonia and Turkey, where her work with various orchestras required her to convince her male counterparts to take her seriously.

The "big gap between the staff and the campers" is also being ironed out with the camp policy of signing up for kafana slots. At the present-day camp, any performing group can sign up for a twenty-minute set. Collaborations between the staff and campers are also more frequent, with an increasing number of campers with a high level of proficiency as instrumentalists or vocalists. As a former member of the EEFC board explained, "The camp became a friendlier place. We on the board have been working to increase the openness and to create a place where people can feel like this is a fun place to be" (David, Interview, 1995). Generally speaking, the policy of the EEFC has been to emphasize equality between its members, and equal representation of different attitudes and individual perceptions of the role and place of Balkan camps in the lives of its members.

Mark Levy's initial vision was to teach only village repertoire at the camp, the music he perceived as community music. When Pitu Guli started playing Bulgarian music they focused primarily on Bulgarian bitov ensemble. It took Levy many trips to Bulgaria to realize his perspective on the country's musical traditions was "warped": "I regarded this gaida, gudulka, tapan thing as traditional Bulgarian music. I was sort of a snob, uneducated actually. I think I was brainwashed by the Bulgarian party line. . . . They did such a job there in terms of representing these instruments as 'Bulgarian,' and the other instruments as not Bulgarian. I really swallowed all of that" (Interview, 1994).

When Americans heard Balkan music for the first time, they were responding to the very sound of it and were not aware of the cultural/historical/political context from which this sound originated. It is taking time for the scene to begin critically evaluating its sources and understanding that various Balkan countries had their own representations of their "folk." Many Balkan music and dance enthusiasts to the present day are not aware of the differences between the regional village styles and the state representations of the same, although this is changing. "We were in a little bubble back then thinking that we knew about the Balkans in general but we only knew select things from specific Balkan traditions, but, you know, the Balkans also changed along with us. . . . We were not dealing only with our own constraints. We were also dealing with the constraints of the Balkans, of what was available when we went to visit" (Silverman, Interview, 2004).

Changes in the music and dance material presented at camp came as a result of an increased awareness and knowledge about Balkan music generated by people's research and travels to the region. As individuals came back from their research trips in the Balkans they brought the new material to camp. Camp offerings have varied from year to year depending on "who went where and studied what." Carol Silverman recalls her first

research trip to Bulgaria in 1971. She would "identify talented singers from recordings, find their villages on maps, and by hook or by crook, get there. . . . I'd go to festivals and meet people, find out where they lived" (Silverman, in Lancaster 2001: 10).

At first all the music at Balkan camps was acoustic. Only village instruments were used and all the singing was done at after-dinner group sings or at the fire circle rather than at the dance hall. The introduction of amplification to the camps brought change on a number of levels. Carol Silverman recalls that when amplification was used for the first time at the Mendocino camp it changed not only the feel of the camp but also what repertoire could be taught and performed at evening parties. "When we started using amplification all these new genres were introduced" (Silverman, Interview, 2004). At first the repertoire expanded to include many regional styles from throughout the Balkans. It was not until much later that musical styles of minorities, such as Roma, were introduced.[13]

Along with an increased understanding of how various musical genres fit into their native cultures came an awareness of contemporary music genres of various parts of the Balkans, particularly from Bulgaria and the former Yugoslavia. For example, Yuri Yunakov, a Bulgarian Rom folk-jazz saxophonist, and Esma Redžepova, a star Macedonian Rom singer, were some of the additions to the camp staff in the 1990s. However, this does not mean that all music from the Balkans is of interest to the campers. On the contrary, there is an invisible line that holds particular musical expressions from the Balkans "in," and for many it needed to be stretched to include even musicians like Yuri and Esma.

Many have embraced the contemporary styles wholeheartedly, and see them as just another piece of the Balkan music patchwork. But the inclusion of Western instruments and electrified, amplified bands has been met with some resistance because of their disjuncture with ingrained ideas about the "folk" and their music. I am often reminded of a lengthy angry letter I received after a concert of Žabe i Babe in Hartford, Connecticut, in which the author pleaded with me not to "destroy traditional music." While this Balkanite loved our acoustic set he was utterly disturbed that as a "native" I would allow both the use of amplification and "westernization" of my music **(CD 8)**. Certainly, some people just plain love the older music and want to be immersed in it. On another level there is a division between people who are interested in learning and experiencing various Balkan cultures and sounds as they continue to change, and people to whom current Balkan realities are secondary either to their imaginations of the culture, or to their personal needs and preferences. While some Balkanites simply do not like this contemporary, amplified music and are passionately opposed to its presence at camp, others love the music but still perceive camp as a place where primarily traditional musical styles and instruments of the Balkans should be cherished. A former member of the board explained to me:

> The board makes decisions: what will be taught here, what our goals are . . . But we are recreating in some ways a village event, a week-

long festival where we have wonderful times and parties. You can get jazz and fusion, and this speediness stuff in America. . . . But, I think the village stuff is much less likely to survive . . . because there is no economic base to support it.

There are, of course, personal preferences involved here, but the EEFC board is obliged to deal with different demands. In order to accommodate the different attitudes toward the decibel levels at camp the board has decided to provide free earplugs for the evening parties.

The expansion of repertoire at Balkan camp has, perhaps, come full circle with the introduction of a class in which choral arrangements of folk tunes are taught. "Mark was always against having Kutev arrangements at camp because he did not think of it as community music. But in the last few years Tzvetanka Varimezova was teaching polyphonic arrangements at the camp and to me that kind of makes sense in a total expansion of what musics are in the Balkans. The most important thing is to help people understand how this repertoire fits into a total picture" (Silverman, Interview, 2004). One might say that the camp is undergoing its own postmodern moment, reflecting on its own place and act of mirroring the Balkans. The trend toward increasing variety continues, with teachers representing an ever greater range of vocal and instrumental styles and backgrounds.

Dance instruction at camps has been diversifying over the years as well. By now, teachers like Yves Moreau, Steve Kotansky, Michael Ginsburg, Larry Weiner, Joe Graziosi, and many others have effectively brought up thousands of Balkan dancers and introduced them to hundreds of regionally specific Balkan dances. While more people know more dances, the major change in dance instruction and participation at the camp is perceived in the domain of the relationship between dancers and musicians. Looking back at the evolution of dancing at Balkan camps Joe Graziosi, a long-time teacher of Greek dance, saw the typical international folk dancer's mentality "'converted' to the idea that we can all do a simple pravo for 20 minutes and have a great time with the music and learn how to dance with the music, and change our whole style of dance to go with the energy of the music. The other big change I notice is that the musicians who grew up and matured and evolved with Balkan camp, like the musicians in Ziyia—they also became increasingly conscious of the energy that was happening on the dance floor and became, more and more, dance musicians" (Joe Graziosi, *Kef Times* Spring/Summer 2003: 7). This kind of synergy between musicians and dancers contributes greatly to the overall camp experience. At camp, and in the scene in general, the level of musicianship is constantly rising, a precondition of the recent increase in collaboration between even top musicians from the Balkans and American Balkanites. Zlatne Uste, formed after the first East Coast camp in New York, has been growing musically since that time and developing its own sound. The band has played several times in Serbia and, more recently, accompanied Šaban Bajramović, one of the best know Romani singers, in

his summer 2004 concerts in New York. Carol Silverman, one of the founding members of Ženska Pesna, has toured and recorded with both Ivo Papasov and Yuri Yunakov. Yuri Yanakov's band has also included Catherine Foster on clarinet, and Lauren Brody, also a founding member of Ženska Pesna. Beyond making possible such professional achievements, the increasing level of musicianship in the scene is making possible the introduction of musical genres that require a significant degree of experience for students to even begin learning. The virtuosity in some of this music is part of its appeal, and the rather high bar set by many Balkan players is a constant source of awe and inspiration **(DVD 12)**.

Balkan camp is now an institution, and in many ways a unique one. A considerable number of camp attendees have been there since the very beginning, dancing and doing music together for a quarter of a century. The camp continues to serve as a meeting place of like-minded people. The original vision of bringing people from near and far has really come to fruition as many fine Balkan musicians and dancers come to revel in this convergence of people joined by a shared love of Balkan music and dance. "What a wonderful thing we have created out of our obsession with these wonderful musics and dances, and our self-made community. How much happiness can the body hold?" writes Leonora (1998: 4), reminiscing about the previous year's Mendocino camp. For many, Balkan music and dance have become not a thing they do but a thing they live. Like any living thing, the Balkanites' village, with camp at its center, continues to change, responding to the changing needs of the villagers, who are themselves changed by the experience.

10

Conclusion

When Tim Rice, an ethnomusicologist and long-time devotee of Balkan music and dance, responded to my 1997 SEM conference presentation on Balkan music and dance in the United States, he began by asking, somewhat jokingly, "Why didn't you interview me?" Rice, echoing others I did not get a chance to interview formally, suggested that his interpretation of the scene as a whole, as well as his explanations for his own involvement in it, would differ from those I had encountered. I am sure this is the case. Each person might amplify a different aspect of the scene, dismiss another, or perhaps suggest a novel interpretation. There are, of course, as many personal perspectives on the Balkan music and dance scene as there are people involved in it. There is no doubt that each individual could have made interesting contributions to this work, but even if it were possible at any given moment to gather every available interpretation, it would be impossible to contain them all, to hold them under one lid. Even those I *was* able to interview sometimes found that sentiments and thoughts they had expressed were no longer representative of their opinion, or even relevant to them, after several years (or a momentary mood) had passed. Individuals' perceptions and understandings of their relationship to Balkan music and dance, as well as their relationship to the scene in general, are constantly being debated, changed, and redefined. Formulating an answer to one of my many questions involved choosing a position and does not necessarily reflect the uncertainty, tensions, and conflicts between different interpretive possibilities. The nature of language is dialogic; it "requires speakers to locate themselves within a social world and permits even a single individual, speaking without interruption, to enact a multitude of contrasting voices. The shared worlds that emerge from dialogues are in a continuous state of creation and recreation, negotiation and renegotiation" (Mannheim and Tedlock, 1995: 3).

These "shared worlds" that emerged as a result of multilayered "dialogues," verbal and otherwise, were the focus of my work. I have chosen

to elaborate on what appeared to be the thickest overlaps, leaving out of focus many strands of conversation and contexts in which they appeared. Thus, this conclusion and the work as a whole is not to be understood as a closure, but an opening. I have documented some of the continuities and discontinuities, agreements and disagreements involved in more than a century's worth of grouping and regrouping segments of American society around international folk dancing (IFD), and later Balkan music and dance. The fact that Balkan and international folk dance and music was predominantly a matter of choice and affinity on the part of its practitioners resulted in an equally long history of explanations and justifications for the activity and its various applications in American society. This necessity for explanation and validation of involvement in this activity created almost laboratory-like circumstances for research. In many cases ideology was foregrounded, being considered at least as attractive as the music or dance content around which it was built.

Those deeply immersed in the scene are often too close to it to be able to see the viewpoints of others, even their contemporaries, as relevant or even related to their own. Furthermore, it is common for people to see the history of a thing as beginning with their own personal involvement in it. Even among Balkanites who are aware that there is a deeper history, there is often a sense that this history has little or nothing to do with them, with their experience of the scene or their interpretation or understanding of Balkan music and dance. "I do not believe in this history. For me it really all started in the sixties, with the counterculture," was a response to the same SEM paper from another ethnomusicologist and Balkan music and dance enthusiast. Of course, when someone stumbles upon Balkan music and dance he or she is not, and cannot be, suddenly aware of the historical background of the American Balkan scene. But being unaware of these ties does not diminish their importance or cultural relevance. It is unlikely that anyone today would join in a kolo because of John Dewey, William Morris, Mary Wood Hinman, or Elizabeth Burchenal. It would be more likely for someone to dance kolos for decades without ever hearing any of these names. How could one know when joining a dance, Seljančica for example, that it was used in settlement houses, the physical education and recreation movements at the turn of the century, was later danced at the New York World's Fair and later still in the 1960s folk movement, all in the service of different social, political, personal, and national goals? Still, this long history of ideas, practices, and values attached to Balkan music and dance is an aspect of American cultural history that current participants are as much a part of as were the early settlement workers. Individual understandings of the "folk" concept, preconceptions of Balkan cultural values, particular responses to unfamiliar music, are culturally grounded, and our lack of awareness of our own "preconditioning" demonstrates the depth of this cultural grounding.

The Balkan music and dance scene exists parallel to the numerous IFD groups still in operation throughout the country, the schools that still include folk dancing in their physical education programs, and even a few

settlements that still use the old IFD repertoire. Although currently synchronic, however, each movement represented succeeded the previous as the most significant and public of its day, and each is no longer the same thing it was. Even if something as physical as a book of music is left sitting on a bookshelf in the same house for over a century, every time it's picked up it will mean something different. And yet its meaning is not completely up for grabs—it remains tied to a history, to a place, to the pathways of the people who run into it and to its immanent qualities, however fading and brittle the paper becomes. Obviously the network of people and ideas I've looked at in this book is much more dynamic. Throughout this historical period folk dancing and music, international or Balkan, has proven to be very fluid and adaptable to a range of circumstances and societal demands. But through all the different time periods and applications, even when it appeared that specific practices stand in opposition to each other, common threads were always present.

In each case, for example, community in some form figured importantly. But, while in the first half of the century folk dancing was used to improve geographic communities (neighborhoods), it came to be used for the creation of a different kind of community, one bound by common interest rather than regional belonging. As American culture in general has seen a shift from the importance of community identification to that of individual self-fulfillment, emphasis in IFD and the Balkan scene has shifted from group and national interests like exercising the nation and improving cross-cultural relationships among immigrants to personal fulfillment and the meaning of community to the individuals involved. Another important change is seen in the steady move towards music and dance material gathered through fieldwork, rather than written descriptions provided in folk dance books by various movements' leaders. Differences in dedication, expectation, utilization, and approach to folk music and dance material have also developed, generally in consonance with the country's social and political climate, and the "availability" of resources in both practical and ideological terms. The continuities are perhaps more interesting in light of these changes, particularly in light of the tremendous social, political, economic, and cultural change over the time span documented. Seemingly very different ideologies have become tied together through their employment of folk music and dance in the various contexts described. Some participants found folk music and dance to be "good, healthy, clean and moral activities," while others saw them as an "escape from the corrupted world of commercial, popular culture." Some understood the activity as an expression of a united world, or affirmation of "family values," others as an "end of couplehood" or "empowerment of women and liberation from patriarchy." For some it has been a refutation of industrial capitalism, for others a convenient illustration of its successes.

What could a current Balkan music and dance enthusiast have in common with William Morris, Jane Addams, Luther Halsey Gulick, Henry Ford, Franklin and Eleanor Roosevelt, or even earlier scene members like Michael and Mary Ann Herman? A major locus of this commonality is in

the strong ideological overtones expressed in their shared perceptions of past and present. All these individuals and movements have to some degree idealized the past as peaceful, pastoral, and rural, with strong communal bonds and happiness expressed through traditional forms of music and dance. The "good old days" are juxtaposed with the present, rapidly changing industrial society, technologically advanced, alienating, violent, and suffering from the degenerative influence of mass media and commercialization. Throughout this period, old, traditional, and valuable dances and songs of peasant cultures have been seen as cultural remedies for the shallowness of American culture. Sentiments that are immanently anti-modern, anti-urban, and anti-commercial are at the heart of each incarnation of these songs and dances. It is no accident that the "most peasant" of the IFD repertoire in the 1950s became the most popular, resulting in the "Balkan craze."

However, the whole nexus of ideas and practice surrounding peasant music and dance has been used, not to dismiss urban, industrial modernity, but to help make it livable—to create a comfortable social space within its borders. The individuals and movements we have looked at have not been choosing between urban/rural, industrial/pastoral dualities, but embracing both. The relationship of Henry Ford to folk music and dance is perhaps the ultimate embodiment of this seeming paradox. His advocacy of wholesome activities, family values, and a back to nature lifestyle could hardly contrast more sharply with his own contribution to industrialization, modernization, and the "plasticity" of American culture. Ford used all his might and access to mass media of every kind to promote or impose cultural values of "the folk" and their relationship, or rather application, to "the American." I was astonished to discover that the Duquesne University Tamburitzans (called the "Balkan Artists Troupe" at the time) made a ten-week Midwest tour for the Ford Motor Company in 1933/34 (Kolar 1986:10). It is somewhat puzzling that such a strong advocate of "American" dance and values would sponsor a "Balkan" group. I can only speculate that, to Ford, the group's status as "peasant" and "folk" may have outweighed its Balkaness. Or perhaps he looked favorably on any tradition that appeared to be white and Christian. He was presumably satisfied, in any case, that the group represented values congruent with those he saw in contra dancing, for example, as opposed to those of the urban "black" and "Jewish" world of popular music.

Whether "Balkan" was another color for the international folk dance palette, whether it was seen as simply peasant or folk, it has been understood as rich, deep, old, and valuable. Engagement in international, folk, peasant, Balkan dances was meant to bring one closer to the truth of living. This engagement has often been more about finding the "peasant within" than exploring another culture. Filmmaker, folklorist, and musician John Cohen told me a fascinating story about his parents, who were active folk dancers in the 1940s in New York City. Whenever they would come to a park or a meadow, his mother would take a deep breath and say: "Oh! It smells like Russia." With such statements, combined with the

costumes his parents wore when they took him on their frequent folk dance outings, he grew up convinced that his mother was raised in a Russian village. He felt that his own involvement in folk music and dance was an extension of this family heritage and, as an adult, was astonished to discover that his mother had arrived in the United States as a baby and was probably born in an urban area. But memories of the smell of the green grass of imagination clearly have real meaning—meaning that can travel the generations.

Through what might almost be considered esoteric magic, involvement in folk dances has been thought to bring one closer to the truth, and the essence of humanity. There is little difference in attitude between, for example, Lillian Wald in 1915 and Ronelle Alexander, an avid Balkan dancer nearly sixty years later, who writes:

> We continue our tireless search for what is called in Serbo-Croatian *izvorni* ("from the source, or spring") culture. In this sense we are both anthropologists . . . and simple human beings who have had enough of progress and plasticity and who want to immerse ourselves in something more real, human, earthy, vibrant, in short, izvorni, before it dies out. (1973: 3–4)

This passage is very illustrative of two notions that persist throughout this historical period. The first is that there is something "earthy," "real," and "true" that Americans are missing, and that it is to be found not here, but far away from home, the notion that Americans have lost, through urbanization and modernization, the truth that can still be found in other parts of the world. That truth is to be regained by drawing on the "source," from the "sacred soil," soil uncontaminated by modernity and commercialism. The second notion is that Americans, although they acknowledge that the true, the real, and the earthy is missing from their lives, can still recognize it, and save it from destruction by people who possess it but are unaware of its value.

These ideas have been passed on from generation to generation. As a part of their cultural heritage, certain segments of American society feel like outsiders to "real, true" experience. Longing and seeking for it, they find it in a symbolic culture of the "sacred soil," or more generally of the "peasant past." The nostalgic feelings give to this activity what James Clifford calls "diasporic dimensions." Fascination with the perceived "antiquity" of folk music and dance, always juxtaposed to the "newness" of American culture and its expressive forms, is deeply rooted in the culture. "The old," as I have shown, transcends boundaries of the culture that created it, and becomes equated with the human and natural.

In 1906, emphasizing the social value of folk festivals in Settlement houses and public schools, Rita Teresa Wallach, wrote, "May we not as a nation, young in art . . . receive from the older civilizations a new impetus and a leavening force to that commercialism which too often deprives mankind of its heritage of beauty?" This sentiment was already so famil-

iar in 1877 to the author of "Annals of the New York Stage" that he could sarcastically comment: "We, as a nation of new civilization, are always trying to be like something old; therefore on Feb. 13th, we may hie us for "ye Concert of Ye Nations of Ye Old Time, at Ye Republican Hall, which is set down on ye cross road, between ye Avenue Five and ye broad Pike," termed in these degenerate days 55 West 33rd St." American fascination with things old reaches far into the past, beyond even the nation's birth. Perhaps one of the oldest American traditions is the feeling that Americans have no tradition.

Numerous cultural tropes persistent in the American mainstream, reaching further into the past than the beginnings of the International Folk Dance (IFD) movement, continue to shape individual responses to Balkan music and dance material. We have seen the ways in which many people stumble upon Balkan music and dance and "recognize" something familiar in it. Although most have never seen or heard anything like it, they have clear images of "peasant" culture in general. Representations of generic, anonymous peasants, specifically Balkan, Slavic, or East European ones, are hard to escape in a variety of media from early travelogues, newspapers, and magazines to Hollywood movies. Associations between the Balkan peasant and the natural and mystical can be seen in figures 10.1 and 10.2. Ideas like those represented in the first, a 1924 engraving, are familiar enough in modern popular culture to be lampooned in the second, a cartoon from 1992.

Even if people do not know where the Balkans are or who lives there, they have most likely been exposed to Eastern European character types,

Figure 10.1. Association of the "peasant," the "Balkan," and the "natural" as represented by the "Spring Dance of the Slav Maidens" (from Horne's World and Its People 1924: 1227)

Figure 10.2 VIZ comic (Issue 56 1992, courtesy of John Fardell)

almost always "peasants." Even if one does not know much about Russians, for example, it is quite likely that one does have an image of a man with furry hat and high boots, with hands crossed on his chest and legs kicking left and right. It is enough to glance at posters, fliers, and record covers within the current Balkan scene to realize that "Balkan" means people (or sometimes bears or puppets) dressed in folk costumes, dancing joyfully either on the village square or in some natural landscape (figures 10.3a, b).

A study of visual representation of the Balkans and Balkan folk would certainly be fascinating in its own right. Deeply rooted in romanticism and nationalism, the representation of a nation through images of its "folk" is practiced in the Balkans as well, as is amply illustrated in promotional materials produced for the American tours of the big folklore ensembles (figure 10.4).

Folk motifs, pieces of embroidery, folk costumes, and pictures of non-Western musical instruments give direct visual clues for the viewer to identify the contents of the presented material, whether in a concert, workshop, camp, or on a recording, as Balkan and peasant. Perhaps the dancing bears and marionettes most clearly divert attention from the people and culture

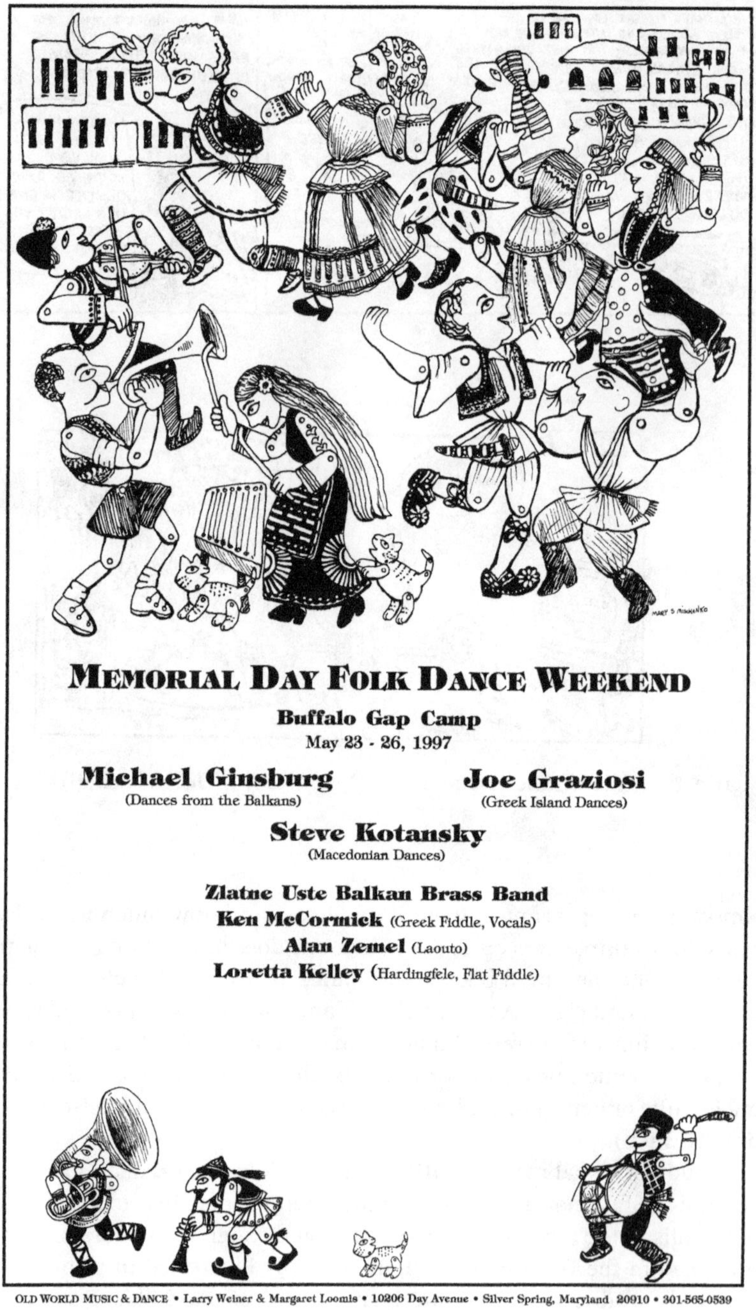

Figures 10.3a, b. Fliers for Memorial Day Folk Dance Weekends (courtesy of Batja Bell)

Memorial Day
Folk Dance Weekend

May 26 - 29, 1995 • Camp Canadensis
(Eastern Pennsylvania)

Georgi Iliev & Jordanka Ilieva
(Bulgarian Šop Village Dances & Singing)

Hector Bezanis	*(Bulgarian Šop Gajda)*
David Bilides	*(Kaval)*
Rachel Johnson	*(Gudulka)*
Petur Iliev	*(Tupan)*

Steve Kotansky
(Vlach & Macedonian Dances)

Walt Mahovlich	*(Clarinet, Accordion)*
Mensur Hatich	*(Accordion)*
Paul Morrissett	*(Violin, Trumpet, Etc.)*
Jerry Kisslinger	*(Tupan)*

Roo Lester
(Scandinavian Dances)

Loretta Kelley
(Hardingfele, Flat Fiddle)

Old World Music & Dance • Larry Weiner & Margaret Loomis
10206 Day Avenue • Silver Spring, Maryland 20910 • 301-565-0539

Figure 10.4. Promotional booklet for "Tanec," a state folk ensemble from Macedonia

represented to the "folkness" of the elaborate peasant costume in which they are dressed.

As in print, on the concert stage of the Balkan scene, folk costumes are the norm. In a most literal way, costumes add color to the performance, and most people I have talked with do not make much of their use on stage. Performers often feel such an outfit is a necessary stage prop—since you cannot perform Balkan music in street clothes or in a tuxedo jacket, why not use beautiful folk costumes. Dressing up, impersonating the other, is part of some people's attraction to the activity. Costumes contribute to the

creation of the "make-believe" world, creating a unique and distinct visual atmosphere. They also help frame the activity, giving it a special place separate from daily life.

"We all have our utopias. Scratch the surface, and we are all striving for something that is beyond our everyday existence," Sonia explained to me in our interview. Ideological issues aside, people are looking for meaning, for a deeper sense of things, for activities that are not mundane. They recognize in Balkan music and dance a powerful artistic expression that is different from any other option in their culture. I can personally relate to perceptions of the music as direct, unpretentious, strong, beautiful, haunting, and visceral. The value given to the music comes in part from the ideological background in which it is contextualized as old, traditional, and proven valuable over centuries, but also from the aesthetic and physical experience of the sound and movement as discussed in chapter 2. In some respects, simply *doing* Balkan music and dance in anything like a customary way encourages attitudes and behavior much like those appreciated within the Balkans. Returning to the girls on Mount Bjelašnica, for example, their vocal polyphony demands close coordination between the singers, focused attention as well as physical and emotional closeness. The bond between singers that sometimes results from musical practice is real and meaningful. Just as dancing in a circle formation, holding each other's hands, moving as one, looking into each other's eyes across the dance floor is an actual, not imagined, joyful social experience. However, through these experiences participants do not "go Balkan," but work to create an artistic outlet and social space for themselves within American culture. Along the road, many encounter and create opportunities to connect with actual people, actual cultures, and actual places in the Balkans. Commenting on over twenty years of playing and directing Zlatne Uste brass band, Michael Ginsburg said, "Commitment to something like this takes you to previously unimaginable places." He has not only traveled with his band four times to Serbia, and partook in Mardi Gras in Brazil, but also played with Esma Redžepova and Ensemble Teodosievski, Šaban Bajramovič, and Zlatni Prsti brass band.

There are many specialty scenes that provide for an alternative music and dance education, enabling people to be actively involved in music-making or dancing, regardless of their age or skills. Segments of American society find there a comfortable social and artistic space, or "cultural home" to use Slobin's (1993) expression. Some of these cultural homes are united under a banner of "folk." For example, Klezmer, Scandinavian, Hungarian, bluegrass, old-time, or Irish music scenes bear much more resemblance to each other than they do to gamelan, African drumming and dance, or Tuvan throat-singing groups. On the other hand, there is much crossover and similarity in organization, infrastructure, and adopted values between various "folk" scenes. An important distinguishing mark of the Balkan scene is the vast and growing number of divergent traditions it gathers under one umbrella, a diversity that is unrivalled even by the global reach of the "world choir" scene.

There are many people one might call "wanderers in affinity" who either cannot or do not want to establish their cultural home in any of the scenes, or perceive them as segments of effectively the same "folk" or "world music" phenomenon. There are people who "build a home" in two or more scenes. Based on my interviews, my impression of the Balkan music scene is that its members frequently cross over into Klezmer, Scandinavian, Hungarian, Middle Eastern (instrumentalists), or Sacred Harp (singers), while Balkan dancers seem to frequent Israeli dances, as well as contra dance and, to a lesser extent, Scandinavian dancing and square dancing. However, a substantial portion of the Balkan music scene is its "hard-core" devotees who, if anything, might only explore related traditions and scenes such as Middle Eastern or Klezmer music. Responses to my inquiries about the choice of the Balkan scene over others included "Klezmer camp is too Jewish for me" (a response from a self-proclaimed WASP); "Israeli dancing was too close to home" (a response from a Jewish man); "nothing else does it for me" (a response from a well-respected musician within the Balkan scene); "Contra dance is just boring, there is no tension there and I don't like the music" (a response from a dancer); "I do contra dancing too, because of that same communal feeling" ; "We do a lot of Sacred Harp singing, it's that same hard edge in the voice" (a leader of a Balkan singing group). Personal preferences are often based on some extramusical aspect of a particular scene, such as feeling a lack of connection with other participants, or feeling it is too serious or competitive. Sometimes, a scene might appear "too ethnic." Even the location of a summer camp can figure in the choice of an affinity group. But for the majority of Balkanites, their scene indeed feels like a cultural home, and they do not find any other to be as aesthetically or socially pleasing.

The Balkan scene is not only a location for crossover with other scenes, but has been influential in generating and influencing them. Klezmer scene participants might not think to look at the relevance of Balkan camps to their music, yet the first "Klez camp" in 1985 was organized by Henry Sapoznik and modeled after the first Balkan camp at Ashokan he had attended the previous year. A Near East camp was also organized by Mark Levy, and 2004 saw the creation of a Balinese music camp, started by Wayne Vitale, director of San Francisco Bay Area-based Gamelan Sekar Jaya, using Balkan camp as a template. The scene has also had an impact on music and dance practice in ethnic communities. For example, Greek Americans followed the lead of folk dancer Joe Kalyonides Graziosi's work with the Orthodox Church and have increasingly introduced previously marginalized regional music and dance into their festivals and dance events.

The scene's relationship to the Balkan region itself generates tension, confusion, and change in the group. Participants often feel a need to explain their lifestyle as well as a need to compare, censor, and evaluate material. They are not seen as such, but issues of preservationism, authenticity, and representation are often more about the Americans themselves than they are about Balkan culture. However, there are actual "live" Balkan

cultures, with live instrumentalists and singers. Village life and community dances actually exist, even if they are harder to find than is usually imagined, and there are real opportunities for firsthand experience of the culture, its music and dance. Even though Americans involved in this activity are not trying to recreate Balkan villages, they are modeling their communities after their personal experiences in the Balkans or village life as they imagine it. Zlatne Uste, again, provides an interesting example. On their first trip to the brass band festival in Guča Serbia, band members experienced a musical intimacy that they found exciting and appealing:

> We went to Guča and there were all these tents set up for the festival. People sit around the tables and they eat and drink, and then the bands come and play around the tables, very close to the people who are listening. And people respond and toast, and lift up their arms. . . . There were these intense social interactions and ways of having fun that were amazing. So, we tried to bring that to the Balkan camp because we liked it. And we found that a lot of other Americans like it. That is why we organize the kafana at the camp. . . . We had to teach people how to tip the musicians, and how to have fun. We also started playing inside the circle, and people loved it. (Matt, Interview, 1996)

Matt describes here how an experience of the home culture of music and dance can stimulate changes in their American incarnations.

For those interested in exploring and discovering new genres, new styles, new teachers, new tunes . . . there are almost unlimited possibilities for "discovery" within the Balkans. A different side of "engagement" with Balkan culture is a desire to bring a "piece" of the Balkans into one's life. One can recognize aspects of the museum mentality in the desire to collect, "to name the objects collected, to order and accumulate, to discover the rare and the new" (Marcus 1991: 10).

The Balkan dancers particularly enjoy naming the dances, using native terms, and accumulating names of tunes, dances, musical instruments, and particular step patterns. Question/answer oriented games often appear in various journals, rewarding this kind of knowledge. A three-page questionnaire to evaluate one's knowledge of international folk dance appears in Duggan, Schlottmenn, and Rutledge, first published in 1946 (1980: 52–55). This example is very illustrative of the type of knowledge appreciated. *The Folk Dancer* also included a section with several questions of this kind with hidden answers. There are over a hundred terms listed in *Balkan Tunes*, Summer 1993, under the text: "Below are some of the words one could use to *describe the musical culture of the Balkans* (emphasis mine). How many of these do you know?" The list contains names of musical instruments, ensembles, and dance and music genres. People take great pride in knowing as many terms as possible, sharing their knowledge with other Balkan dancers and distinguishing themselves from the uninitiated: "You know, folk dancers are like stamp collectors or any other kind of collectors; they want all the paraphernalia that goes along with the dance.

It is a very materialistic way of looking at things, but we live in very materialistic times" (Anonymous, Interview, 1995). I believe one reason people want to gather so much information and material goods from the Balkans is to establish a relationship with the world of their fascination; to make something imagined real through contact with objects and names, tangible and measurable things. It is a phenomenon Lyotard described: "An imaginary world is thus an ensemble of names. These names interlock with other systems (chronological, topographical, etc.) which all contribute to the establishment of the "reality" of a particular imaginary world" (Lyotard 1983: 67). There is a desire to make "the Balkans" something graspable, and preferably portable:

> It was a very common thing for Folk Dancers to buy costumes. Part of it is because they were just so beautiful . . . part of it is just feasting your eyes on them. There was also that "I've been there and here is my evidence" kind of a thing, on everyone's part. It's almost like a badge: "My interest is so serious." There was that kind of mentality. Part of it is the American collecting thing. Part of it is "I want to know," it's a new field of knowledge. And then part of it is utilitarian for performances. (Jane, Interview, 1994)

The desire to accumulate is probably most evident in the hunger for new step patterns, dance tunes, and songs. In this way a certain hierarchy of authority is built into the scene, helping in the establishment of goals and parameters for potential future achievement. In this way and others, one can establish authority, not necessarily above someone else, but in one's own eyes, making it possible to quantify and assess one's own dedication and knowledge.

Concern with the authenticity of music and dance material is another aspect of the need for a means of evaluating one's dedication, knowledge, or authority. This concern goes side by side with preservationism, itself a result of a perception that Balkan music and dance are valuable but vanishing. How should a dance or song be evaluated? What criteria should be used? There is often a lack of trust in one's own judgment and taste, and a desire to find external, extra-musical reasons for liking or disliking a particular musical piece.

The fact that the music is "borrowed" rather than "inherited" makes the process of evaluating and justifying musical choices more complicated. Even in making a musical choice clearly outside of "inherited" options, some people are reluctant to let go of "heritage," looking to concepts including reincarnation to find a genetic tie to the Balkans. Issues of ethnicity and musical choice were made even more complex and given a sense of urgency by the conflict in the former Yugoslavia. In many conversations with Balkanites on this subject I detected a deep belief that culture, at least for Balkan people, is indeed genetic. While the conflict put the region on the map for Americans, it added another level of frustration to the

Balkanites' attempts to explain why they would want to be involved with music from such a place. Many accepted the widespread representation of people from the region as "ethnically" a certain way and concluded that the music of those people must somehow contain elements of that ugliness. For some this meant questioning whether or not they should be doing the music of "bad people." Rather than trying to understand the circumstances, economic, political, and ideological, that led to the war, they came to feel that Serbs and Croats, in particular, were "like this" all along, waiting to betray the American lovers of their music, and to pollute their choice of Balkan music and dance. The following is an excerpt from an interview with a long-time Balkan dancer:

> C It is a very hard thing for me to accept that people who I have cherished and appreciated their background and their attitudes and their lifestyles completely betrayed me. Suddenly there is this aspect of their personality that they were hiding from me. I was so naive. I think I could no longer even *talk* to a Bosnian.
>
> M Well, I am a Bosnian.
>
> C Oh, no, dear, you are an artist.

Perhaps better than anything else the conflict in Bosnia and later Serbia made many Americans realize the implications of cross-cultural borrowing and made them grapple with issues of representation of the other. For many, involvement with Balkan music and dance has been attended by a thirst for a deeper understanding of Balkan cultures, which, for a number of scene participants, has led to academic pursuits in ethnomusicology, anthropology, folklore, linguistics (Tim Rice, Sonia Seaman, Jane Sugarman, Mark Levy, Bob Leibman, Carol Silverman, Ronelle Alexander, to name a few). However, a deep understanding of a culture does not come automatically with even the most precisely executed dance step or sequence of notes, but comes as a result of continued contact and thoughtful engagement with the culture and people. Many in the scene do not realize that they do not love "Balkan people" but their own constructed or "inherited" images of them.

The Balkan music and dance scene has essentially been about the "Balkanites," not about the Balkans—about "us" not about "them." Yet an unwillingness to claim the music and dance as theirs, as in the here and now, prevents many scene members from making the repertoire believable. However true one wanted to remain to the "original" renderings of steps and tunes, this very intention changed the relationship between the individual and the repertoire. Music and dance can never be reduced to notes, rhythms, and step patterns. In any type of cross-cultural learning/borrowing there is by default much that has to be invented in a different cultural context. The very fact that in the United States Balkan music and dance are rather unusual options for artistic expression leads to the

placement of this repertoire in a radically different web of meaning. Meanings, connections, and associations must constantly be discerned, invented, and negotiated within a particular group as well as individually.

Still, despite a wilderness of ideological pitfalls developed over more than a century (preservationism, idealization of "the folk," and the like), there is much to be said for just being around Balkan music and, increasingly, Balkan people and culture. The Balkanites intentional proximity and openness to their chosen music creates space for something that has not happened elsewhere in American culture: seeing the Balkans as an actual place inhabited by actual people. In the West in general "the Balkans" are synonymous with chaos, fragmentation and frenetic action without direction. A suitable metaphor can be found in the example of the Guča festival, in which several brass bands simultaneously play different songs full bore in a small tent. From the outside it appears to be utter chaos (**DVD 13**). But when one assumes the position of an insider, takes a place at one table and commits oneself to the experience, a whole different world of meaning and action opens up (**DVD 14**). This zooming in, getting literally closer, begins to resolve the apparent chaos into understandable human behavior. The resulting intimacy can be thrilling, as well as potentially uncomfortable. This may be additionally true for Americans who, despite their hunger for the closeness of village life, are in many ways quite comfortable with the disconnection and privacy of mainstream America.

While by design and circumstance the Balkan scene is a village that can appear and disappear as is convenient, the longer one spends there the greater the family ties, figurative and actual. Participants have ever more in common with each other as marriages, births, deaths, and other rites of passage become more tied to the scene. They also have ever more in common with Balkan musicians who, in the context of American culture, also find themselves on the fringe. In the Balkan scene they, too, are finding a comfortable place in an alternative mainstream and license to reinvent themselves to a degree. Balkan scene participants, increasingly in collaboration with these Balkan musicians, continue to create a liminal space: a village both real and imagined, in which men can lock arms and sing about yearning love, a woman can comb and braid a friend's hair without attracting attention, and where men and women, young and old can dance and play together on an equal footing. While the imaginative nature of the scene can mask real problems it also creates space for real solutions. Whatever the fictions of its relationship to some village somewhere in southeastern Europe, the Balkan scene, its joys and sorrows, obligations and community ties are very real—more real to many, perhaps, than the American culture that is its deepest cultural wellspring. The richness of what the Balkanites have created and its proven resonance with segments of American society is likely to ensure its continuing vitality well into the future. Those who stumble upon the scene will continue to weave Balkan music and dance into their own lives, social, cultural, artistic and political spheres as they see fit. New generations of "villagers" will surely

find their own reasons and meanings, will have their own needs and vision for maintaining the "village." And, most likely, they will interleave these new ideas and practices with recycled materials and "inherited folk culture" to create an American home of their own design as did the generations before them.

Appendix
Sample Questionnaire
Questionnaire for Balkan Music and Dance Lovers and Practitioners

1. Sex ________ 2. Age _________ 3. Name/phone # (optional) __________
4. Place of Birth____________ State _________ Country ________________
5. Ethnic Background(s)____
6. My highest level of education is_____________________________________
7. My profession is____
8 a. I grew up in:
   1. urban area 2. suburbs 3. small town 4. rural area
   b. I am currently living in:
   1. urban area 2. suburbs 3. small town 4. rural area
9. How many times have you moved from one town to another?________
10. In what states did you live? ____________________________________
11. Did you live abroad longer than three months? __________________
12. Where? ____
13. When and where did you get introduced to Balkan music and dance for the first time? ____
14. How did you get introduced to Balkan music?__________________
15. a. You have started your involvement with Balkan music as a:
    1. dancer 2. singer 3. instrumentalist
    b. Circle the activities in which you are (or have been) involved:
    1. dancing 2. singing 3. playing
16. How many Balkan camps have you attended? ___________________
17. List any Balkan languages you've studied, indicating your level of proficiency. ____
18. Are (were) you a member of a performing group? Yes No
    a. If yes, for how long? ____________________________________
    b. How often do you perform Balkan music? ___________________
    c. Do you ever get paid for performing Balkan music? Yes No
    d. Why do you perform this music? ___________________________
    e. How do you acquire the repertoire. Please list in order of importance. ____
    f. What are your goals as a performer (regarding the material you are working from, as well as the audiences you are presenting it to)? ____

19. Please list three of your favorite recordings of Balkan music.
    a. ______________________________
    b. ______________________________
    c. ______________________________
20. Name three persons that have influenced you the most.
    a. ______________________
    b. ______________________
    c. ______________________
21. What kinds of Balkan music have you studied (Bulgarian, Albanian, Serbian, Bosnian, etc.). Please start with the one you have learned first!
    ____
    ____
22. What instruments do you play?______________
23. Do you specialize in music/dance from a particular region?
    Yes No If yes, which one is it?
    ____
24. List in order of preference any other music/dance in which you are actively engaged.
    ____
25. a. Have you visited the Balkans?______________
    b. If yes, how many times? ______________
    c. Which Country(ies) ______________
    d. The longest stay ______________
    e. Do you have folk costumes, instruments you do not play, etc.?_____
    f. How did the visit to the Balkans change your understanding of Balkan culture? ______________
26. a. What aspects of Balkan culture attract you?
    ____
    b. What aspects of Balkan culture do you dislike?
    ____
27. Are you attracted only to traditional Balkan music? ____ If yes, why?
    ____
28. What does Balkan music mean to (provide for) you personally?
    ____
29. Why Balkan and not some other kind of music?
    ____
30. How important is the Balkan camp to you? What does the camp provide for you?
    ____
31. Are majority of your friends people involved in the Balkan music and dance scene?
    ____

Thank you!

Notes

Introduction

1. Jane Sugarman, an ethnomusicologist and long-time enthusiast of Balkan music and dance, wrote in an e-mail message (EEFC list, Sat. 29 Nov. 1997) that the song was "recorded by Slobodan Ilić, Muharem Serbezovski (RTB [Radio-Televizija Beograd] 16 3060), and others; the Muharem Serbezovski recording lists: 'Indijska narodna—B. Milivojević [Indian folk—[arr.] B. Milivojević." Sugarman also explains that she has "tried in vain to find the song in the Indian film it is supposed to be from," whose English translation is *The Blind and the Lame*, and she has "personally concluded that B. Milivojević wrote the song, based on the sound of Indian film music and with lyrics based on the plot of the film."

2. Žabe i Babe performs largely Bosnian traditional and popular music genres. I formed the group in 1992 with friends and colleagues from Wesleyan University. The band has performed in a wide variety of venues, and in 1997 recorded a CD, "Drumovi," with the Ansambl Teodosijevski.

3. Notable exceptions are more recent issues of *Kef Times*, which feature series of interviews with prominent individuals and groups in the scene.

Chapter 1

1. For example, see Slobin's *Fiddler on the Move*, Hast's *Music, Dance, and Community: Contra Dance in New England*, and Levin's *Where Rivers and Mountains Sing*.

2. Jane Wieman, a longtime folk dancer who has been living and dancing in Japan since 1983, provides a concise history of Balkan folk dancing in Japan in *Kef Times* (Fall 2001/Winter 2002: 8, 9, 20). While Michael and MaryAnn Herman taught international folk dance in Japan as early as 1956, Wieman sees 1975, the year when Yves Moreau was invited to Japan to teach specifically Balkan dances, as a pivotal year in the development of the Balkan scene. Most of the dancing is still done to recorded music and

the Balkan music scene has yet to take off. The first Japanese Balkan Music and Dance Camp was held in 2001 in Makino.

3. I did not exert any control over the final sample in terms of asking a specific group of people to fill out the questionnaire. The sample is thus random and the results are subject to sampling variability. The calculations are based on eighty-one responses from both the teaching staff and the students.

4. Since the large portion of my research was done on the East Coast it is probable that these percentual relationships reflect the more substantial presence of people of Jewish origin on the East Coast.

5. However, if we consider the fact that Moreau gives us only 72 percent of his sample divided into the three categories (East European background 32 percent, WASP 25 percent and Anglo-Saxon 15 percent), we can recalculate his sample taking his 72 percent as 100 percent, i.e., excluding the 28 percent of assumed foreigners (people from Canada and twelve other countries). The results are now almost identical to mine (i.e., 35 percent would be identified as WASP, 21 percent as Anglo-Saxon, and 44 percent as East European, including 15 percent Jewish).

6. This is especially interesting when contrasted with the memories of embarrassment, even shame, expressed to me by people whose parents were "colorful" immigrants.

7. There were 10 percent of women and 3 percent of men in the twenty-three to twenty-nine age group, 29 percent of women and 17 percent of men were between the ages of thirty and thirty-nine, 51percent of women and 53 percent of men were between the ages of forty and forty-nine, and 10 percent of women and 27 percent of men were fifty or older.

8. Miller used different age categories and did not calculate the average age of the campers. However, the data that show forty to fifty-four to be the largest age group in her sample (56.7 percent) are strikingly similar to mine.

9. While 30percent of the campers were raised in urban areas, 42 percent in a suburb, 22 percent in a small town, and 6 percent in a rural area, 37 percent currently live in an urban area, 40 percent in a suburb, 17 percent in a small town, and 6 percent in a rural area.

10. While 14 percent of men have master's degree, and 39 percent bachelor's degrees, only 4 percent listed high school as their highest level of education. The distribution among women is 12 percent PhD, 39 percent master's degree, 47 percent bachelor's degree and 2 percent high school.

11. Jane Sugarman suggested to me that this might be a recent development and that there was a greater difference between camp attendees and staff members. According to Sugarman, some of the early staff members were "working class" people.

12. Music and dance camps are also not a novelty or invention of any of the above mentioned scenes. Their format has been inherited from the late 1800s, when the first summer camps were created in the United States. Summer camps organized to foster and teach particular ethnic repertoire have been around for at least a century, and international folk dance camps have been going on for at least half a century.

13. A large wooden dance floor is one of the most important prerequisites for a successful campsite.

14. Although a large number of students prefer learning from sheet music or transcriptions if provided by the teachers at the camp, they still memorize the songs and use written music primarily as a learning aid.

15. For a compiled list of 264 bands and analysis of the acquired data, see Laušević 1998: 490–501.

16. Greece, Turkey, and Romania were listed as visited Balkan countries by 15percent, 8percent, and 5percent, respectively.

17. In an EEFC list message (Dec. 19, 1997), David writes, I suppose ironically, "I have the greatest respect for the wonderful people who do the folkdance research for the rest of us—no matter what the personal hardships and privations, tramping through soggy villages, eating questionable parts of chickens and other farmyard animals, scratching discreetly at previously unexperienced zoa, smiling bravely through the cigaret haze all the while."

Chapter 2

1. For a fascinating discussion related to this practice, see Leo Lemay's *New England's Annoyances*. This literary analysis of the earliest known folk song written in New England, ca. 1630, details what the author argues is the celebration of the settlers' values and personality through mock criticism of their shortcomings and the region's hardships.

2. There are, doubtlessly, many Americans who were exposed to Balkan music and dance, but, whether touched by that experience or not, never thought of pursuing this activity.

3. "Kafu mi draga ispeci" is largely considered to be a Bosnian song, both in the Balkan scene and in its homeland. The song actually originated in the Sandžak region of Montenegro and was made popular throughout the former Yugoslavia by the Serbian singer Predrag Gojković-Cune in the early 1960s.

Chapter 3

1. There is a substantial body of literature on the settlement movement, written both by insiders, i.e., heads of settlements, and outsiders. Jane Addams's *Twenty Years at Hull-House* (1910) and Lillian Wald's *Windows on Henry Street* (1934) are considered "classics" of literature on the activities of the settlement written by its leaders. For a quick and clear survey of the activities carried out by settlements at the turn of the century one can consult the *Handbook of Settlements* edited by Robert Woods and Albert Kennedy (1911). Some of the most informative contemporary critical views of the settlements are provided in Mina Carson's *Settlement Folk* (1990) and Ann Trolander's *Settlement Houses and the Great Depression* (1975).

2. From a letter written in 1883 by Samuel A. Barnett, quoted in Gordon, 1964: 137.

3. Mina Carson provides a brief and insightful critique of the idea of organic unity:

> On one hand, it was part of an assertion of human brotherhood and spiritual equality: one aspect of the beneficent humanitarianism of the nineteenth century, pointing toward increasing political and social democracy. On the other hand, the organic metaphor offered a kind of license to philanthropists and politicians to exercise far-reaching social control over those large and threatening segments of society outside the pale of the moral law and social codes that nominally governed the behavior of the middle and upper classes. (1990: 7)

4. The larger public was for the first time introduced to the life of the American poor through Jacob Riis's 1890 book *How the Other Half Lives*. With a series of photographs taken in the slums of New York City the author documented the conditions of immigrant life, vividly introducing the poor to the rich.

5. After returning from London, where he had visited Toynbee Hall (the first settlement house in the world) Stanton Coit first organized a boy's club in 1886 in New York City. In 1887 the club turned into the neighborhood guild, and was in 1891 named University Settlement. This settlement is still active.

6. While U.S. cultural politics at this time involved the imposition of the Asian Exclusion Acts, the settlement movement did not, a priori, exclude African Americans or Asian immigrants. The racial politics of the settlement movement can be perceived as largely inclusive in the ideological domain, although a large portion of the settlement work was focused on white European immigrants.

7. Felix Adler was the head and founder of the Ethical Culture Society founded in New York City in 1860. In an attempt to deal with the ethnic, cultural, and religious diversity of Americans, Adler established universal human ethical values as a foundation for the society. The Ethical Culture Society also had international folk dance programs and was inspired by and was an inspiration to settlement leaders.

8. Twenty-Fifth Annual Report of the University Settlement Society of New York, 1911, p. 15 (NYPL, microform).

9. For more information about the relationship and mutual influence between Jane Addams and John Dewey see "John Dewey and Hull-House" in Deegan (1988: 251–253) and Farell's *Beloved Lady*, pp. 80–103.

10. By "race history" Hall implies the history of white people, or what he generically calls the history of the human race.

11. Beginning in the early 1800s, temperance organizations sprang up throughout the United States with the goal of moderating or even eliminating the use of liquor. American women were particularly active in these local, national, and international organizations. The temperance movement had much in common with the settlement house movement in terms of its dedication to the improvement of family and community life.

12. Much of the dance hall repertoire came out of minstrel and vaudeville traditions. The dance hall music can loosely be identified as rags. It is often referred to as "syncopated" music. Many critics of the dance hall found the dance rhythms to be dangerous and to stimulate improper physical behavior. The earliest dances were two-steps and waltzes. In the teens a whole series of so called "animal dances," such as the Bunny Hug, Grizzly Bear, Camel Walk, Foxtrot, Jitterbug, etc., became popular. It was not the steps per se that bothered the dance hall critics but the dance etiquette and body language of the dancers. Couple dances in which dancers embraced each other, with their hips touching and their arms draped over each other, were scandalous enough at the time. The fact that dancers constantly changed partners made this public display of physical intimacy even worse. Chicago Hull House residents even organized the Juvenile Protective Association in 1907 in an attempt to prevent youth from being, among other things, enticed into the dance hall. For more information on dance practices at the turn of the century see Dance History Archives at streetswing.com, as well as Paul Cressey, *The Taxi Dance Hall* (1932), and Randy McBee, *Dance Hall Days* (2000). Linda Tomko's *Dance Class* (1999) addresses the settlement movement's revisionist practices towards social

dancing of the time. I am particularly grateful to Susan Cook from the University of Wisconsin for her insight on dance hall musical practices.

13. So-called taxi dance halls enabled male customers to "rent" female dancers at a "dime-a-dance." Taxi dancers often engaged in prostitution.

14. Rita Teresa Wallach, "The Social Value of the Festival," *Charities and the Commons* 16 (2 June 1906), as quoted in Carson 1990: 108.

15. For a more detailed analysis of different applications of folk dancing in settlements see Tomko's 1999 book *Dancing Class.*

16. It would demand an extraordinary amount of research in settlement houses' archives to determine how many settlements had folk dance programs.

17. Felix Adler, "The Ethics of Neighborhood," University Settlement Studies, July 1906; Roy Lubove (1974) *The Progressives and the Slums.*

18. Report of the Henry Street Settlement, 1893–1914, p. 20 (microfilm, NYPL, Humanities).

19. The Social Settlement of Hartford defines as one of its aims "to provide a center for the social life of the neighborhood, and to serve as a common ground for all classes of society where they may meet to know and understand one another" (in Woods and Kennedy 1911: 27). The reader needs to perceive the importance given to the active participation in learning about each other through contact, exposure, and engagement, so crucial in understanding the role of folk dance programs in the settlements.

20. Just as there is not much about racial relationships in settlement workers' writing there is not much about relationships between immigrant groups themselves at the turn of the century. Animosities between members of different immigrant groups, as described by Asbury (1927) in *The Gangs of New York,* were not the primary concern of settlement workers. Jean Ritchie, a traditional Appalachian singer and recording artist who taught at the Henry Street Settlement in the1940s told me that fights between older and newer immigrant groups were frequent and often taken out to the streets (Interview, 2004).

21. Follett, *Creative Experience,* as cited in Addams (1930: 199).

22. There is no date on the cover of this document. I believe that the report was for 1915–1916, although it might have been for the year 1914–1915.

23. The issue of Americanization was not viewed uniformly even by residents and settlement leaders. A limited insight into the insiders' writings on this issue suggests a gender-based difference in opinion with regard to the role of settlements in the Americanization of the foreign-born. While the assimilationist standpoint was most strongly advocated by male settlement leaders, women appear to have been more supportive of the idea of cultural pluralism. I have not come across a similar conclusion in the current writings on the settlement movement. Making a strong case out of this observation would demand additional research. Since my interest in the settlement house movement developed only as a byproduct of research on folk dance programs, I suggest this as a further avenue of pursuit for scholars whose primary interest is the history of the settlement movement.

24. Carson (1990: 159) writes that after "the Immigration Act of 1917 had imposed a literacy test designed to exclude the southern and eastern European groups most feared by American nativists . . . the National Federation of Settlements opposed any requirement that foreign-born people 'learn English with a view to enforcing the suppression of their native speech.'" Pointing to the settlements' long-time practice of offering voluntary classes

in English and citizenship, the NFS insisted that coerced acculturation would only breed "misunderstanding and bitterness" in the immigrants, who would be reminded of the silencing of linguistic minorities by Old World autocracies. Carson quotes the National Federation of Settlements' Statement of Policy [May 1918 as a source for these citations.

25. Henry Street Settlement Music School, papers, NYPAL at Lincoln Center.

26. Simkhovitch, "The Universities and Preparedness," n.p. (written during World War I).

27. Describing the purposes of the Neighborhood Playhouse, associated with the Henry Street Settlement, Lillian Wald wrote in *The House on Henry Street*: "It is our hope that the playhouse, identified with the neighborhood, may capture and hold something of the poetry and idealism that belong to the people, and open the door of opportunity for messages in drama and dance and song and story" (as quoted in "Report of the Henry Street Settlement, 1893–1918" under "Art and our Neighbors").

28. Jane Addams's 1892 speech, "The Subjective Necessity for Social Settlements," in *Twenty Years of Hull House*, pp. 260–65.

29. Following the example of the Henry Street Labor Museum, many settlements organized displays of immigrant folklore. On display to visitors were not only products, but actual immigrants and their labor. What these programs hoped to achieve was a public appreciation of immigrants' arts and crafts and the respect of immigrants' children for their parents' artistic achievements.

Chapter 4

1. The author gives for reference another work of his own, the article "The Conservation of the Nation's Most Valuable Resources," in *Educational Review* 56, 4, November 1918.

2. Dr. William T. Harris (in Barrows 1890: 3), U.S. Commissioner of Education, made a distinction between the old system of physical education that prevailed until the 1860s, whose aim was solely muscular development and training of the body, and the new physical education, whose concern was the spirit as much as the body. According to the author, "the new physical education began with the work of Dr. Hitchcock at Amherst, and was followed up by Dr. Sargent in the Hemenway Gymnasium at Cambridge, Dr. Hartwell at the Johns Hopkins, and their coworkers in the various colleges and universities."

3. The Sokol society was founded in Bohemia in 1862. As a part of the Czech national movement, this organization was meant to perpetuate and celebrate the ethnic heritage and national character of the Czechs. In the words of its co-founder, Miroslav Tyrs, the goal of the organization was "to educate our people to the highest physical efficiency, to nobleness and morality. . . . When we address a Sokol the response will come from a man in the truest sense of the word, a man physically, mentally and morally, a patriot who is ever ready to respond to the call of his country, ever ready to draw the sword in defense of Democracy, Liberty and Humanity" (Tyrs, in Chadima 1990: 24). The first Sokol group in the United States was founded in 1865 in St. Louis. To the present day Czech Sokols (Polish Falcons as well) exist throughout the States in areas that have a substantial Czech (or Polish) population. Like Turner societies, the Sokols organized athletic games and "national festivals" that included folk dancing.

4. Research on European folk dance programs could provide insight into the origin of folk dance repertoire in the United States at the beginning of the century, as well as an understanding of the ideological and dance background of some of the early immigrant folk dance teachers in the United States.

5. The founder of the first Turner society in Germany was Friedrich Ludwig Jahn (1778–1852). His students Charles Beck, Charles Follen, and Francis Lieber organized the first Turnverein in the United States upon immigrating in 1820s. With massive German immigration after 1848, Turnvereins became quite popular. According to Henry Metzner (1974: 25), by 1867 there were 148 societies with ten to two hundred members. Betty Spears (1978: 121) sees the Turnverein as "a social center affording a bridge between the old culture and the new." Along with classes in English language and American citizenship, Turner societies organized folk dancing and other programs to help preserve German culture and lore.

6. Betty Spears (1978: 121) has come to a conclusion that the Turner movement affected not only thousands of German Americans, but that it also "aided the acceptance of Physical Education in the public schools of several cities with large German-American populations." The German system of physical education fell in disfavor after World War I. It became criticized as a system that was good only for building strong bodies but not for imprinting strong ethical values or enabling the spiritual growth of the youth.

> The essential unity of the child, the tremendous need today for men and women possessing fine qualities of citizenship, the growing appreciation of the importance of play-forms in education indicate the poverty of the muscle-building program. . . . The splendid physical bodies of the German people and the poverty of their moral possessions, as shown in 1914–1918, illustrate perfectly the thought here. More important than muscles, or muscular strength, are the way the muscles are used and the mental content revealed by all action. (Williams 1922: 12)

7. Numerous older publications contain various "national" dances (Fanny Elssler dances, for example, "La Cachucha"). However, I perceive this repertoire and the contexts in which it occurs as separate from both the physical education movement and the settlement movement. Social dancing was extremely popular at the turn of the century, and the latest dancing fads reached ballrooms and dance halls across the United States. The "exotic," "national" dances that were occasionally a part of the popular dance repertoire cannot be placed in the same category as "folk" dances, even though they might belong to the same category stylistically. It would be interesting to explore the possible crossover between the "folk," "national," or "exotic" dance repertoire as it appeared in different contexts within American society.

8. For the first time "Folk dancing" appears in the list of courses of instruction at the Boston Normal School of Gymnastics in 1908–09 (BNSG 1890–1909, Annual Catalogue of the Instructors, Students, and Graduates, with a Statement of the Course of Instruction, pp. 16–17). Since the new instructor is not listed, it is most likely that M. B. Gilbert was teaching this course.

A firsthand account of a teacher who independently decided to introduce folk dance in her class was provided in a letter written by Anne Barr

Clapp, University of Nebraska, Lincoln (Clapp, in Gulick 1911: 72): "I have used them [folk dances] constantly in our gymnasium with university girls since I returned from Sweden in 1898 and I have had nothing but the best results." It is not clear whether the Swedish dances were the only folk dances Clapp taught. It is possible that she had learned other folk dances from Swedish Physical Education teachers.

9. This program was established in 1887 to train male gymnasium directors.

10. In her 1999 book *Dancing Class*, Linda Tomko provides a more detailed account of Hinman's work, analyzing her contribution in the context of gender and class issues in American dance of the Progressive era.

11. The girls "do actual assisting every day at all the big classes, read books and write papers on how this work applies to the education of the child, also learning where each dance comes from, its history, [what influences the different countries in their social life, etc.,] and each carries a class of her own in some settlement" (Hinman, in Gulick 1911: 94–95).

12. The inconsistency of these references, both in terms of the type of information they carry, as well as their placement on the printed page, makes it quite hard to discern their real meaning. In some cases the name of a person (presumably the name of the person she learned the dance from) would be followed by a date (possibly the date when Hinman learned the dance, although it might also be the date when the dance was first taught), in others the name of a place (city and country in which Hinman learned the dance?) would be followed by a date (year when she was there?). There are dances that have references to both a person and a place, but the dates that follow them are different. This type of information is quite confusing, as it could be pointing to multiple origins of Hinman's sources for the same dance, or to Hinman's creation of a new dance based on two previously described and perhaps published folk dances.

13. The Girls Athletic League, as Betty Spears points out, was until 1909 "run by a group of prominent women in the city rather than by the school system." It was not until Burchenal became the Inspector of Girl's Athletics that the GAL was brought under the full control of the school system.

14. James E. Sullivan and Superintendent of New York public schools William H. Maxwell were involved in forming this organization. The secretary of the PSAL, C. Ward Crampton, was also a strong advocate of folk dancing. Crampton had published one of the first folk dance books for use in schools and playgrounds. Gulick was also the head of the Playground Association of America and the leader of the Camp Fire Girls. Through numerous articles and conference appearances he contributed much to the popularization of folk dancing throughout the United States. He brought the benefits of folk dance programs to the attention of both the general public and wealthy businessmen. At the St. Louis Exposition in 1903 Gulick gave a talk on PSAL. It was common for the national conferences of physical educators to be held at the world fairs. This was the beginning of the relationship between folk dancing and world fairs.

15. Rogers (1941: 315) explains: "Louis Chalif began studying ballet dancing at the age of nine in Odessa, Russia, in the Government Theatre under Thomas L. Njinski, the father of the great artist, Vaslav. Later he traveled as a dancer with the Imperial Moscow Ballet, under the supervision of Lidia M. Gerten, the prima ballerina of the day. . . . Mr. Chalif then traveled through Europe and became ballet master of the Odessa Government Theatre." In this as well as in other biographical accounts there is no information provided on any kind of international folk dance training.

16. The school was at first located at 5–9 West 42nd Street. In 1913–1914 the school was relocated to a building commissioned by Chalif, the "Temple to Terpsichore" on West 57th Street, across the street from Carnegie Hall. By 1937 Chalif was teaching at the International Building at Rockefeller Center, 630 Fifth Avenue. Catalogs and announcements (1911–1938) of the Chalif Russian Normal School of Dancing are located at the New York Public Library for the Performing Arts at Lincoln Center.

17. It would be illuminating to find out where and how Chalif learned the folk dances. The phenomenon of international folk dancing might have been truly international in its inception. It is also possible that Chalif learned the dances while traveling with the ballet troupe. Judging by the highly stylized material he taught, it is unlikely that he learned the dances from peasants in the countries he visited.

Mark Slobin informed me in a personal conversation (1996) that "Russian gentry was producing folklore for export to world's fairs by this time and had earlier formed serf ensembles on their estates."

The only account I have found that refers to possible sources of Chalif's dance material is provided by Chalif himself in Prospectus, 10, Chalif Russian Normal School of Dancing, 1911/1912, p. 17: "Mr. Chalif has spent many years on the Continent studying the characters of the people of the various European countries, which enables him to create types in Pantomime and Dances that are fascinating to execute and charming to behold." This statement still does not provide us with precise data on the acquisition of actual dance material. One could even be misled by Chalif's words to believe that all of his dances were impressionistic interpretations of the people he encountered on his travels through Europe. However, while Chalif's material is extremely stylized, it is generally related to actual folk dances of the national groups to whom the dances are attributed.

18. In an article written by Eve Stebbins, probably around 1930 (NYPL, Clippings, Chalif, Louis Harvy, 1876–1948), the following evaluation of Chalif's managerial work was provided: "Mr. Chalif's specialty, indeed, seems to be the printing and distribution of his booklets. He has hundreds of letters testifying to their excellence. Some of his publications are in their sixth edition and about 25,000 are in circulation."

19. The title of the dance is misspelled. Most likely the title of this particular kolo, circle dance in Serbo-Croatian, is *Srbijanka*, "A Serbian Woman." Hence Cola Serbianka is from Kolo Srbijanka.

20. Chalif taught folk dancing at the School of the Ethical Culture Society in New York, founded by Felix Adler. He was the director of the Grand Harvest Festival of All Nations held under the auspices of the Playground Association of America at Van Cortlandt Park in New York in September 1908. Chalif also taught "athletic dancing" at YMCAs, and became the Director of the Historical, Pantomime, National, and Folk Dances of the Hudson-Fulton Celebration in New York in 1909.

21. In NYPL, Catalogs, announcements, etc., 1911–1938, Chalif Russian Normal School of Dancing, N.Y. Prospectus (10, 1911/12).

22. Chalif proudly declared in 1914 (1914: 173) that his students and their pupils teach "in the gymnasia of universities, Turnvereins, private schools, etc., in every city of America and in Europe as well." While the remark might sound pretentious it is true that Chalif's school had a tremendous impact on the development of dance in the United States.

23. In a letter written by Mary Stewart, Supervisor of Children's Playground Association in Baltimore, Maryland, Miss Hofer was mentioned as the instructor who gave a course in folk dancing to the members of a

training class for playground directors. According to Stewart the dances taught in the winter of 1908 were used on playgrounds the following summer (quoted in Gulick 1911: 69–70). There is no account of the actual dances taught, nor is there more information provided on Miss Hofer herself.

24. One of the most comprehensive folk song collections of the time, *Folk Songs of Many Peoples*, was copyrighted by the YWCA in 1921. This impressive two-volume collection contains over three hundred folk songs with lyrics in the native language and in English translation. The compiler and editor, Florence Hudson Botsford (1921), acknowledges the "Members of the Foreign-Born Department of the National Board of the Young Women's Christian Association," as well as the "field, local and foreign language secretaries of the International Institutes of the Young Women's Christian Association" for furnishing material for the compilation. As an organization with posts in many parts of the world, the YWCA possibly contributed to the "import" of folk dance material as well. In any case, the idea of collecting folk materials from various parts of the world was not foreign to this organization.

25. The first Normal School for female physical education teachers was established by Dudley A. Sargent at Harvard in 1881.

26. Helen Ely, 1920–21, "Industrial Recreation," in *Bulletin of the Mary Hemenway Alumnae Association*, Department of Hygiene, Wellesley College.

27. Examples are numerous, ranging from the desire to accumulate tunes and steps to what Tim Rice describes in *May It Fill Your Soul* as the conceptual separation of melody from ornamentation that prevented him from "getting" the music. See also related discussions in chapter 1 and the conclusion of this book.

28. From "A May Day Festival 1924," *Bulletin of the Mary Hemenway Alumnae Association*, Department of Hygiene, Wellesley College, 24–37.

29. Music from different lands was not a foreign concept to brass bands. *National, Patriotic and Typical Airs of All Lands*, collected by the Bandmaster of the United States Marine Corps, John Philip Sousa (1890), is an example of "world music," including Balkan, intended for brass band performance.

30. Although European hurdy-gurdy is not the same instrument as the street-organ or the organ-grinder, the terms are often used as synonyms in the United States. In Gulick's writing, hurdy-gurdy refers to the mechanical instrument (organ-grinder, street-organ) used for the accompaniment of folk dances.

31. An undated article titled "Louis H. Chalif," written by Ann Barzel, can be found in NYPL, Chalif, Louis Harvy, 1876–1948, Clippings.

32. NYPAL, Chalif, Louis Harvy, 1876–1948, Clippings.

33. Gulick most clearly expresses the commonly shared perception of folk dances as the survival of the strongest and the purest. "These stories, told both by word of mouth and by body movement, were repeated by the common people through the countless ages of man's early history, until they gradually developed coherency and uniformity, each of its own kind. In every case—as is also true of folk music—the most effective form of presentation survived. A folk dance represents, then, the long history of human activity embodied in a specific art form" (Gulick 19–11: 205). Gulick's fascination with the long "survival" of folk dances reflects his application of social Darwinism to the history of dance.

Chapter 5

1. Hinman provides a whole list of appropriate quotations to use in program notes or read to audiences at folk dance performances and festivals.

2. The periodization of the IFD history as offered in this work needs to be understood in terms of the dominant direction of developments, rather than the simple replacement of one ideology and manner of use with another. It is particularly difficult to bracket the time frame of a given period since it does not end abruptly but only loses dominance.

3. From an article published in the San Rafael daily paper, November 1941, SFPAL.

4. A substantial increase in the number of articles concerning Balkan countries is also noticeable. Various Balkan nations gained visibility in the American press with the onset of Balkan wars, but much more so with the beginning of World War I. Along with political news, attention was given to Balkan culture as well.

5. Whether it is a grand march led by the Stars and Stripes, or a military band playing "Russian, Chinese, German, British, Italian, Spanish, Finnish, Japanese, Jugo-Slavian, Polish and Mexican national songs" (*San Francisco News*, July 1928), there was an interesting mixture of military and national imagery at the international dances and concerts.

6. Also see Knott 1939 and 1949, Lears 1981, Susman 1984, and Meyer 1950.

7. An extremely interesting article "The Dance: Aiding Folk Culture" written by John Martin (*New York Times*, April 16, 1933) discusses the contributions of each of the three major folk dance organizations in New York City. The English Folk Dance Society of America is, in his words, an organization that "treats the folk dance as 'a modern recreation and art': it takes its materials from traditional sources, but devotes itself less to scholarship than to social practice." On the other hand the American Folk Dance Society, headed by Elizabeth Burchenal, "delves into the obscurity of folk communities and emerges with research data which are in every sense scholarly." The Folk Festival Council had a broader perspective, incorporating elements of both of these positions, and thus had a potential for unifying the folk dance movement.

8. Mary Wood Hinman, "Educational Possibilities of the Dance," presented at the Mid-West Physical Education Association Convention, March 1933, in Wichita, Kansas. [In NYPAL, Doris Humphrey, Mary Wood Hinman, Swedish Book, Miscellany, Articles written by and about Mary Wood Hinman.]

9. Ibid.

10. Ibid.

11. While the substantial presence of people of Jewish origin was felt on the East Coast and particularly in New York City—both in the settlement house programs and international folk dancing in general—this is not necessarily the case in the rest of the country. Also, a substantial percentage of immigrants in tenement dwelling, again on the East Coast, were also Jewish.

12. This dynamic is further complicated in the recent Balkan scene in which mainstream Americans were initially instructed by other mainstream Americans. As we will see in chapter 8, ethnic teachers were sometimes less "authentic" than Americans who did firsthand research in Balkan villages.

13. Gurzay was an international folk dance enthusiast and teacher in New York in the 1920s. She taught folk dancing, particularly Italian repertoire, at the YWCA and also taught for the Folk Festival Council. Gurzay's papers are deposited at the Balch Institute for Ethnic Studies Library in Philadelphia and include "diaries, correspondence, writings, pamphlets, brochures, photographs, records relating to her early life in NYC and to numerous Italian-American folkdance organizations in New York and Philadelphia."

14. For example, in the 1932 Seasonal Festival of the Homelands twenty-four ethnic groups were represented: Polish, Spanish, Norwegian, Yugoslav, Scotch, and Finnish groups presented Summer dances and songs; Slovak, Irish, Greek, German, Italian, and Czech groups presented Autumn dances and songs; Lithuanian, Danish, Ukrainian, Bulgarian, Swedish, and Basque groups presented Winter dances and songs; and Alsatian, Armenian, English, Welsh, Hungarian, and Russian groups presented Spring dances and songs.

15. Herman's typewritten notes given to me at the time of our interview in 1994. From here on I will cite them as Herman, Notes.

Chapter 6

1. Short biographies of these folk dance teachers can be found in Betty Casey's *International Folk Dance U.S.A.*, as well as on Dick Oakes's detailed Web site: www.phantomranch.net.

2. This lengthy paragraph is included here for two reasons. One is that the information is relevant to our understanding of possible sources of Vyts's repertoire, and the other is to introduce the reader to his peculiar style of writing, in which certain aspects of the story, such as the location of the home of two sisters, are amplified with great detail. The reader gets the impression of sincere documentary writing. At the same time, as we can see in the above example, Vyts frequently omits details like the sisters' names, the year, or other facts that would be relevant to an understanding of how, and from whom, he learned the dances.

3. Crum's experience as a translator has enabled him to recognize text that has been translated from another language. "I am sure," Dick Crum told me in our interview, "that Vyts had an old Russian dance manual or possibly a Lithuanian recension, and that he had taken all these dances out of these books and had translated them and taught them" (Interview, 1997).

4. Over the years *Viltis* carried many stories on Vyts's youth, travel, and arrival in the United States. These autobiographical sketches were primarily concerned with telling an engaging, personal story, rather than providing exact dates and facts on Vyts's life and the study of folk dance. For example see "Researching America" (1994/54, 2: 13–15), "Girl Trouble" (Summer 1950/8), "Comment via Interview" (March–April 1949/6), and the series of articles published beginning in December 1990 titled "Life During World War I."

5. Dick Crum once inquired about the sources of kolos such as "Seljančica" and "Nebesko kolo" that Vyts published in his book without any references. Vyts's answer was that a woman in the settlement house taught him these dances (Crum, Interview, 1997).

6. Vyts explored not only the dances but the religions of different cultures. Apparently, he knew so much about Judaism that many people in the folk dance world believed that he was a convert. Mary Bee Jensen

observed, "For two successive years he was engaged by the main Zionist organization for their annual fundraising spectacles held at the Civic Opera Theater" (Mary Bee Jensen, in Casey 1981: 11). But Vyts was also interested in Buddhism, Hinduism, and various types of mysticism.

7. In the late 1920s Vyts joined Kar's concert, danced in the Hindu Arts Ensemble, choreographed the anniversary concert on March 21, 1937, and trained other dancers in the group consisting of "one Anglo, one Pole, a Hindu and six Lithuanians."

8. I have been unable to determine whether or not the Lithuanian Folk Dance Club "Ateitis," also organized and directed by Vyts, was part of the Lithuanian Youth Society or an independent organization.

9. See *Viltis* 6 (March–April 1949). There are numerous reports in *Viltis* on the "Ateitis" Lithuanian folk dancers and their concerts and tours.

10. Beliajus explains (in Casey 1981: 92) how "*Lore* resembled the current *Viltis*; in a way it was a forerunner of *Viltis*. When PA was eliminated, so was *Lore*."

11. There is some conflicting information with regard to the dates of the establishment of *Viltis*. I have used the date printed in earlier issues of *Viltis* itself. The 1947 issue contains an article written by Vyts titled "Fifth Year of *Viltis*," in which it is stated that the first Service Letter was issued in May of 1943. However, some later issues of *Viltis*, such as vol. 33, no. 1 (1974) give 1942 as the year when *Viltis* was established. For more information on the beginnings of the magazine, see "Fifth Year of *Viltis*" and "The *Viltis* Story" written by Vyts and published in the May 1947 (vol. 5, no. 1) and May 1954 (vol. 13) issues of *Viltis*.

12. The original official title of the group was "Chang's International Folk Dancers." The later omission of the apostrophe was intended to indicate that the group neither belonged to Chang nor was it led by him any longer.

13. The most extensive information on Song Chang and international folk dancing in California in the 1930s is to be found in Virgil Morton's Collection deposited in the San Francisco Performing Arts Library. There are several articles typewritten by Morton in the 1960s and 1970s that provide valuable data on pre–World War II folk dancing in California and Song Chang's contribution to its development. Dick Crum's long-standing involvement with IFD and research of historical sources helped this historical data come to life through interviews I conducted with him in 1997. Finally, there are published articles in *The Folk Dancer*, the newsletter of Changs International Folk Dancers, and articles in other folk dance magazines and San Francisco daily papers.

14. Submitted to the Department of Physical Education at College of the Pacific, Stockton, in 1947.

15. Presumably the groups referred to included the Swedish Applied Arts organization.

16. Although Frye does not cite the source of this information, she likely knew Chang personally, or at least interviewed him. To the best of my knowledge, no one has written about Chang's early days in greater detail.

17. In his article "Folk Dance Federation of California, Inc." (in Casey 1981: 48–49), Vi Dexheimer claims that Song Chang "became interested in folk dancing in 1931 while touring Europe. Feeling the warmth and the friendship surrounding him during these visits he wondered why there weren't more organizations devoted to this form of recreation." I cannot attest to the reliability of Dexheimer's source of information for this claim. In the introduction to his article he identifies Virgil Morton's notes and

early issues of *Let's Dance* magazine as his sources, which suggests that this is perhaps his own interpretation of the data rather than presentation of new information.

18. Morton recalls two such groups preceding Changs led by a Miss Patzell for the San Francisco Recreation Department, one on Sacramento Street near Fillmore and the other at the Capp Street Recreation Center (Morton, letter written to Robert Chevalier, August 11, 1969).

19. I am not certain whether the Swedish Applied Arts was indeed the only folk dance hub in San Francisco at the time, or if its importance in the development of folk dance became exaggerated as a result of the fact that most of the information on the early history of folk dance in San Francisco comes from Virgil Morton, a person who started folk dancing at Gravanders'. Swedish Applied Arts became known among folk dancers as a place in which folk dance originated, but it is my impression that this is largely because Morton's perspective became a part of oral history.

20. Swedish Applied Arts was located at 2020 and 2016 Pacific Avenue in San Francisco.

21. A typewritten article titled "Some Personal Notes on the Founding and Early Years of Changs International Folk Dancers" written in May 1962.

22. They met at 15 Hotaling Place in the studio of Beryl Wynnick and Max McCarthy (Morton, 1962).

23. Among the people present at the first meeting of Changs International Folk Dance group attended by Morton were Max McCarthy, a sculptor and painter in the primitive style; Beryl Wynnick, one of the first women artists to work in the medium of stainless steel; Harry Dixon, nationally known coppersmith, and brother of the artist Maynard Dixon; Stillman Clark, engaged in sandblasting designs in plate glass; Harriet Roudebush Chang, recent bride of Song Chang, and an outstanding artist in the field of etching; Mary Ann White, actress with the S. F. Theatre Union; Nairn Abbott, dancer with Veronica Pataki; Jose Ramis, primitive painter and world traveler; and the aforementioned Patricia Holmberg and Vivika Timirasieff, weavers and craft students from the Swedish Applied Arts (Morton, 1962).

24. Chang may have been an artist himself, as Morton recalls Song and Harriet making Christmas cards in their San Francisco studio apartment (Morton, 1962).

25. Ideologically loaded, Glass's statement is also an example of a problem that frequently occurs in interpreting IFD in the United States: a lack of distinction between the various segments of society involved in folk dancing and their different agendas and uses of the activity. Conclusions that might apply to one group of people involved in IFD are often applied to other segments without distinction.

26. In 1942 Chang's International Folk Dancers moved to the Italian Athletic Club, 1630 Stockton Street.

27. The organization consisted of Song Chang, president; Pete Bryant, vice-president; Stillman Clark, secretary; Beatrice Jenkins, treasurer; and Jack Kaufman, financial secretary.

28. The editor of the first bulletins, Stillman Clark, was assisted by Peggy Kranz, Eileen Kosloff, Keith Titmus, and Virgil Morton. In the fall of 1941 Virgil Morton became a temporary editor of the bulletin after the previous staff resigned. Several months later Bonnie Guinee became the regular editor.

29. Ralph Piper was one of the organizers of the Folk Dance Federation of Minnesota in 1947. His account of the growth of the Federation provides a valuable document of the growth of the folk dance movement in general. The FDF of Minnesota started with thirty-four chartered clubs and held monthly festivals in various parts of the state. In 1950 the membership included over 100 clubs (Griffith, Betty Rose, transcript of interview with Ralph Piper, NYPAL).

30. According to Morton about two hundred folk dance enthusiasts attended this picnic and the folk dancing that followed was filmed by Mr. Roland K. Abercrombie. "Not only is this film an important document of an historical occasion, but it should help prove to the detractors of Changs that there was an intense awareness of correct folk dance instruction and interest in authentic national dress prior to the formation of the Federation" (Morton, 1964, letter). As of this writing I do not know if or where this historically valuable document can be found.

31. According to the Folk Dance Federation of California Web site: http://www.folkdance.com/html/folk_dance_federation_of_california.html (accessed on July 26, 2004), by 1946 there were close to one hundred groups in the federation.

32. For more information on the history and current activities of Folk Dance Federations of California see their Web sites at: http://folkdance.com and http://us.geocities.com/FDFedSouthInc or http://www.socalfolkdance.org.

33. Most of Michael Herman's work has been well documented. Particularly useful sources are his own publications, books, booklets, and issues of *The Folk Dancer* magazine and *Folk News* as well as articles that appeared elsewhere. Herman's obituary, written by Dick Crum, who knew him personally for many years, is certainly indispensable for any researcher. My interviews with folk dance teachers such as Dick Crum and Michael Ginsburg who knew Michael Herman at the height of his career as well as through the later years proved to be a valuable source of information. I was able to interview Michael Herman at the age of eighty-four in Bayshore, Long Island, at which time he gave me a ten-page autobiography he said he had typed to refresh his memory for the interview. Judging by the appearance of this manuscript I believe that it was compiled long before we scheduled our meeting.

34. The fact that Herman was also trained as a classical violinist suggests that he may have attended a settlement music school as a child in Cleveland.

35. Vasile Avramenko, who immigrated in 1925 to Canada, devoted himself to the establishment of Ukrainian folk dance and ballet schools throughout Canada and the United States. As a charismatic leader, dancer, and public speaker, Avramenko was very successful in organizing Ukrainian communities, as well as in drawing the attention of the general American public to Ukrainian issues. After the spectacular Ukrainian Festival at the Metropolitan Opera House in New York (April 25, 1931) Henry Beckett advocated in the *New York Evening Post* for unrestricted immigration from the Ukraine: "What this country needs is more Ukrainians. Through them Americans may learn to play."

36. Herman became a member of many ethnic folk dance groups in New York. As a member of the French Folklore Society he danced under Jeanine Dawson's direction. The Danish Folk Dance Group was the first to take Herman in, where the Sorensons acted as a second family to him. He

became a member, and not only danced with them, but also played for their dances along with group leader Carl Hanson (Herman, Notes).

37. "Chester Junek was responsible for acquiring him for these sessions" (Herman, Notes).

38. The complete set of *The Folk Dancer* can be found at the NYPAL at Lincoln Center. The magazine provided news and advertisements of folk dance events, dance directions, music transcriptions, as well as articles on folk costumes and crafts. At the present day the magazine serves as a valuable source for historical research, as most of the writing was done by Michael Herman.

39. The Kentucky Dance Foundation's Folk Dancer Record Center in Brandenburg, Kentucky, (http://www.folkdancer.org) acquired the Folk Dancer label record stock and record archives from the Michael Herman Estate in 1997. The organization transfers the recordings onto compact discs and makes them available to current folk dance teachers.

40. Herman was proud of the "international" constituency of the orchestra members; Walter Ericksson was Swedish, Svend Tollefsen, Norwegian (accordionist), Walter Andersen, Danish (bass), Francis Witkowski, Polish (clarinet), Anthoni de Bartolo or John Cali, Italian (guitar), Leo Pleshkow, Jewish, and Michael Herman, Ukrainian on violins (Herman, Notes).

41. Altogether Michael Herman made "about 600 records, some for the Methodist church, and some for Victor. The Methodist Church made 21 records, 2 dances on each side, and Victor made 84 dances" (Herman, Interview, 1994).

42. For brief histories of the most popular folk dance camps—University of the Pacific, Stockton, CA (1948), Texas Folk Dance Camp (1949), Mendocino Folklore Camp, CA (1962), and Buffalo Gap International Folk Dance Camp, WV (1969), to name only a few—see chapter 3, "Selected Camps and Organizations," in Casey's *International Folk Dancing U.S.A.*

43. Jean Ritchie (Interview, 2004) told me that when she worked at Henry Street Settlement in the 1940s they would often organize trips to Herman's Folk Dance House.

44. When Beliajus expresses his opinion that "the Easterners are more careful to avoid mutilation of folk dances," while "the general run of the Western folk dancer feels no scruples about mutilating dances," he is, first of all, drawing attention to himself as a leader who knows the danger of "mutilation" and who is going to save his followers from falling into this trap.

Chapter 7

1. "A Brief History of the USA Folk Dance," Denis Heenan, in *Viltis* May 1992/51, 1.

2. John Martin, "The Dance: Folk Art as Inspiration," *The New York Times* January 8, 1932.

3. "Brotherly love and understanding between nations was the single most laboured aspect of exhibition diatribe," Greenhalgh (1988:17–18) writes, "the sentiment usually being ridiculed by displays of military technology, imperial conquest and abject racism on the sites themselves." Greenhalgh also warns us of the sentiment that underlay the World's Fair "that whenever different peoples came together to show off the achievements of their respective cultures, this would result in a reduction of differences and the growth of fellowship . . . but mostly generated bitterness and hatred" (Greenhalgh 1988: 18).

4. "The Dance Situation—1955," *Viltis* December 1955/14.
5. In *Viltis* March–April 1949/6.
6. This line of thinking was perpetuated throughout Europe by "national folklorists."
7. Although "folk" and "popular" are essentially the same word they are often used as opposites. The term "popular" is given the negative connotations of being without value, commercial, and short-lived.

Chapter 8

1. As we already know, Vyts "became fascinated by Jugoslav dances during the mid 30s" (*Viltis* Oct.–Nov. 1954/13). According to Filcich, Beliajus was the first one to teach kolos in 1949 to the folk dance communities in Oregon and Washington. "Since then he has made Southern California quite kolo conscious, with San Diego virtually kolo-crazy!" (Filcich, in *Viltis* Oct.–Nov. 1955/14).
2. In a brief history of the development of kolo dancing in California, John Filcich (*Viltis* Oct.–Nov. 1955/14) writes, "Folk dancers first learned about kolos in 1945 through the efforts of two service men stationed at Treasure Island, Marine Phil Hodak and Milan Palaski, who was in the Navy. They came from two good kolo cities, Detroit and Chicago respectively, and missed in California the usual kolo dancing they enjoyed at home. After attending some local affairs they gathered together a group of young Yugoslavs—mostly girls, since the men were in the service—and met at the Slovenian Hall in San Francisco once a week."
3. For those interested in the actual expansion of repertoire and introduction of particular Balkan dances, I recommend consulting Dunin's (1979) "South Slavic Dances in California: Compendium for the Years 1924–1977." Also, Dick Crum's article "Some Background on the Kolo in the United States," in *Viltis* Oct.–Nov. 1954/13, provides valuable information on the origin and development of particular kolos among the Serbian and Croatian immigrant communities in the United States, and their penetration into the folk dance community.
4. *Viltis* December 1957/16:17.
5. A "Kolo Federation" was formed, but by Yugoslav immigrants rather than folk dancers. See Crum 1954: 5.
6. Mary Ann Herman. "'Kolo'-nizing America," *Dance Magazine* October 1956(10): 46, 68, and 70.
7. Koleda was formed in Seattle in 1967 by Dennis Boxell, one of the pioneering teacher-ethnographers who traveled to the Balkans in order to learn the dances firsthand. Yves Moreau, another important figure in the Balkan dance world, also danced in Koleda at this time.
8. Although the writer obviously does not know how these regions relate to each other in geographic, cultural, and political terms, she has an idea of there being a connection between them which gave her a sense of being in the "Balkan world."
9. In 1957 Dick Crum published a collection titled *Vranjanka and other Jugoslav Songs and Dances*.
10. Officially established in 1963 by Anthony Shay and Leona Wood as artistic directors and Philip Harland as music director, Aman Folk Ensemble was one of the largest and most influential international music and dance performing ensembles.
11. Dunin (1979: 71) adds that "only three of the ten (Kolarovski, Joukowsky and Gajicki) lived in Yugoslavia for a major part of their lives and later

immigrated to the United States. . . . the above listed teachers (except for Engler) taught dances that were never before danced in California, taking into consideration even the South Slavic communities and their dance repertoire in California."

12. Beliajus's article "Why Folk Dancing?" originally appeared in *Recreation* 1937, published in New York City but it was reprinted in *Viltis* May 1980/39, 1.

13. A biography of Robert Leibman can be found on Dick Oakes's Web site, www.phantomranch.net/folkdanc/folktchr.htm. See also *Kef Times* (2003–2004/9, 1: 5, 7, 16) for an interview with Leibman.

14. For those interested in biographies and individual contributions of these teachers to the Balkan scene, Dick Oakes's Web site provides a wealth of information (www.phantomranch.net/folkdanc/folktchr.htm). Interviews with some of the most prominent Balkan dance teachers can also be found in the EEFC publication *Kef Times*.

15. For more information see http://www.phantomranch.net/folkdanc/perform/dolinacygany.htm.

16. See Mark Forry's 1990 dissertation on tamburitza music.

17. There were also folk clubs such as Ashgrove in Los Angeles that were catering to the folk movement in general and would occasionally include Balkan programs.

18. Dick Oakes's website carries a number of articles about the folk dance coffeehouses (http://www.phantomranch.net/folkdanc/coffee.htm). The site includes photographs, fliers, reminiscences and articles submitted by old-time patrons.

19. Pirated recordings are usually recognizable by the inscription "for non-commercial use only" and almost never carry the name of the original record label.

20. Although it mostly covers an earlier period, an extensive discography of Balkan music imported or released in the United States can be found in *Ethnic Music on Records: A Discography of Commercial Ethnic Recordings Produced in the United States 1894 to 1942* compiled by Richard Spottswood (1990). Volumes 2 and 3, out of the seven volumes of *Ethnic Music on Records*, are devoted to Slavic and Eastern European music. The information is cross-referenced under the name of the artist(s), song title, and name of the record company. *Ethnic Recordings in America* is another useful source of information on the availability and role of ethnic recordings in the United States. Of particular interest in *Ethnic Recordings in America* are the articles by Pekka Gronow, "Ethnic Recordings: An Introduction," and Richard Spottswood, "Commercial Ethnic Recordings in the United States."

21. Krilčić also published three volumes of Yugoslavian song lyrics that were popular at sing-alongs (Ethel Raim, Interview, 1994).

22. After their partnership was broken, Kramers continued to operate a store in San Francisco while Filcich opened a store in Los Angeles.

23. The different record labels did not necessarily divide their "territories," but rather competed with each other for their share in the market, often doubling recordings of the same dances. For example, Moreau talks about a "little war going on between the Folk Dancer label and Folkraft" (Moreau, Interview 1994).

24. In his 1990 article "Observations on the recent widespread adoption and adaptation of Bulgarian folk music and dance in North America and elsewhere," Yves Moreau (1990: 114) points out that "Many folk dance and music adepts in North America got their first introduction to Bulgarian folk music in the late 1950s and early 1960s through a few LP record-

ings then available on the market . . . among them the album of the Bulgarian State Folk Song and Dance Ensemble directed by Filip Kutev (Angel Records), Lloyd/Lomax's *Bulgaria* (Columbia World Library of Folk and Primitive Music, XLP 45607) and *Folk Music of Bulgaria* (Topic 12T 107)."

Chapter 9

1. Pitu Guli at that time featured Mark Levy and Stewart Mennin on gaida, Lauren Brody and Stuart Brotman on gudulka, Chris Yeseta on tambura, and Ed Leddel on tapan.

2. Ethel is currently working and performing with "Urban Women, Village Songs" in New York and directing the Center for Traditional Music and Dance (originally called the Balkan Arts Center and later the Ethnic Folk Arts Center).

3. Describing this type of a strong attraction to unfamiliar sound, Slobin (1993: 56) offers the "conversion story" of a woman who "after simply hearing a Highland bagpipe band outside her window, became so attracted to the music that she became a professional piper."

4. After the Harvesters stopped singing together in 1960, Ethel started the Pennywhistlers in 1961. This group was singing Russian, American, Yiddish, and Bulgarian repertoire.

5. *Le Mystère des Voix Bulgares* is the title of an LP record of Filip Kutev and Bulgarian Radio women's choir that had several incarnations on the Western market. In 1958 the Chant du Monde label recorded a concert of the choir in Paris and issued it on a ten-inch record. In 1965 Albert Grossman, Bob Dylan's manager, obtained the rights to release this recording in the United States after hearing it in Paris. This recording reached a number of Americans long before the "Mystère" craze. According to Joe Boyd this was "a cult classic that cognoscenti appreciated, but which did not sell particularly well" (Boyd 2003). Twenty years later, another incarnation of the Radio Sofia Women's Choir, *Le Mystère des Voix Bulgares*, "sold a hundred thousand lps in Britain . . . [and] another half million copies in the U.S. Todora is Dozing . . . provided the background music for tv commercials around the world" (Boyd 2003). The recording from Radio Sofia and Balkanton archives was released by a Swiss musicologist Marcel Cellier in the mid 1970s. For more information see also Buchanan's 1997 article "Bulgaria's Magical Mystère Tour" in *Ethnomusicology*.

6. I understand that my use of the term differs from the ways it is used in *Subcultural Sounds*. The reason I prefer this term over "recontextualization" is that while the whole musical genres are "recontextualized," only certain codes, and only in certain genres, are actually being switched.

7. A number of women sang in this group at different times, but Lauren Brody, Carol Freeman, and Carol Silverman were the core of the group singing together for ten years.

8. Koenig is still active as a Balkan dance teacher and is currently on the board of directors of the Center for Traditional Music and Dance (formerly BAC).

9. Dick Oakes provides a more detailed biography of Martin Koenig on his Web site, http://www.phantomranch.net/folkdanc/teachers/koenig_m.htm (accessed on July 2004), along with the discography of records Martin and Ethel produced and a description of video material Martin recorded in the Balkans. Ethel and Martin also worked on two documentary films, *The Popovich Brothers of South Chicago* about Serbian-American community and *Pericles in America* about Greek-Amercian community.

10. For more information about the history of this organization see http://www.ctmd.org.

11. When a scene has become so integral to participants' lives, the desire to celebrate life-cycle events with the community comes as a natural extension of the desire to belong and foster the newly found/constructed community. In a firsthand account of the development of KlezKamp, Henry Sapoznik (1994: 184) notes how "KlezKamp's resonance in the extended Jewish community has been made tangible in the explosion of registrants wishing to celebrate life-cycle events at Kamp. Over the last few years, participants have opted to share these very personal and community based events in the context of KlezKamp. Over the years we have hosted baby namings, an *opshern* . . . , even a wedding." Though somewhat different in form, an ideologically similar integration of musical affinity and life-cycle celebrations occurred in the early days of Russia's Pokrovsky ensemble, which held group members' weddings in a village so the peasants could join in. While the Balkan scene is not based on ethnic heritage, it is interesting to note its ideological crossover with European heritage movements like the Pokrovsky ensemble and Hungarian tanchaz.

12. In an article titled "Where Our $ Comes From—Where Your $ Goes," Rachel MacFarlane reports that the majority of the EEFC income comes from workshop tuition (85percent in 2000), 13 percent from membership fees and donations (*Kef Times* Fall 2000–Winter 2001/6, 2).

13. It is true, though, that Pomak songs were an integral part of Ženska Pesna repertoire in their performances and teaching throughout the 1970s.

Bibliography

Acocella, Joan Ross. 1993. *Mark Morris*. New York: Farrar Straus Giroux.

Addams, Jane. 1898. "Women's Work for Chicago." *Municipal Affairs* 2 (September): 502.

———. 1910. *Twenty Years at Hull-House with Autobiographical Notes*. New York: Macmillan.

———. 1916 [1909]. *Spirit of Youth and the City Streets*. New York: Macmillan.

———. 1930. *The Second Twenty Years at Hull-House, September 1909 to September 1929 with a Record of a Growing World Consciousness*. New York: Macmillan.

Adler, Felix. 1906. "The Ethics of Neighborhood." *University Settlement Studies,* July 1906.

Alexander, Ronelle. 1977. "*Izvorni*—From the Source." *Spring Folk Festival 1973.* New York: Balkan Arts Center. Alford, Violet. 1951. *Handbook of European National Dances.* New York: Chanticleer Press, with the Royal Academy of Dancing and the Ling Physical Education Association.

Allen, Catherine *Pocket Full of Fun. Np, nd.*

Amos, Karin S. 1995. *Alexis de Tocqueville and the American National Identity*. Komparatishe Bibliothek. Comparative Studies Series. Band 5. Jürgen Schriewer, ed. Frankfurt am Main: Peter Lang Gmbh, Europäischer Verlag der Wissenschaften.

Appadurai, Arjun. 1990. "Disjuncture and Difference in the Global Cultural Economy." *Public Culture* 2(2): 1–24.

Asbury, Herbert. 1927. *The Gangs of New York: An Informal History of the Underworld.* New York: Knopf.

Barrows, Isabel C., ed. 1890. *Physical Training: A Full Report of the Papers and Discussions of the Conference Held in Boston in November, 1889.* Boston: Press of George H. Ellis.

Begenau, Don. 1972. "Exploring Social Dance in New York." *Focus on Dance* 6: 60–62.

Beliajus, Vytatus. 1940. *Dance and Be Merry; Thirty-One Folk Dances with Variations Representing Seventeen Nations*, vol. 1. Chicago, New York: Clayton F. Summy Co.

———. 1951. *The Dance of Lietuva: Fifty-four Circle and Folk Dances from Lithuania.* Chicago, New York: Clayton F. Summy Co.
———. 1955 [1951, *Let's Be Merry*]. *Merrily Dance.* Delaware, Ohio: Cooperative Recreation Service, Inc.
Bernstein, Elizabeth. 1957. "Folk Dance Activities in New York City." *Viltis* 16 (Summer).
Blumenthal, Laura. 1999–2000. "Ramblewood Highlights." *Kef Times* 5(2): 6, 7.
Boston Normal School of Gymnastics. 1890–1909. Annual catalogue of the instructors, students, and graduates, with a statement of the course of instruction, 1897–1898. Wesley College Archive.
Boston Public Schools. 1910. "Health Day Program." Wesley College Archive.
Botsford, Florence Hudson. 1921. *Folk Songs of Many Peoples; with English Versions by American Poets.* 2 vols. New York: The Woman's Press (The National Board of the Young Women's Christian Associations of the USA).
Bourdieu, Pierre. 1984. *Distinction: A Social Critique of the Judgement of Taste.* Richard Nice, trans. Cambridge, Mass.: Harvard University Press.
Boyd, Joe. 2003. "How Stalin Invented World Music, or Le Mystère de Voix Sovietique." http://www.netrhythms.co.uk/articles_p1.html#boyd (accessed on July 2004).
Boyes, Georgina. 1993. *The Imagined Village: Culture, Ideology and the English Folk Revival.* Manchester: Manchester University Press.
Brace, Charles Loring. 1872. *The Dangerous Classes of New York and Twenty Years' Work Among Them.* New York: Wynkop and Hallenbeck.
Buchanan, Donna. 1997. "Bulgaria's Magical Mystère Tour: Postmodernism, World Music Marketing, and Political Change in Eastern Europe." *Ethnomusicology* 41(1): 131–157.
Cantwell, Robert. 1993. *Ethnomimesis: Folklife and the Representation of Culture.* Chapel Hill: University of North Carolina Press.
Carson, Mina. 1990. *Settlement Folk: Social Thought and the American Settlement Movement, 1885–1930.* Chicago: University of Chicago Press.
Casey, Betty. 1981. *International Folk Dancing U.S.A.* New York: Doubleday.
Chadima, Helen. 1990. "The Beseda: The Czech National Dance in Cedar Rapids, Iowa." *Dance Research Journal* 22(2): 23–28.
Chalif, Louis Harvy. 1876–1948. Clippings, New York Public Library of the Performing Arts at Lincoln Center
———. 1914. *The Chalif Text Book of Dancing, Book 1.* New York: Louis H. Chalif.
———. 1926. *Folk Dances of Different Nations*, 3 vols. New York: Louis H. Chalif.
———.1911–1938. Chalif Russian Normal School of Dancing catalogs, announcements, etc., New York Public Library of the Performing Arts at Lincoln Center (MGZ).
———. n.d. Chalif-Swoboda Ballet Company clippings, New York Public Library of the Performing Arts at Lincoln Center.
Chicago Park District. 1942. *Folk Tunes Including Square and Round Dances and Specialties.* Compiled by Workers of the Writers' Project of the Work Projects Administration of the State of Illinois. Chicago: WPA, Chicago Park District, Burnham Park.
Clifford, James. 1994. "Diasporas." *Cultural Anthropology* 9(3): 302–338.
Clippings from the Catalogues of Colleges, Normal Schools, Private Schools, Public Schools and Universities. Wesley College Archive.

Cohen, Selma Jeanne. 1967. "Project Rocket." *Dance Magazine* (February): 39–41, 73.
———. 1990. "4th World Conference on Folkdance: Dance-music in Folk Culture" (International Organization of Folk Art, Larissa, Greece, 16–20 May 1990). *Dance Research Journal* 22(2): 47–48.
Condon, Yvonne M. 1990. "St. Louis 1904 Louisiana Purchase International Exposition." *Historical Dictionary of World's Fairs and Expositions, 1851–1988*: 178–186. John E. Findling and Kimberly D. Pelle, eds. Westport, Conn.: Greenwood Press.
Cowdery, James R. 1995. "The American Students of Balasawaswati." *UCLA Journal of Dance Ethnology* 19: 68–76.
Crampton, Charles Ward. 1937 [1909]. *The Folk Dance Book for Elementary Schools, Class Room, Playground, and Gymnasium.* New York: A. S. Barnes.
———. 1922. *The Second Folk Dance Book*. New York: A. S. Barnes and Co.
Crawford, Caroline. 1908. *Folk Dances and Games.* New York: A. S. Barnes.
Cressey, Paul Goalby. 1932. *The Taxi-Dance Hall: A Sociological Study in Commercialized Recreation and City Life*. Chicago: University of Chicago Press.
Crum, Dick. 1954. "Some Background on the Kolo in the United States." *Viltis* 12: 4–5.
———. 1957. *Vranjanka and Other Jugoslav Songs and Dances: The Dick Crum Book*. Hargail Music Press. New York.
———. 1996. "Michael Herman (1910–1996)." *Sing Out!* 41(2): 27–28.
Czarnowski, Lucile K., and Jack B. McKay. 1953. *How to Teach Folk and Square Dance*. Oakland: Triangle Printing Company.
Davis, Allen Freeman, and Mary Lynn McCree, eds. 1969. *Eighty Years at Hull-House.* Chicago: Quadrangle Books.
Deegan, Mary Jo. 1988. *Jane Addams and the Men of the Chicago School, 1892–1918.* New Brunswick, N.J.: Transaction Books.
Deutsch, Leonhard. 1942. *A Treasury of the World's Finest Folk Song*. New York: Howell, Soskin.
Dewey, John. 1902. "School as Social Settlement." *National Education Association Proceedings:* 373–383. N.p.
———. 1939. *Freedom and Culture.* New York: Putnam
Dudley, H.W. 1898. "Women's Work in Boston Settlements." *Municipal Affairs* 2 (September): 493–496.
Duggan, Anne Schley, Jeanette Schlottmenn, and Abbie Rutledge. 1980 [1948]. *Folk Dances of European Countries.* New York: Books for Libraries, Arno Press.
Dunham, Patricia. 1948. *Work and Sing,* 2d ed. Delaware, Ohio: Cooperative Recreation Service.
Dunin, Elsie Ivancich. 1979. *South Slavic Dances in California: A Compendium for the Years 1924–1977*. Palo Alto, Calif.: Ragusan Press.
Dweyer-Shick, Susan. 1975. "The Development of Folklore and Folklife Research in the Federation Writers' Project, 1935–1943." *Keystone Folklore* 20: 5–31.
Eaton, Allen H. 1932. *Immigrant Gifts to American Life: Some Experiments in Appreciation of the Contributions of Our Foreign-born Citizens to American Culture.* New York: Arno Press with the *New York Times.*
Ely, Helen L. 1920–1921. "Industrial Recreation." *Bulletin of the Mary Hemenway Alumnae Association.* Department of Hygiene, Wellesley College.

Ericson, Jane Harris, ed. 1972. *Focus on Dance 6: Ethnic and Recreational Dance.* Washington, D.C.: American Association for Health, Physical Education, and Recreation

Evanchuk, Robin J. 1987–88. "Inside, Outside, Upside-down: The Role of Mainstream Society Participants in the Ethnic Dance Movement." *Folklore & Mythology Studies* 11 and 12 (special issue): 115–129.

Farwell, Jane. 1960. *Folk Dances for Fun: 25 Folk Dances and Singing Games.* Delaware, Ohio: Cooperative Recreation Service.

Feld, Steven. 1984. "Communication, Music, and Speech about Music." *Ethnomusicology* 16: 1–19.

Filcich, John. 1953. *Igra Kolo. Dance Kolos with John Filcich*. Oakland: Slav-Art Music Co.

Findling, John E. 1990. "Chicago Fair 1933–34: 'The Century of Progress.'" *Historical Dictionary of World's Fairs and Expositions, 1851–1988*. John E. Findling and Kimberly D. Pelle, eds. Westport, Conn.: Greenwood Press: 266–274.

Finnegan, Ruth. 1989. *The Hidden Musicians: Music-Making in an English Town*. Cambridge: Cambridge University Press.

Forry, Mark Edward. 1990. "The Mediation of 'Tradition' and 'Culture' in the Tamburica Music of Vojvodina (Yugoslavia)." PhD diss. University of California, Los Angeles.

Franklin, W., and Michael Steiner, eds. 1992. *Mapping American Culture*. Iowa City: University of Iowa Press.

Frye, Grace Tener. 1947. "The Revival of the Folk Dance as Social Recreation in Northern California." Master's thesis, Department of Physical Education, College of the Pacific, Stockton, California.

Gagnon, V.R. 1955. "In Denver, a Life Dedicated to Folk Dance." *Dance Magazine* (April): 35–36.

Getchell, Larry. "A History of the Folk Dance Movement in California." http://www.folkdance.com/html/history.htm (accessed on July 2004).

Gillespie, Angus. 1976. "Pennsylvania Folk Festivals in the 1930's." *Pennsylvania Folklife* 26 (1): 2–11.

Ginsburg, Michael. 1998. "The Balkans Return to Camp." *Kef Times* 4 (1): 1.

———. 2001. "A History of Zlatne Uste." *Kef Times* 7(1): 8.

Glass, Henry Buzz. 1972. "Folk Dance-Dimension '70." *Focus on Dance* 6: 68–70.

Glassberg, David. 1990. "Philadelphia 1926." *Historical Dictionary of World's Fairs and Expositions, 1851–1988.* John E. Findling and Kimberly D. Pelle, eds. Westport, Conn.: Greenwood Press: 239–249.

Gordon, Milton M. 1964. *Assimilation in American Life.* New York: Oxford University Press.

Green, Charles, and Lee V. Eastman. n.d. *The Yugoslav National Folk Nallet-Tanec First American Tour.* Promotional booklet, 23 pp. New York: Consolidated Concerts Corporation.

Greenhalgh, Paul. 1988. *Ephemeral Vistas; the Expositions Universelles, Great Exhibitions and World's Fairs, 1851–1939.* John M. MacKenzie, general ed. Manchester: Manchester University Press.

Griffin, Claudius W. 1981. "Physical Fitness." In *American Popular Culture*. Thomas M. Inge, ed. Westport, Conn.: Greenwood Press.

Gronow, Pekka. 1982. "Ethnic Recordings: An Introduction." *Ethnic Recordings in America: A Neglected Heritage.* Washington: American Folklife Center, Library of Congress: 1–50.

Gulick, Luther H., and Harry J. Smith. 1907. "Dancing as a Part of Education." *The World's Work* (October): 9445–9452.

Gulick, Luther Halsey. 1909. "Folk and National Dances." Reprinted from *Proceedings of the Second Annual Playground Congress for the Playground Association of America.* New York City and the Playground Extension Committee of the Russell Sage Foundation.
———. 1911. *The Healthful Art of Dancing.* New York: Doubleday, Page & Co.
Hall, G. Stanley. 1905. *Adolescence: Its Psychology and Its Relations to Physiology, Anthropology, Sociology, Sex, Crime, Religion and Education,* 2 vols. New York: D. Appleton.
Hast, Dorothea E. 1994. "Music, Dance, and Community: Contra Dance in New England." PhD diss., Wesleyan University.
Hering, Doris. 1965. "In our Discontent," part 1. *Dance Magazine* (October): 54–58.
———. 1965. "In our Discontent," part 2. *Dance Magazine* (November): 54–55, 63.
Herman, Mary Ann. "Americans Dance Foreign Folk Dances." *Focus on Dance* 6.
Herman, Michael. 1947. *Folk Dances for All.* 5th printing 1956. New York: Barnes and Noble.
———.1953. *Folk Dance Syllabus.* New York: Folk Dance House Publications.
———.1994. Notes. Typewritten by the author.
Haywood, Charles. 1966. *Folk Songs of the World.* New York: The John Day Co.
Hinman, Mary Wood. 1916. *Hinman School of Gymnastic and Folk Dancing.* Chicago: Studio.
———. 1916–1919. *Gymnastic and Folk Dancing,* 4 vols. *Solo Dances, Volume I (1916); Couple Dances with Description, Volume II (1918); Ring Dances with Descriptions, Volume III (1919); Group Dances, Volume IV (1916).* New York and Chicago: A. S. Barnes and Co.
———. 1919. *Gymnastic and Folk Dancing,* vols. 1–4. Chicago: Mary Wood Hinman.
———.1919–1937. *Gymnastic and Folk Dancing,* 5 vols. *Solo Dances, Volume I (1923); Couple Dances with Description, Volume II (1928); Ring Dances with Descriptions, Volume III (1919); Group Dances, Volume IV (c1926); Tap Dances, Clogs & Jigs, Sword Dances, and Gymnastic dances for boys, Volume V (1937).* New York and Chicago: A. S. Barnes and Co.
———. 1929–1930. *Gymnastic and Folk Dancing,* 5 vols. New York: A. S. Barnes and Co.
———. 1932. *The New York Times,* September 25.
———. 1933. "Educational Possibilities of the Dance." Paper presented at Mid-West Physical Education Association Convention, March 1933, Wichita, Kansas.
Hofer, Mari Ruef. 1925. *All the World a-dancing.* Piano arrangements rev. by Stella Roberts. Chicago: Clayton F. Summy Co.
Homans, Amy Morris. 1929. "A Message from Miss Homans, Given at the Luncheon of the Mary Hemenway Alumane Association, June 15, 1929." *Bulletin of the Mary Hemenway Alumane Association, Department of Hygiene, Wellesley College.* (September): 3–4.
Horne, Charles F. 1924, 1925, 1934. "Jugoslavia." In *The World and Its People,* vol. IV, chapters 10 and 11, pp. 1225–1240, New York: Ira R. Hiller.
Indreika, Petras. 1972. "The East Chicago Lithuanians." Aldona Indreika, trans., from Lithuanian; Rose Levan, ed. *Program for the Study of Ethnic Publications,* Kent State University, Kent, Ohio.

James, Jack, and Earle Weller. 1941. *Treasure Island: "The Magic City" 1939–1940.* San Francisco: Pisani Printing and Publishing.
Joukowsky, Anatol M. 1980. *The Teaching of Ethnic Dance.* J. Lowell Pratt & Co., 1965. Reprint, New York: Books for Libraries, Arno Press.
Horosko, Marian. 1989. "Hoopla! Put on Your Boots and Let's Go." *Dance Magazine* (June): 84–85.
Hunt, Yvonne. 1989. "3rd World Conference on Folk Dance: Folk Dance in Education (Larisa, Greece, 17–21 May 1989)." *Dance Research Journal* 21(2): 43–45.
Kalaidjian, Walter. 1993. *American Culture Between the Wars: Revisionary Modernism & Postmodern Critique.* New York: Columbia University Press.
Kelley, Florence. 1898. "Hull House." *New England Magazine* 18 (July): 550.
Kelly, David. 1995. *The Czech Fascist Movement 1922–1942*. East European Monographs, New York: Columbia University Press.
Kimmins, C.W. 1919. *Peasant Dances of Many Lands.* 2d ed. W.C.I. Montague House, Russell Square, London: Evans Brothers Ltd.
Kirshenblatt-Gimblett, Barbara. 1991. "Objects of Ethnography." In *Exhibiting Cultures: The Poetics and Politics of Museum Display.* Ivan Karp and Steven D. Lavine, eds. Washington, D.C.: Smithsonian Institution Press: 386–443.
———. 2002. "Sounds of Sensibility." In *American Klezmer: Its Roots and Offshoots.* Mark Slobin, ed. Berkeley: University of California Press: 129–173.
Knott, Sarah Gertrude. 1939. "The Traditional in Recreation." *Recreation* 32: 643–646, 680–681.
———. 1949. "To Each His Own." *Viltis* 6 (January–February).
Kolar, Walter, W. 1986. *Duquesne University Tamburitzans: The First Fifty Years Remembered.* Pittsburgh: Tamburitza Press.
Kraus, Richard. 1972. "Dance in the Age of Aquarius." *Focus on Dance* 6: 56–59.
———. 1985. *Recreation Leadership Today*. Glenview, Ill.: Scott, Foresman and Co.
Kraus, Richard, Sarah Chapman Hilsendager, and Brenda Dixon. 1991 [1969]. *History of the Dance in Art and Education*. 3rd ed. New Brunswick, N.J.: Prentice-Hall.
Kulbitsky Olga. 1972. "Dance: A Sport for Men." *Focus on Dance* 6: 63–64.
Lancaster, Julie. 1999–2000. "Mendocino Impressions, 1999." *Kef Times* 5(2): 4–5.
———. 2000–2001. "Many Threads: History of the Balkan Music & Dance Workshops."
Kef Times 6(2): 1, 6, 7.
———. 2000–2001. "Interview with Carol Silverman." *Kef Times* 7(1): 1, 10, 11.
———. 2001–2002. "History of the Balkan Music and Dance Workshops, Continued. Balkan Camp Branches Out: East Coast Camps." *Kef Times* 7(2): 1, 10, 11,17.
———. 2003. "Interview with Joe Kaloyanides Graziosi." *Kef Times* 8(2): 1, 7.
———. 2003. "Interview with Polly Tapia Ferber." *Kef Times* 8(2): 5, 7, 9.
———. 2004. "Interview with Bob Leibman." *Kef Times* 9(1): 5, 7, 16.
Lancefield, Robert Charles. 2005. Hearing orientality in (white) America, 1900–1930 PhD dissertation. Wesleyan University 2005.

Larson, Donald G. 1990. "San Francisco 1939–1940, Golden Gate International Exposition." *Historical Dictionary of World's Fairs and Expositions, 1851–1988.* John E. Findling and Kimberly D. Pelle, eds. Westport, Conn.: Greenwood Press: 301–303.

Lears, T. J. Jackson. 1981. *No Place of Grace: Antimodernism and the Transformation of American Culture, 1880–1920.* New York: Pantheon.

Lemay, Leo. 1985. *New England's Annoyances: America's First Folk Song.* Newark, Del.: University of Delaware Press.

Leonora, Suzanne. 1998. "Mendocino Highlights." *Kef Times* 4(2): 4.

Levin, Theodore with Valentina Süzükei. 2006. *Where Rivers and Mountains Sing: Sound, Music, and Nomadism in Tuva and Beyond.* Bloomington: Indiana University Press.

Levine, Lawrence W. 1986. *Highbrow/Lowbrow: The Emergence of Cultural Hierarchy in America.* Cambridge, Mass.: Harvard University Press.

Lidster, Miriam. "Teachers Can Make It Live." *Focus on Dance* 6: 75–77.

Lincoln, Jennette Emeline Carpenter. 1913. *The Festival Book. May-Day Pastime and the May-pole: Dances, Revels and Musical Games for the Playground, School and College.* New York: A. S. Barnes and Co. Lomax, Alan, foreword, and Botkin, B. A., preface. 1948. *The People's Song Book.* Waldemar Hille, ed. New York: Boni and Gaer.

Lubove, Roy. 1974. *The Progressives and the Slums: Tenement House Reform in New York City, 1890–1917.* University of Pittsburgh Press, 1962. Reprint, Westport, Conn.: Greenwood Press.

Lyotard, Jean François. 1983. The Postmodern Condition: A Report on Knowledge. Translation from the French by Geoff Bennington and Brian Massumi. Minneapolis: University of Minnesota Press.

MacFarlane, Rachel. 2000–2001. "Where Our $ Comes From—Where Your $ Goes." *Kef Times* 6(2): 13.

———. 2003–2004. "Delving into the Heart of Brass: Zlatne Uste Goes to Serbia." *Kef Times* 9(1): 1, 8, 9, 13.

Marcus, Julie. 1991. "Postmodernity and the Museum." *Social Analysis No. 30* (December 1991): 10–19.

Martin, John. 1980. *The Dance: The Story of the Dance Told in Pictures and Text.* Reprint, Books for Libraries, Arno Press.

McBee, Randy D. 2000. *Dance Hall Days: Intimacy and Leisure among Working-Class Immigrants in the United States.* New York: New York University Press.

McLaughlin, John. 2004. "Bill Vanaver: A Conversation in Mt Airy." Reprinted from *The Folk Life Quarterly* 1 (November 1977). http://www.thedigitalfolklife.org/vanaver.html (accessed on July 30, 2004).

Mendonça, Maria. 2001. "Gamelan II: Outside Southeast Asia" *The New Grove Dictionary of Music and Musicians II*, eds. S. Sadie and J. Tyrell, New York: Macmillan.

Metcalf, Eugene W. Jr. 1986. "The Politics of the Past in American Folk Art History." *Folk Art and Art Worlds,* John Michael Vlach and Simon Bronner, eds. Ann Arbor: University of Michigan Research Press, 27–50.

Meyer, Robert Jr. 1950. *Festivals USA: A Comprehensive Guide to Over 1200 Annual Celebrations Throughout the Country.* Binghamton, N.Y.: Vail-Ballou Press.

Miller, Arthur George, John T. F. Cheffers, and Virginia Whitcomb. 1974. [1st to 3d ed. by A. G. Miller and V. Whitcomb, published as *Physical Education in the Elementary School Curriculum,* 1957, 1963, 1969, 1974.]

Physical Education: Teaching Human Movement in the Elementary Schools. Englewood Cliffs, N.Y.: Prentice-Hall.

Miller, Melissa E. 1994. "Who Are These People, and Why Are They Here? A Survey of Attendees at Mendocino Music and Dance Camp, June 1994." Research paper, Santa Clara University.

Moreau, Yves. 1990. "Observations on the Recent Widespread Adoption and Adaptation of Bulgarian Folk Music and Dance in North America and Elsewhere." *Ethnomusicology in Canada, Proceedings of the First Conference on Ethnomusicology in Canada Held in Toronto 13–15 May, 1988*. Robert Witmer, ed. Toronto: Institute for Canadian Music: 113–119.

Mullen, Michael. 1990. "New York 1939–1940, New York World's Fair." *Historical Dictionary of World's Fairs and Expositions, 1851–1988.* John E. Findling and Kimberly D. Pelle, eds. Westport, Conn.: Greenwood Press: 293–300.

Monahan, Kathleen. 1977. "Yugoslav-American Records." *Journal of American Folklore* 90 (358): 497–501.

Monroe, Lewis B. 1869. *Manual of Physical and Vocal Training for the Use of Schools and for Private Instruction*. Philadelphia: Cowperthwait and Co.

Narodny, Ivan. 1913. "Music of the Balkan Nations." *Musical America* 3 (May): 27.

New York Historical Society, The. 1995. *The Encyclopedia of New York City.* Kenneth T. Jackson, ed. New Haven, Conn.: Yale University Press.

Nunnes, Theodore. 1897. *The Sponsor of Folk Songs.* Temple Bar, n.p.

Oakes, Dick. www.phantomranch.net. (accessed July 2004).

Pellegrini, Angelo M. 1956. *Americans by Choice.* New York: Macmillan.

Perry, Clarence A. 1910. *Organized Athletics, Games and Folk Dancing.* [Reprint of *The Wider Use of the School Plant,* chapter 10, by C. Perry.] New York: Department of Child Hygiene of the Russell Sage Foundation.

Petrill, Jack. 1957. "Dancing in Recreation." *Dance Magazine* (May): 53–54.

Physical Training, Report of Conference. 1889. Published by Boston Normal School of Gymnastics.

Porter, James. 1977. "Recordings of European, Canadian, and Euro-American Music." *Journal of American Folklore* 90 (355): 98–106.

Reid, Georgia (compiler). 1973. *Dance Directory: Programs of Professional Preparation in American Colleges and Universities.* 8th ed. Washington, D.C.: American Association for Health, Physical Education, and Recreation.

Rice, Timothy. 1987. "Toward the Remodeling of Ethnomusicology." *Ethnomusicology* 31(3): 469–489.

Riis, Jacob. 1890. *How the Other Half Lives: Studies Among the Tenements of New York.* New York: Macmillan.

———. 1903. *The Making of an American*. New York: Macmillan.

Rogers, Frederick Rand. 1941. *Dance: A Basic Educational Technique: A Functional Approach to the Use of Rhythmics and Dance as Prime Methods of Body Development and Control, and Transformation of Moral and Social Behavior.* New York: Macmillan.

Rosenberg, Neil, ed. 1993. *Transforming Tradition: Folk Music Revivals Examined.* Urbana: University of Illinois Press.

Royce, Josiah. 1908. "Some Relations of Physical Training to the Present Problems of Moral Education in America." Ph.D. diss., Boston Normal School of Gymnastics. Wesley College Archive.

Rydell, Robert, W. 1993. *World of Fairs: The Century-of-Progress Expositions.* Chicago: University of Chicago Press.

Sapoznik, Henry. 2002. "KlezKamp and the Rise of Yiddish Cultural Literacy." *American Klezmer: Its Roots and Offshoots.* Mark Slobin, ed. Berkeley: University of California Press: 174–186.

Schimmerling, H. A. *Folk Dance Music of the Slavic Nations.* New York: Associated Music Publishers.

Scrapbook (III) on Health and Gymnastics in America (album, newspaper articles about conference held at M.I.T., correspondence, and fliers on Chicago World's Fair and Columbia Exposition and physical education associated with it). Wesley College Archive.

Scrapbook (IV) on Health and Gymnastics in America. 3L Department of Hygiene and Physical Education, Boston Normal School of Gymnastics. Wesley College Archive.

Scrapbook (V) on Health and Gymnastics in America. 3L Department of Hygiene and Physical Education, Boston Normal School of Gymnastics. Wesley College Archive.

Sefton, Alice Allene (compiler). Collection of Dances, Various Places, Various Dates. 1 box, 127 pieces. New York Public Library (*MGV 79–3909).

Shambaugh, M. Effie. 1927. "Research Study of Folk Dancing." *Bulletin of the Mary Hemenway Alumane Association, Department of Hygiene, Wellesley College* (September): 15–17.

———. 1929. *Folk Dances for Boys and Girls.* New York: A. S. Barnes and Co.

———. 1929. "The Place of Folk Dancing in the Program of Physical Education for Elementary and Secondary Schools." *Bulletin of the Mary Hemenway Alumane Association, Department of Hygiene, Wellesley College* (September): 13–15.

Shay, Anthony. 2002. *Choreographic Politics, State Folk Dance Companies Representation and Power.* Middletown, Conn.: Wesleyan University Press.

Shochat, Lisa. 2000–2001. "Interview With Eran Fraenkel." *Kef Times* 7(1): 3, 13.

Slobin, Mark. 1979. "Code Switching and Code Superimposition in Music." *Working Papers in Sociolinguistics* 63. Southwest Educational Development Laboratory, Austin Texas.

———.1993. *Subcultural Sounds: Micromusics of the West.* Hanover, N.H.: University Press of New England.

———. 2000. *Fiddler on the Move.* Oxford: Oxford University Press.

———. 2002. *American Klezmer: Its Roots and Offshoots.* Berkeley: University of California Press.

Society for International Folk Dancing, London. 1966. *A Selection of European Folk Dances,* book 3. Oxford: Pergamon Press.

Sousa, John Philip. 1977. *National, Patriotic and Typical Airs of All Lands, with Copious Notes.* 1890. Reprint, New York: Da Capo Press.

Spears, Betty. 1986. *Leading the Way: Amy Morris Homans and the Beginnings of Professional Education for Women.* Contributions in Women's Studies 64. Westport, Conn.: Greenwood Press.

Spears, Betty, and Richard A. Swanson. 1978. *History of Sport and Physical Activity in the United States.* Elaine T. Smith, ed. Dubuque, Iowa: Wm. C. Brown Co. Spottswood, Richard C. 1982. "Commercial Ethnic Recordings in the United States." In *Ethnic Recordings in America: A Neglected Heritage.* Washington, D.C.: American Folklife Center, Library of Congress: 51–84.

———. 1990. *Ethnic Music on Records: A Discography of Ethnic Recordings Produced in the United States, 1893–1942.* Vols. 1–7. Urbana: University of Illinois Press.
Stebbins, Genevieve. 1902. *Delsarte System of Expression*. New York: Edgar S. Werner Publishing & Supply Co.
Summers, Victoria Frances. 1939. "The Historical Development of the Undergraduate Program in Health and Physical Education at Wellesley College." Submitted for Hygiene 323, graduate seminar in Hygiene and P. E., Wellesley College.
Susman, Warren. 1984. "The Culture of the Thirties." *Culture as History: The Transformation of American Society in the Twentieth Century*. Warren Susman, ed. New York: Pantheon: 150–183.
Tawa, Nicholas. 1982. *A Sound of Strangers: Musical Culture, Acculturation, and the Post-Civil War Ethnic American.* Metuchen, N.J.: Scarecrow Press.
Taylor, Margery FitzStephen. 1938. "An Historical Study of Professional Training in Hygiene and P. E. in the BNSG and at Wellesley College." Submitted for Hygiene 323, graduate seminar in Hygiene and P. E., Wellesley College.
Tedlock, Dennis, and Bruce Mannheim. 1995. *The Dialogic Emergence of Culture.* Urbana: University of Illinois Press.
Tomko, Linda. 1990. "The Settlement House and the Playhouse: Cultivating Expressive Dance in Early Twentieth-Century New York City." *The 5th Hong Kong International Dance Conference. Conference Papers.* Vol. 2: K–Z: 274–294. Hong Kong: The Hong Kong Academy for Performing Arts.
———. 1999. *Dancing Class: Gender, Ethnicity, and Social Divides in American Dance, 1890–1920.* Bloomington: Indiana University Press.
Torp, Lisbet. 1990. *Chain and Round Dance Patterns: A Method for Structural Analysis and its Application to European Material.* Vol. 1–3. University of Copenhagen: Museum Tusculanum Press.
Trolander, Judith Ann. 1975. *Settlement Houses and the Great Depression.* Detroit: Wayne State University Press.
Tuan, Yi-Fu. 1992. "Place and Culture: Analeptic for Individuality and the World's Indifference." In *Mapping American Culture.* Iowa City: University of Iowa Press: 27–49.
U.S. Bureau of the Census. 1990. *Census of Population, Social and Economic Characteristics.* Department of Commerce, Economics and Statistics, Bureau of the Census, Washington, D.C.
Vice Commission of Chicago. 1970. *The Social Evil in Chicago: A Study of Existing Conditions.* 1911. Chicago: Gunthorp-Warren Printing Co. Reprint, Arno Press.
Wald, Lillian D. 1915. *The House on Henry Street*. New York: Henry Holt.
———. 1934. *Windows on Henry Street.* Boston: Little, Brown, and Co.
Wallach, Ritta Teresa. 1906. "Social Value of the Festival." *Charities and the Commons* 16(June): 315–320.
Waters, Mary, C. 1990. *Ethnic Options: Choosing Identities in America.* Berkeley: University of California Press.
Weaver, Rikki. 1997. "The Art of Balkanalia!" *Kef Times* (Fall): 6.
Weinstein, Gregory. 1928. *The Ardent Eighties: Reminiscences of an Interesting Decade.* Foreword by Lillian D. Wald. New York: The International Press.
Whisnant, David E. 1983. *All That Is Native and Fine: The Politics of Cul-*

ture in an American Region. Chapel Hill: University of North Carolina Press.

Wieman, Jane. 2001–2002. "Balkan Folk Dancing in Kansai, Japan." *Kef Times* 7(2): 8, 9, 20.

Williams, Jesse Feiring. 1922. *The Organization and Administration of Physical Education.* New York: Macmillan.

Wollter, Kim. 2000–2001. "Balkan Village in the Redwoods." *Kef Times* 7(1): 6, 7.

Wood, Thomas Denison, and Rosalind Frances Cassidy. 1927. *The New Physical Education.* New York: Macmillan.

Woods, Robert A., and Albert J. Kennedy, eds. 1911. *Handbook of Settlements.* New York: Russell Sage Foundation, Charities Publication Committee.

———. 1990. *The Settlement Horizon, with new introduction by Judith Ann Trolander.* [1922, Russell Sage Foundation] Reprint, New Brunswick, N.J.: Transaction Publishers.

YMCA of the USA. 1914. *Physical Education in the Young Men's Christian Associations of North America.* Copyright, International Committee of Young Men's Christian Associations. New York: Association Press.

Index

Key to Video Selections on Website

www.oup.com/us/balkanfascination

All CD/DVD tracks are the author's field-recordings unless noted otherwise.

DVD 1: Page 6, "Ramo, Ramo, Druže Moj" performed during the student concert, West Coast Balkan Music and Dance Workshops, Mendocino, California, 1995.

DVD 2: Page 31, "Student Concert Sampler," West Coast Balkan Music and Dance Workshops, Mendocino, California, 1995.

DVD 3: Page 32, "Little Campers," Students of Petar Iliev dance at the student concert, West Coast Balkan Music and Dance Workshops, Mendocino, California 1995.

DVD 4: Page 42, "Zlatne Uste Golden Festival, New York City:" Hungarian set in the large hall, and Bulgarian set in small room.

DVD 5: Page 42, "Boston Balkan Night," Zornitsa men's group.

DVD 6: Page 48, "Zlatne Uste at the Guča festival, Serbia, 2003." Zlatne Uste performs "Lipe Cvatu" (9:10–13:58) and "urevdan" (14:11–18:15) on the mainstage. This track begins with the emcee reminding the audience of the unexpected appearance of an orchestra from New York at the festival in the late 1980s. "As the press wrote in those days," he continues, "'this group of endearing Americans plays as if they were born under these skies.' Our guests from New York are with us again to remind us of those days and to remind us that Guča the trumpet capital." Here the booing and whistling from the audience increases, to which the emcee responds "dear attendees, I know that you love everyone who plays the trumpet," and urges the audience to welcome the band. Courtesy of Mr. Aleksandar Tijanić and RTS (Radio Televizija Srbije).

DVD 7: Page 49, "Ansambl Teodosievski, Esma Redžepova and Šani Rifati" (dancing with a glass on his head) join forces to augment the party atmosphere, West Coast Balkan Music and Dance Workshops, Mendocino, California, 1997.

DVD 8: Page 60, "Lesno Oro/ Mome Odi Niz Livada," Izvorno Ensemble: Carol Silverman and Ruth Hunter (voice), Mark Levy (gajda), David Bilides (kaval), Bill Cope, Lew Smith, and Al Murray (tambura), Dan Auvil (tapan). West Coast Balkan Music and Dance Workshops, Mendocino, California, 1997.

DVD 9: Page 60, "Ganga: Ako Dragi Poljubac Dobiješ," sung by Azra Lučkin, Mevla Lučkin, and Emsija Tatarević. Mount Bjelašnica, Bosnia and Herzegovina, August 2000.

DVD 10: Page 61, "Delem, Delem," performed by Esma Redžepova and Ansambl Teodosievski, West Coast Balkan Music and Dance Workshops, Mendocino, California, 1997.

DVD 11: Page 61, "Dance Class." Michael Ginsburg teaches the Macedonian dance Žensko Pušteno Oro to a recording by Pece Atanasovski. West Coast Balkan Music and Dance Workshops, Mendocino, California, 1995.

DVD 12: Page 224, "Ivo Papasov." Ivo Papasov's name has become synonymous with both sensitive musicality and extreme virtuosity. Here he shows his complete control of his instrument, making it sound like several different instruments and playing it in various stages of disassembly. Finally the band demonstrates the breakneck tempos for which they are known. Ivo Papasov with Yuri Yunakov Ensemble: Ivo Papasov (clarinet), Yuri Yunakov (saxophone), Neshko Neshev (accordion), Kalin Kirilov (bass), and Salif Ali (drumset), Cedar Cultural Center, Minneapolis, Minnesota, 2005.

DVD 13: Page 240, "Chaos" at the Guča Festival. Four bands play in one space in an evening party under a tent at the Guča Brass Band Festival, Serbia, 2002.

DVD 14: Page 240, "A Table at the Guča Festival." As perspective changes, apparent chaos resolves into to an intimate musical experience with Orkestar Bobana Salijevića, Guča, Serbia, 2002.

Audio Selections on Website

CD 1: Page 29, "Camp Soundscape." West Coast Balkan Music and Dance Workshops, Mendocino, California, 1997.

CD 2: Page 56, "Kafu mi Draga Ispeci," Ljubomir Živkov leads a tamburitza set in the kafana, East Coast Balkan Music and Dance Workshops, Ramblewood, Marryland, 1995.

CD 3: Page 62, Epirótika Medley performed by Ziyiá : George Chittenden (clarinet), Christos Govetas (laouto & voice), Beth Cohen (violin), Lise Liepman (santouri), and Dan Auvil (defi). From their CD *"From the Mountains to the Islands,"* Courtesy of Ziyiá.

CD 4: Pages 101, 160, 206, "Seljančica" performed by Banat Tamburitza Orchestra in the ca. 1950-1958. Originally published as a 78 rpm disc by The Folk Dancer Record Service, Flushing, New York. MH-1006; Courtesy of Kentucky Dance Foundation, Folk Dancer Record Center, Brandenburg, Kentucky.

CD 5: Page 161, "Milanovo Kolo (Serbia)" performed by Michael Herman's Folk Dance Orchestra, Walter Ericksson, arranger; originally on a 45 rpm disc "Happy Folk Dances," RCA Victor; EPA-4129, 1958; Courtesy of Kentucky Dance Foundation, Folk Dancer Record Center, Brandenburg, Kentucky.

CD 6: Pages 207-213, "Ke Pomine Tano" performed by Pitu Guli/Ženska Pesna (Carol Silverman, Carol Freeman, Jane Sugarman, Michael Alpert – voice: Mark Levy – clarinet, Miamon Miller – violin, Stewart Brotman – ud, Jane Sugarman – kanun, Ed Leddel – tarambuka), McCabe's, Los Angeles, July 1978. Courtesy of Mark Levy.

CD 7: Page 213, "Shto Si, Goro, Povyakhnala?" performed by Kitka, Women's Vocal Ensemble. From their 1999 CD *Nectar.* Courtesy of Kitka.

CD 8: Page 222, "Visoko Drvo" performed by Žabe i Babe. From their 1997 CD *Drumovi*. Courtesy of Bison Publishing.